THE SEX TALK

A Muslim's Guide to Healthy Sex & Relationships

First Edition

Written By: Nadiah Mohajir, M.P.H.
Navila Rashid, M.S.W.
Haddijatou Ceesay, Ph.D.

Edited By: Asifa Quraishi-Landes, S.J.D.
Illustrated By: Lohitha Kethu, M.A.
Designed By: Mat Schramm

ISBN (Print): 978-0-578-37744-5
Cover art illustrated by Lohitha Kethu

Dedication

This book is dedicated to all the Muslims who had questions
about sex and their bodies and didn't know whom to ask;

To all the Muslims who navigated relationships and intimacy
by themselves, without access to information or someone
trustworthy to turn to during a crisis;

To all the Muslims who have survived on the margins of their
communities for far too long because of their lived experiences;

We see you. We hear you. And, we hope you see yourselves
represented in the pages of this book.

Acknowledgements

Bismillah. We begin the name of God. Our gratitude first and foremost is to God, the Most Compassionate, the Most Wise, who has allowed us to advance this important work for the last decade and has blessed us with the sustenance to continue this work moving forward.

This book has been years in the making and has been a collaborative effort by so many people across the country. We pray that God accepts all of their efforts and hard work. Our eternal gratitude and prayers are due to:

Nadiah Mohajir, Navila Rashid, Haddijatou Ceesay
Our team of writers who have written content for this publication. Your willingness to tackle challenging sections, push beyond your comfort zone, and continued commitment to never stop learning is unparalleled.

Dr. Asifa Quraishi-Landes
Our wonderful teacher, mentor, advisor, and editor who pushed us with love and compassion and gave us more hours than she ever had.

Lohitha Kethu
Our brilliant medical illustrator who translated our vision better than we could ever have imagined.

Mat Schramm
Our long-time friend and colleague who helped bring this project to completion with his eye for design.

Aliza Kazmi, Aisha Ismail, Sabreen Mohammed, Kiran Waqar, Sahar Pirzada
Our HEART team that has worked tirelessly to market, promote, and launch the book. Your creativity is unmatched, and your thought partnership was critical to bring this work to completion.

Dr. Laila al-Marayati, M.D.; Dr. Sameena Rahman, M.D.; Zeenat Hussein, medical student; Noor Khalil, medical student
The medical professionals and medical professionals-in-training who have reviewed our work.

Dr. Alia Azmat, Sahar Pirzada, Dr. Julianne Hammer, Deonna Kelli Sayed, Huda Al-Marashi, Dr. Sabahat Adil, Golden Sage Editing, Aliza Kazmi, Yusra Ahmed, Sirajum Sandhi, Isatou Bah, Chaplain Seher Siddiqee, Yasmeen Khayr, Nazihah Adil Siddiqui, Amal Killawi, Sarah Hasan, Dr. Tasneem Mandivala, Yasmeen Shaban, Sadia Arshad, Marianna Castro, Sameeha Khan, Aminah Habib, Sabreen Mohammed, Shazia Pappa
Our team of volunteers, interns, and colleagues that gave their time to help edit, provide feedback, and help with research over the years for this publication.

Nura Maznavi, Ayesha Mattu
The Love, Inshallah team who originally brought us this idea.

Wajiha Akhtar-Khaleel, Shirley Ma, Mahdia Lynn, Jessica Athens, Saira Rasheed, Saara Hafeez, Kimya Fourozan, BettyRose Green, Kafia Ahmed
Our board of directors, members of which continue to be our biggest advocates and a collective resource as we develop our organization.

Dr. Asifa Quraishi-Landes, Dr. Kameelah Rashad, Dr. Shabana Mir, Dr. Julianne Hammer
Our scholars advisory board, whose members have generously provided us with guidance and support as we continue to deepen our work. We are grateful for the labor and the hard work they put in to produce scholarship that has provided us with the foundation we need to build communities that are gender equitable and free of violence. Many of them have been quoted in this publication.

Move to End Violence, Muslims for Just Futures (formerly Justice for Muslims Collective, Peaceful Families Project, FACE, KARAMAH, Black Women for Reproductive Justice, Sistersong, Sisterlove, National Asian Pacific American Women's Forum (NAPAWF), Muslim Women's League, Queer Crescent, @ VillageAuntie, Muslim Wellness Foundation, Advocates for Youth, Family and Youth Institute, *Breaking Silence* (film), Hijabi Monologues, Hurma Project, Muslim ARC, Dr. amina wadud, Dr. Shabana Mir, Dr. Alia Azmat, Dr. Kecia Ali, Dr. Laury Silvers, Dr. Zahra Ayubi, Dr. Asma Barlas, Dr. Debra Majeed, Dr. Saadia Yacoob, Dr. Shehnaz Haqqani, Dr. Ingrid Mattson, Dr. Sobia Ali-Faisal, Dr. Azizah al-Hibri, Dr. Kameelah Rashad, Mahdia Lynn, Kamilah Pickett, Dr. Olubunmi Basirat Oyewuwo, Aisha Rahman, Qudsia Raja, Nadya Ali, Dr. Laila al-Marayati, Muslim Women's Organization, Dr. Sameena Rahman, Muslim Youth Leadership Project, Mariame Kaba, Loretta Ross, Shira Hassan, Urooj Arshad, Tarana Burke, Sarah Jawaid, Michelle Gislason, Center for Urban Research and Learning, Nadia Khansa
Our movement family and brilliant Muslim women scholars: those who came before us and those who work alongside us. Women—particularly Black, Indigenous, brown, Muslim, queer, and trans women and femmes—have been at the forefront of this work for centuries. We are indebted to so many of our sisters in the movement for laying the groundwork for us to do what we do. While there are too many to name in the pages of this book, we want to extend our sincere gratitude to some of our organizational partners and teachers who have been particularly critical in our learning as we deepened our analysis of the reproductive justice and anti-sexual violence movements.

These amazing thought leaders, many of whom are Muslim—as well as many more not mentioned here—have laid the groundwork for us to do what we do, and for that we will forever be grateful.

Our many funders, individual donors, supporters, and organizational partners who have continued to make this work possible year after year. We are forever grateful for your trust in our leadership and your investment in this work. Naming all of you would span many pages in this book, but know that you are appreciated and we are grateful to be in partnership.[1]

Tariq, Iman, Noor, Rumi, Jenan, Sarah, Alia, Aisha, Seher, Alexa, Knickerbocker, Nasiha, Neneh, Sukai, Jenny, Sage... And so many more who are not named here
And finally, we're eternally grateful for our beloved life partners, babies, (and fur babies!), and families—biological and chosen—who cared for us, our homes, and our people, as we poured hours—which turned to years—into this project. Who held space for us as we struggled with writer's block, and who celebrated us as we got closer to the finish line. You are the core of our hearts, and you are our daily reminders that the world we are seeking to build is very much possible.

---

[1] For a full list of our funders, please visit https://hearttogrow.org/our-supporters/

Table of Contents

CHAPTER FOUR: KEEPING UP WITH YOUR SEXUAL HEALTH   101

CHAPTER FIVE: RELATIONSHIPS
THE GOOD, THE BAD, AND THE IN-BETWEEN   141

Before You Begin

We anticipate that some of our readers will be uncomfortable with the opinions and suggestions offered in this book. If you find yourself in that position, we ask you to be patient and take this as an opportunity to learn about perspectives and lived realities that are different from yours. We hope that you can see in these pages a journey for self-reflection and gaining new information, and above all a tool to deepen your compassion for the people you love.

Not everything in this book will resonate with you. We have done the best we can with the skills God has gifted us, and we pray that it is helpful. We ask you to read this book in the spirit of service in which it was written. Please take what is useful to you, and set aside that which is not.

Introduction

Muslims are having sex. Married Muslims. Single Muslims. Queer and trans Muslims. Straight Muslims. They're having healthy sex and unhealthy sex. And, sadly, like all other communities, many Muslims are also experiencing forced or nonconsensual sex, also known as sexual violence, along with other forms of violence. Yet, unfortunately, there are virtually no resources addressed to Muslims on this topic presenting accurate medical information that also take seriously all the nuances and complexities of being a Muslim in America. We think it's time to change that. It's time to have some honest conversations about sex in a comprehensive and positive way that promotes healthy, thriving, sexual relationships that are spiritually fulfilling as well as physically and emotionally satisfying.

This book is for the Muslim who is waiting until marriage to have sex. It's for the Muslim who has already had sex. It's for the Muslim who is looking to be in a healthy relationship, and it's for the Muslim looking to get out of an unhealthy one. It is meant to be a resource that addresses the emotional, physical, spiritual aspects of sexuality in order to finally address the things that have too often remained unsaid. The advice offered here goes beyond first-time sex and covers a variety of topics, particularly about having long-term healthy sexual relationships and taking care of your body. We hope it helps promote informed decision-making grounded in a deep understanding of the self, body, and spirituality.

Ultimately, we wrote the book that we wished we had when we were young adults. We wanted a guide for pursuing healthy sexual relationships from a Muslim lens. We felt let down by white feminist sex-positive frameworks that were often dismissive of our Islamic values.[2] We were frustrated with the lack of accurate reproductive and sexual health information—both from mainstream sources and from Muslim authors—that was empowering, gender equitable, and free of judgment and blame.

The everyday lived realities of Muslims can often be messy, complicated, and nuanced. We believe that people of all ages can and do make informed decisions about their sexual health when they have accurate, culturally- and religiously-sensitive information and systems that promote agency and choice. This sort of information allows us to carefully think about how our faith, identities, and sexuality intersect to live out all aspects of our lives—including our sexual lives—in ways that are informed and fully consistent with our values.

We anticipate that many of our readers will be uncomfortable with some of the opinions and suggestions offered in this book. If you find yourself in that position, we ask you to be patient and take this as an opportunity to learn about perspectives and lived realities that are different from yours. We hope that you can see in these pages a journey for self-reflection, for gaining new information, and above all a tool to deepen your compassion for the people you love.

This book is intended to be helpful to readers who are having sex for their first time or their hundredth time. We hope it presents non-judgmental information about what it means to love, experience partnership, and to engage in sex as a Muslim and as a person, and recognizes how often those identities intersect and cannot be separated. Not everything in this book will resonate with you. We have done the best we can with the skills God has gifted us, and we pray that it is helpful. We ask you to read this book in the spirit of service in which it was written. Please take what is useful to you, and set aside that which is not.

---

[2] See Laws, M. (2020). Why we Capitalize 'Black' (and not 'white'). *Columbia Journalism Review.* Available at https://www.cjr.org/analysis/capital-b-black-styleguide.php.

Who Are We?

Founded in 2010, HEART is a national nonprofit that builds power with survivors, communities, and institutions in Muslim communities to promote sexual health, uproot gendered violence,[3] and advance reproductive justice[4] by establishing choice and access for the most impacted Muslims. By offering accurate sexual health and violence education, advocacy, research, and training, HEART mobilizes people to become agents of change in their own lives and communities and connects them to a network to sustain their empowerment. Our vision is ambitious: To build a world where all Muslims are safe, can exercise self determination over their reproductive lives and thrive in the communities they live, work, and pray.

As such, HEART is working to dismantle the silence and stigma that looms around talking about sexual and reproductive health and violence within Muslim communities. Without dismissing the values of faith, HEART uses a public health framework and makes sexual and reproductive health information accessible to the community, helping Muslims to reclaim sex and sexuality as positive experiences. Though Muslim-led, HEART is not affiliated with any particular religious school of thought, nor does it offer religious guidance on what is Islamically permissible or not. The organization's leaders firmly believe that every Muslim has the right to choose what version of Islam by which they want to live, that these decisions are personal and complex, and ultimately the business of each individual Muslim and their relationship with God.

Over the years, many individuals have shared their sexual and reproductive health narratives with the HEART team, bringing to our attention several recurring issues. These issues include individuals not being familiar with their own anatomy, individuals not knowing symptoms of common medical problems such as yeast infections and therefore letting them go untreated, young individuals struggling with painful sexual intercourse in their relationships, struggling with their sexuality, and, all too often, violence and abuse.

HEART programming does not just offer sexual health and violence information, but also guides participants to explore their personal and cultural biases, and challenges them to assess their privilege, teaching them strategies to dismantle systems of oppression, and makes sexual health and violence information and services more accessible to all.

---

[3] This expansion of language allows us to look at the following levels and forms of violence: 1) state violence 2) communal violence 3) sexual violence 4) interpersonal violence 5) violence that is power-based in relation to gender dynamics.

[4] We are grateful to Loretta Ross, founder of SisterSong, who turned this concept into a movement. SisterSong (sistersong.net) defines reproductive justice as "the human right to maintain personal bodily autonomy, have children, not have children, and parent the children we have in safe and sustainable communities." We believe this includes examining the multiple intersections that individuals cross every day that can have a profound impact on one's reproductive and sexual health such as access to culturally and linguistically appropriate health care, a living wage job, quality education, freedom from discrimination, violence, and other systems of oppression, and communities that support healing, empowerment, and self-determination.

These are the values at the foundation of HEART's work:

WE ARE **FAITH-DRIVEN.**

Compassion, justice, accountability, and gratitude are core Islamic values that drive our work. We are inspired by our faith tradition's commitment to equity and justice and uplift these values throughout the book.

WE PRACTICE **EMPATHY.**

Non-judgmental support is essential for individuals to heal, live authentically, and reclaim their stories. We know that the lived experiences of Muslims are diverse and nuanced, and so we are committed to offering information in a way that is objective, inclusive, and empowering.

WE CULTIVATE **BELONGING.**

Everyone—including Muslims—of all races, sexual orientation, gender identities, economic backgrounds, abilities and religious practice should feel welcome, seen, and heard. We have worked hard to make this book as inclusive as possible, and we recognize that there is still work to do.

WE ARE COMMITTED TO **COMPASSIONATE TRUTH TELLING.**

Challenging harmful narratives is critical to achieving equity and freedom. Throughout the book, we will challenge dominant attitudes, beliefs, and interpretations of our faith tradition that are harmful and ask you to reflect on how this messaging may or may not inform your own attitudes and behaviors.

WE APPROACH OUR WORK WITH **HUMILITY.**

We are lifelong students working to deepen our understanding of gender, sex, violence, and faith. We ask that you offer us grace for the mistakes we make in this book and in our work, and reach out to us to engage in dialogue about how we can do better and be in partnership to tell your stories more authentically. Reach out to us using the QR code on the back of this book to engage in a dialogue about your experience with the content.

Why did we write this book?

In 2015, *Love, Inshallah* and HEART teamed up to create the survey "#TheFirstTime," to allow participants to anonymously submit their questions and concerns about first-time sex. Following are the questions that were used as prompts and summaries of the responses.

What questions did/do you have about first-time sex?
For some respondents, first-time sex concerns centered around, "Will it hurt?" or "Where does it go?" or "Will it bleed or be messy?" Others wondered how long it would take to experience orgasm, what was considered a "normal" experience, and whether the act of having sex would change someone in a fundamental way. Still others shared a desire to please their partners, but were unsure of how to do that.

What piece of advice would you give your best friend on his/her first time and/or wedding night?
Most respondents listed the need for patience, the ability to communicate with one's partner, not becoming consumed with body image, and taking your time. Others insisted that people not feel pressured to have sex on the wedding night, as alleviating this pressure will help with being relaxed and ready for one's first physically intimate experience with their spouse.

What resources do you wish you had access to before your first time having sex or at the initial stages of becoming sexually active?
A number of participants wanted more nuanced information and conversation about the mechanics of sex, including sex toys, sexually transmitted infections, and the difference between real sex versus pornographic sex. Almost every participant listed a desire to approach someone they knew—an older relative, friend, or someone in the community—who could provide nonjudgmental advice and insight.

#TheFirstTime survey results highlighted the reality that Muslims are thinking about sex and have questions about it, whether or not they are sexually active. It is important to take these questions seriously and provide these answers. It is notable that research indicates Muslims are having sex: The Family and Youth Institute estimates that more than 50% of never-before-married Muslim college students are engaging in some form of sexual activity, including having sexual intercourse.[5] Canadian researcher Sobia Ali-Faisal, estimated the number to be even higher. Her study indicated that more than two-thirds of 407 study respondents reported that they had had sex before marriage; of the remaining who didn't, 50% had considered premarital sex at some point.[6]

At HEART, we have noticed that the Muslim cultural norm of discussing sex only within the context of marriage and/or heterosexual relationships excludes the lived experiences of many Muslims. The resulting lack of open, nuanced conversation has long-term negative consequences for healthy Muslim intimacy: Silence can instill shame and negative attitudes toward sex. This can lead to uninformed or even risky decision-making, which many people carry into their sexual relationships. For example, it can result in:

[5] Family & Youth Institute. *Premarital Sex Among Muslim Youth*. Infographic. Available at: https://www.thefyi.org/infographics/pre-marital-sex-among-muslim-youth/.
[6] Ali-Faisal, S.F. (2014). *Crossing Sexual Barriers: The Influence of Background Factors and Personal Attitudes on Sexual Guilt and Sexual Anxiety Among Canadian and American Muslim Women and Men*. Electronic Theses and Dissertations. Paper 5051; Ali-Faisal, S.F. (2015). *What Does the Research Say? That Muslim Youth Need Sex Education*. Blog post. Available at: https://hearttogrow.org/what-does-the-research-say-that-muslim-youth-need-sex-education/.

- the inability to identify common medical problems, or worse, unhealthy or abusive relationships,

- staying in unhealthy or abusive relationships because of the spiritual guilt people may feel for being in premarital relationships,[7]

- shame, or serious mental health and spiritual crises, causing people to leave the faith, and/or inflict self harm.[8]

In #TheFirstTime survey, we saw that people struggled to find resources within Muslim circles that offered a nonjudgmental tone, accurate information, and that also considered the nuances and complexities of being a Muslim in America. One survey participant's response put it bluntly: "Go ask your non-Muslim friend." This disappointing, though likely accurate, sentiment should serve as a call to action for all Muslims concerned with the wellbeing of our communities.

In the spirit of our Muslim responsibility to do the good with our hands, tongues, and hearts, it is important for us to ask: Have we created a safe, judgment-free space in our communities in which individuals can explore their values and expectations about sex, while still feeling a sense of belonging to their Muslim community? Is it possible to have a values-based conversation on sex, while still honoring personal agency? Is it possible to be sexually empowered and committed to upholding Islamic guidelines? How can we frame conversations around sex in a way that instills positive, healthy attitudes about sex rooted in the faith and free from cultural baggage, patriarchy, and shame?

At HEART, we invite and facilitate these tough, uncomfortable conversations daily—in Muslim spaces as well as secular spaces with Muslims present. In secular spaces, we have noticed that certain aspects of white sex positive feminism often presume that healthy sexual awareness conflicts with living by the guidelines of one's faith. This is the idea that women are not sexually free until they have sexual freedom even from religious guidelines.[9] This movement often dismisses religious laws, as if they are always the problem. One example of this is presuming that practicing abstinence is oppressive. Compounding this with the reality that immigrant and Black Muslims continue to be racialized within the current geopolitical contexts of the United States and Muslim communities, it becomes even harder for young Muslims to make sense of their religious identity, alongside personal identity, relationships, and societal expectations.[10] Age-old stereotypes of sexually aggressive Muslim men and submissive Muslim women often skew the conversation into caricatured versions of Muslim family life rather than informed discussion of real-life Muslim relationships. Most notably, the white sex positive movement pressures women to "perform" to prove their feminism: The pressure to be sexually active, openly talk about their sex lives, show interest in porn and other sexualized media become a type of "passport to feminist legitimacy."[11] This need to perform to prove one's liberation and freedom, ironically, is also tied to capitalism and patriarchy by commodifying women's sexual freedom and objectifying their bodies to satisfy the male gaze.[12]

[7] Mohajir, N and Qureshi, S. (2020). *Responding with RAHMA: Removing Roadblocks for Muslim Survivors.* Hurma Project Conference. Retrieved from: https://hurmaproject.com/wp-content/uploads/2021/03/Responding-with-RAHMA-Removing-Roadblocks.pdf.

[8] HEART Women & Girls. (2011). *Let's Talk about Sex Education: A Guide for Effective Programming for Muslim Youth.* Retrieved from: https://hearttogrow.org/resources/lets-talk-about-sex-education-a-guide-to-effective-programming-for-muslim-youth/.

[9] Zakaria, R. (2021). *Against White Feminism: Notes on Disruption.* W. W. Norton & Company.

[10] Mu'Min, K. (2019). *I'm Proud to be Black, I'm Proud to be Muslim. I'm Good, but Everybody Else is Trippin'!: Identity & Psychological Well-Being among Black American Muslim Emerging Adults.* Ph.D. dissertation, Chestnut Hill College, Philadelphia, Pennsylvania, USA; Ahmed, S, and Maha E. (2009). Challenges and Opportunities Facing American Muslim Youth. *Journal of Muslim Mental Health* 4(2): 159-174; Azmat, A. et. al. "They Sit with the Discomfort, They Sit with the Pain instead of Coming Forward": Muslim students' Attitudes and Challenges Mobilizing Sexual Violence Education on Campus. *Religions.* Manuscript submitted for publication.

[11] Zakaria, Rafia. (2021). *Against White Feminism: Notes on Disruption.* W. W. Norton & Company.

[12] Ibid.

This pressure to uphold certain expectations and perform according to certain identities is also ever present in Muslim spaces, as Dr. Shabana Mir explains, "More in public than in private, many Muslim American students adhered to stereotypically "Islamic" identities. Male-female interaction was often wooden and evasive, evoking images of traditional, sex-segregated Muslim communities."[13] Dr. Shabana Mir explains the dichotomy between these two worlds further in her book about college womens' experiences:

> Muslim women's overall gendered behavior is characterized by a fusion of resistance and conformity—resistance and conformity to majority stereotypes and to Muslim expectations. Muslim women forge public and private gendered and sexual discourses and identities within the social spaces of campus culture where their sexual conduct often fits neither mainstream nor Muslim sexual discourses regarding male-female interactions, friendship, romance, dating, courtship, and sex.[14]

On the other hand, Muslims often approach this topic with loads of cultural baggage, often stemming from the after-effects of Western colonialism, which imported attitudes of shame, stigma, and silence around gender and sexuality—attitudes that were not the norm in pre-modern Muslim societies.[15] All of these spaces tend to dismiss the possibilities of more nuanced and creative ways to enhance and celebrate sex positivity for Muslims. This book deliberately challenges the notions that Islam is sexually oppressive on the one hand, and that open discourse about sexuality is a product of white feminism on the other.

The responses to #TheFirstTime survey re-emphasized to us the need for relevant, culturally-appropriate literature about sexual health and emotional intimacy in Muslim communities. Such literature must take seriously the lived realities of American Muslims, including the fact that some Muslims' sexual experiences can be considered non-traditional according to dominant social expectations in Muslim communities. This prompted us to conduct our own extensive research on the existing literature on sexuality. We discovered some Muslim-focused resources on sexuality such as *The Muslimah Sex Manual: A Halal Guide to Mind Blowing Sex* and *Birth Control & Abortion in Islam*. We also located numerous articles and websites that explored issues such as birth control, abortion, sexuality, and relationships. While these resources certainly have elements and information that readers may find useful, we felt that they were inadequate because these resources were either too academic or did not acknowledge the nuances of diverse lived realities of American Muslims. Similarly, a number of these resources, such as *Sex and Society in Islam* by Basim Musallam, tend to report only classical opinions (some of which were influenced by patriarchal attitudes of the time) and not enough attention to whether and how those might evolve with changed circumstances. Many of the classical sources include elements of misogyny, anti-Blackness, homophobia, transphobia, and are centered on male pleasure and satisfaction as the end goal. They often do not include in-depth, medically accurate information—let alone a women's perspective—on consent, decision making, unplanned pregnancy, sexually transmitted infections, and sexual violence. In short, we concluded that these resources may be useful for many in our communities, but they may not speak to all those needing help and support.

---

[13] Mir, S.(2014). *Muslim American Women on Campus: Undergraduate Social Life and Identity*. University of North Carolina, Chapel Hill.
[14] Ibid.
[15] Carrasco-Miró, G. (2019). Encountering the Colonial: Religion in Feminism and the Coloniality of Secularism. *Feminist Theory*, 21(1):91–109.

All this considered, we noticed in our research that the number of relevant resources is starting to grow: numerous initiatives and resources have emerged that center women's pleasure, emphasizing it as a part of Islamic tradition, including the @VillageAuntie, a sex educator and author whose work includes offering workshops for women on sexuality and pleasure with an Islamic lens, and Habeeb Akande's book *Kunyaza: The Secret to Female Pleasure.*

But there is still much more needed, and it is this gap that we hope to fill with this book. With it, we hope to provide a resource that challenges some of the unhelpful presumptions, prioritizes women's pleasure, and empowers our readers with medical and Islamic information to be fully in control of their sexual health decision-making. We pray that this book helps to create healthier lives—for individuals, and for their partners, loved ones, and communities.

Who is this book for?

Of the many important themes from #TheFirstTime survey, the most important is that Muslims' experiences with sex and relationships are extremely diverse, and that lack of open dialogue, shame, and stigma has limited how we talk about sex in our communities. As an organization rooted in public health promotion, it is critical for us to uphold our commitment to work for Muslims of all lived experiences, and we have tried our best to develop content that speaks to the diversity of Muslims realities. To that end, we would like to take a moment to address all of our very different readers directly.

For those of you abstaining from sex until marriage: We see you and honor the commitment you are making to yourself and God. We hope that you find the information in this book useful as you deepen your understanding of yourself, and what you ultimately want in your significant other in order to prepare for a healthy, intimate, sexually-fulfilling marriage.

For those of you who already have experienced sex: We know that your experiences are more common than our communities would like to believe, and your questions and concerns are valid. We recognize that talking about sex exclusively in the framework of marriage can leave a lot of people out. Most people likely have (or will have) the same fears, questions, and curiosities about sex. This book offers information without judgment. It is not a religious treatise on matters relating to sex and intimacy.

If you identify as a member of the LGBTQ+ (lesbian, gay, bisexual, trans, queer, etc.) community: Your questions about sex and love may feel impossible to address, especially in Muslim communities that only recognize cis-heterosexual intimacy. We hope you feel that this book is different, and that you find guidance and support here. At the same time, we realize that in order to truly reflect and represent the LGBTQ+ experience, an entirely separate publication needs to be written. However, you are not forgotten in these pages, and many themes discussed in this book overlap regardless of sexual orientation and gender identity. We kept you in mind as we wrote it, as this effort is an evolving one that hopes to acknowledge all the various ways in which love and companionship are experienced in our communities.

In order to respect the wide range of Muslim experience and identities, we have worked to incorporate inclusive language in this book as much as possible. For example, whenever possible and appropriate, we use:

- "Partner," "significant other," or "spouse" instead of "husband" and "wife" to acknowledge that relationships can take many forms. Moreover, the word "partner" reflects the spirit behind the relationships we are promoting: a mutually fulfilling partnership;

- They/them pronouns instead of s/he pronouns;

- "Cisgender" or "cis," which refers to a person whose gender identity corresponds with the sex they were assigned at birth. At times, we may also use "people with vaginas" or "people with penises" to acknowledge that the sex someone is assigned at birth may not reflect how they identify with respect to gender.

- "Non-binary" or "genderqueer" refers to people whose gender is not male or female or don't identify with any gender.[16]

- "Transgender" or "trans," which refers to a person who has a different gender identity than the sex that they were assigned at birth.

If these terms are not your usual way of speaking, we appreciate that the language in this book may be unfamiliar to read. We hope you can be patient, understand the intentions behind our choices, and try to focus on the meaning and not the semantics of our message.

We hope that you will find guidance as you make comprehensive decisions around sexual and reproductive health. While we will not take a deep dive into Islamic rulings regarding consensual sex, we will take strong positions against practices or traditions that we believe actively harm, oppress, or lend to violence: Because we belive that is in direct violation of Islamic tenets that promise integrity and safety to all of God's creation.

How do you use this book?

This book offers a lot, but it doesn't do everything. We have tried our best to address the topics in this book using as comprehensive lens as possible, while also being intimately aware that Muslims in America are as diverse in every way that they can get. We know we will fall short and not be able to provide a fully representative picture for any one community. Specifically, we hope that future editions can more authentically incorporate writers and voices from Black, Shia, Queer, Transgender, and Gender Non-Conforming, Indigenous, Convert/Revert, and Disabled Muslim communities.

We have tried to mention topics pertaining to all of the above communities, and we know that we must have the conversations led by these directly impacted communities in order for the most authentic inclusion. Our vision is to build sustainable programming alongside these diverse Muslim communities and engage them for future editions. Any errors made in this book are unintentional, and we hope you reach out to us so that we can correct misinformation. As you read, please keep in mind what we are seeking to do, and what we specifically are not trying to do:

---

[16] National Center for Transgender Equality. (2018). Understanding Non-Binary People: How to Be Respectful and Supportive. Available at: https://transequality.org/issues/resources/understanding-non-binary-people-how-to-be-respectful-and-supportive.

WHAT THIS BOOK IS	WHAT THIS BOOK IS NOT
Information presented in a nonjudgmental way, encouraging critical thinking	A sex manual or a how-to
A resource of foundational knowledge	An encyclopedia with comprehensive information
An opportunity for reflection	A religious treatise[17]
Committed to gender-neutral and inclusive language	A book presuming heteronormative relationships
A resource that is medically accurate	A substitute for a healthcare professional
Appropriate for a slightly more mature audience	A replacement for first-time sex education[18]

Chapter Summaries

For a bit more detail, here is a summary of each chapter:

CHAPTER ONE: WHAT DOES ISLAM HAVE TO DO WITH IT?

This chapter addresses the ways that Islam, *sharia* (Islamic law), and norms within Muslim communities impact the topic of sex and intimate relationships for Muslims. It also explains the approach that HEART takes on these issues, and why.

CHAPTER TWO: SEX ED 101

This chapter is similar to what you'll learn in sex education class, but meant to be a quicker overview. It covers anatomy, the menstrual and reproductive cycle, contraception, and sexually transmitted infections. It includes illustrations and diagrams to accompany the information as well as prompts for reflection along the way and resources for further learning.

CHAPTER THREE: WHAT TO EXPECT

This chapter offers readers an idea of what to expect with sex. Topics include decision-making, consent, preparing for sex, preparing for the first time as well as common roadblocks to having sex.

CHAPTER FOUR: KEEPING UP WITH YOUR SEXUAL HEALTH

This chapter offers readers information on how to keep up with their sexual health. Topics include preventative care such as pap smears and gynecological exams, attending to circumstances that may occur after becoming sexually active (pregnancy, sexually transmitted infections, infertility, pregnancy loss and abortion) as well as tools to prepare for your routine medical visits.

---

17 We do not offer religious guidance on issues regarding sex, including the permissibility or impermissibility of particular sexual practices. Rather, we share some of the diverse opinions and perspectives that exist in the world of fiqh (Islamic legal doctrine), to empower people to better inform their own decisions. There are also numerous resources from the literature of Islamic jurisprudence, which we have included at the end of each chapter as well as in our Works Cited section at the end of the book.

18 We believe this book is meant for a slightly older audience that is starting to think about being in relationships; because the age in which people begin navigating relationships can vary, we encourage you to determine with your family the appropriate age to read this book, as a way to begin open conversations about sex.

CHAPTER FIVE:
RELATIONSHIPS: THE GOOD, THE BAD, AND THE IN-BETWEEN

The final chapter addresses the various types of intimate relationships and the elements of healthy, unhealthy, and abusive relationships. Readers will learn about the different types of violence that may occur in a relationship, how to identify it, seek help, or help another person. Also covered in this section are marriage, divorce, and infidelity.

Chapter Contents

Each chapter includes:

- **Foundational information:** This includes background information, such as medically accurate and evidence-based information, on topics related to sexual health and violence.

- **Personal reflections:** Opportunities to journal about what you are learning.

- **Try it out boxes:** Interactive sections to help integrate what you're learning with your lived experiences

- **Did you know boxes:** Interesting facts you may or may not already know that we want to highlight.

- **Points of interest (POI):** Analysis from history and research that challenges mainstream or dominant understandings of a topic.

- **In your own words:** Direct quotes from the respondents who took "#TheFirstTime" survey to offer additional context to the information presented

- **Resources for further study:** The information found in this book can be considered a foundational introduction to a lot of the topics, and so we have offered some of our favorite resources through which you can take a deeper dive into those topics.

- **Glossary:** The end of this book contains a list of terms, definitions, and concepts for your reference.

There is no right or wrong way to read this book. Feel free to go cover-to-cover, or jump to sections most relevant to you, or skip around to what you find most interesting. We have presented information in a number of different ways, so that you can approach this work in whatever way works best for you.

Chapter 1: What Does Islam Have to Do With It?

L. KETHU

In This Chapter

This chapter addresses the ways that Islam, *sharia* (God's law), and norms within Muslim communities impact the topic of sex and intimate relationships for Muslims. It also explains the approach that HEART takes on these issues, and why.

Quick Snapshot

Setting the Stage

The Quran and *sunnah* (life example of the Prophet Muhammad, peace be upon him) are quite frank about sex. In fact, they even treat sex as an act of worship between married partners.[19] The Prophet Muhammad, peace be upon him, encouraged everyone to ask questions and to take care of their bodies, emphasizing that seekng accurate information about the body and sex is natural and nothing to be ashamed of. Thus, getting better informed about sex and sexual health is an Islamic thing to do.

The Quran and *sunnah* create a framework around sex and sexuality that emphasizes:

- Abstinence until marriage
- Privacy around sex
- Mutual pleasure between partners and a right to sexual pleasure for everyone—regardless of gender.

Unfortunately, many Muslims mistakenly think that the Islamic principles of privacy and modesty around sexuality mean shame and secrecy. This is partly due to the aftermath of centuries of colonialism, which caused many Muslims to adopt European cultural norms such as Victorian notions of shame attributed to feeling sexual desire.[20] These Victorian notions of shame have contributed to what today is the white sexual liberation movement as a response to dismantling puritan notions of repressed sexuality. Yet, among the pitfalls of this movement is that it proposes that there is only one way to be sexually liberated—i.e. through performing ones' sexuality to prove one's feminism.[21] Coupled with expectations from families and Muslim communities to maintain stereotypical gendered norms and ideals of chastity, young Muslims find it challenging to navigate this new world of freedom, dating, and relationships as they enter college.[22] As a result, a binary is produced: "sexually repressive societies that denied women sexual liberation and choice, and supposedly sexually liberated societies like the United States that expect women to perform their sexual identity.[23]" This binary not only is not reflective of Muslims' diverse experiences with sex, but it also reinforces the harmful narrative that the idea of being sexually empowered is a purely western concept and in conflict with Islamic tradition, or not applicable to Muslims who also want to practice their faith. Because this narrative is far from true, it is necessary to turn to our tradition to understand how Islam fits into healthy sexuality and relationships.

---

[19] Learn Islam. (n.d.). *Intimacy in Islam*. Retrieved from https://learn-islam.org/class3-intimacy-in-islam.
[20] Hussein, J. Ferguson, L. (2019). Eliminating Stigma and Discrimination in Sexual and Reproductive Health Care: A Public Health Imperative. *Sexual and Reproductive Health Matters*, 27(3): 1-5.
[21] Zakaria, R. (2021). *Against White Feminism: Notes on Disruption*. W. W. Norton & Company.
[22] Mir, S.(2014). *Muslim American Women on Campus: Undergraduate Social Life and Identity*. University of North Carolina, Chapel Hill, p. 157.
[23] Zakaria, R. (2021). *Against White Feminism: Notes on Disruption*. W. W. Norton & Company.

The Nuanced Nature of *Fiqh*
(Islamic rules of behavior)

To build a better understanding of how Islamic rules of behavior can influence our sexual health and intimate relationships, it is first important to understand a bit more about *sharia* (God's Law) and *fiqh* (Islamic rules of behavior).

Many Muslims have heard of the words *haram* (impermissible) and *halal* (permissible)—especially in the context of sexual activity—but most don't really know where those words came from and why. This is all part of the big topic of *sharia*. Sharia (God's Law) is interpreted in books of *fiqh*—individual rules of human behavior interpreted by Muslim legal scholars (*fuqaha*). The *fiqh* rules are developed through the process of *ijtihad*, interpretation of the Quran and *Sunnah*, with the goal of providing Muslims with guidelines for living a spiritually-fulfilling life.[24] Moreover, because *fiqh* is ultimately the human interpretation of God's law, "no *fiqh* rule can demand obedience because every such rule is the product of human (and thus fallible) interpretation. This pluralism allows the divine *sharia* 'recipe' to be tangible enough for everyday Muslim use, yet flexible enough to accommodate personal choice."[25]

Accordingly, these guidelines are fairly user-friendly because the *fiqh* scholars categorized all human action into five categories. That is, every human behavior can be identified as either *wajib* (required), *mandub* (recommended), *mubah* (neutral), *makruh* (discouraged) or *haram* (prohibited).[26] In other words, the *fiqh* takes very seriously not just what we could call "legal" behavior, but also "ethical" behavior too.[27] This means that there will be many behaviors that the *fiqh* recommends, but does not require (such as extra charity), and also actions that the *fiqh* allows, but still very much discourages (such as wasting money).

To make things even more complex, the *fiqh* rules come in a diverse range of *fiqh* opinions—organized into schools of thought (*madhhab*). These opinions often disagree with each other, but they are all still equally valid. We will not, of course, be able to address all of these opinions on every topic in this short book, but we will refer to them as best we can, with suggestions for where you can go for more information.

In short, *fiqh* is not "law" in the western sense of how a government will monitor your behavior.[28] Instead, it is a set of guidelines designed to help Muslims who are seeking guidance on how to live their lives. That guidance, naturally, has to cover a lot more than just what is mandatory and prohibited. It also means guidance on what will enhance one's character. That is why the *fiqh* scholars addressed all the gray areas in between the mandatory and the prohibited. In other words, the *fiqh* shows us very clearly that **just because you can, doesn't mean you should**.

Unfortunately, this is not the attitude taken by many Muslims, especially in their intimate relationships. For example, imagine these hypotheticals—all based on real-life situations:

- An Imam advises a divorced couple that the minor children must stay with their father until puberty according to *fiqh*, dismissing safety concerns about the children living with an abusive father.

---

[24] Quraishi-Landes, A. (2018). Sharia and Diversity: Why Some Americans Are Missing The Point. Institute for Social Policy and Understanding. Retrieved from https://www.ispu.org/sharia-and-diversity-why-some-americans-are-missing-the-point/.

[25] Ibid.

[26] Siddiqui, S. Z. M., & Quraishi-Landes, A. (2019). Legislating Morality and Other Illusions about Islamic Government. *Locating the Sharīʿa* (pp. 182–182). Brill.

[27] Ibid.

[28] Quraishi-Landes, A. (2016). Five myths about Sharia. *The Washington Post*. Retrieved from https://www.washingtonpost.com/opinions/five-myths-about-sharia/2016/06/24/7e3efb7a-31ef-11e6-8758-d58e76e11b12_story.html.

- A man marries multiple wives, but does not tell his first wife.

- A woman is seeking divorce from her abusive husband after discovering that she is a second secret wife; she presents her situation to an imam, she is told that she does not have grounds for an Islamic divorce, leaving her stuck in the marriage.

- A husband divorces his wife of 30 years, simply with a thrice-declaration of *talaq*,[29] with no notice, no attempt at reconciliation, and against the desires of his wife.

- A father arranges the marriage of his virgin daughter, without consulting her, due to the belief that he is acting in her best interest.

The above examples all illustrate someone choosing to do something that is discouraged, but may still technically be allowed by the rules of *fiqh*, depending on the interpretation. All of them can cause serious harm and disruption in people's lives, and yet this is difficult for Muslims to acknowledge because none of these behaviors are technically prohibited by the rules of *fiqh*.

This phenomenon occurs in the many of the sexual health topics that we will address in this book—such as details of married life, the nature of consent, and identifying and recovering from physical abuse, sexual violence, and marital rape. As we review these topics, we will emphasize the importance of paying attention to all of the *fiqh* guidelines—the recommended and discouraged as well as the mandatory and prohibited. Through our research, we deduce that a lot of what causes harm in Muslim intimate relationships stems from too much attention on the "can" and not enough on the "should."

In our research for this book, we have faced a challenge: it is difficult to find gender equitable rules about sexual health and intimacy in mainstream contemporary Islamic discourse, not because they don't exist, but because they have not been taught consistently, or even translated into modern texts. As a result, the more gender-equitable opinions are not part of established majority *fiqh* rules. We have identified some scholars who have articulated alternative *fiqh* interpretations, but we recognize that most do not have the classical *fiqh* training credentials of the more mainstream scholars. The smaller numbers of classically-trained female *fiqh* scholars is, in large part, due to the many obstacles placed in front of women seeking traditional classical training. As Kecia Ali explains:

> [i]f mastery of classical tradition is required in order to be considered credible, women are likely to be marginalized, if not excluded from interpretative reforms, and it matters deeply that women, whose concerns and perspectives differ from men's, be among those engaging in renewed ethical thought on topics including marriage and sex.[30]

In this book, we have worked hard to find and uplift as many women scholars as possible, even if they lack traditional training, because we believe that they have expended sincere effort and skill in search of truth and justice, and we believe that we can all benefit from their perspectives, analysis, and insights.

As you read this book, you will notice that we will note where we believe a *fiqh* opinion reflects a patriarchal norm that we do not believe is best suited to the lived experiences and needs of Muslims today, especially those living in the United States. As an alternative to those opinions, we will try to point to other *fiqh* interpretations and sometimes new reform ideas that more closely align with the RIDHA framework that

---

[29] A divorce initiated by the husband, without the wife's consent, which you can learn more about in Chapter 5.
[30] Ali, K. (2016). *Sexual Ethics and Islam: Feminist Reflections on Qur'an, Hadith, and Jurisprudence*. Oneworld Publications; Expanded, Revised edition, London.

HEART has developed, explained below. Thus, you will read some opinions that may be new to you because they are not the mainstream and more dominant *fiqh* opinion in circulation. Please do not be unsettled by this. Even unpopular minority *fiqh* opinions are just as valid as the more well-known majority opinions. We believe, therefore, that it is appropriate for us to point in the direction of alternative *fiqh* opinions in those areas when we see harm arising from Muslims following the dominant *fiqh* opinions.

As you read, you may find some of the opinions presented here appealing, and others distasteful: we are not insisting that you follow any particular *fiqh* opinion. Muslims always have the right to select whatever *fiqh* interpretation feels right to them. In this book, we seek only to provide you with tools to help you make your own decisions about how to live your life as a Muslim, including in your intimate relationships. Our recommendation is that you try to connect with God in the best way you can, and then listen to your heart and follow that. After all, each of us ultimately will answer to God alone for our actions, and that includes behavior in our intimate relationships.

 POINT OF INTEREST

There are a variety of factors that should be considered when it comes to translating and interpreting Islamic historical texts, such as the Quran and Sunnah, including

- who is translating the text (and who is missing from that discourse),
- their historical and social context, AND
- what approach they are using.

These elements can make a significant difference in the conclusions they draw. This is as true of those interpreting scripture as it is of those interpreting a poem.

Dr. Kecia Ali offers this reflection in her introduction to *Sexual Ethics and Islam* when she says:

in making value judgments, people are influenced not only by religious texts and teachings but also by their own social, cultural, and religious backgrounds. The early jurists were no exception to this rule; like contemporary Muslim thinkers, they could not help but be influenced by their own sense of what was right and wrong, natural, and unnatural. In engaging with Muslim texts in the past, it is important to consider the ways the authors' base assumptions differ from those in the present.[31]

Dr. Ingrid Mattson also explores this in depth in her paper titled "Gender and Sexuality in Bioethics" when she explains:

It is not only the curriculum, but the presence or absence of women along-side of men in teaching circles, mosques, seminaries, universities, and medical schools of each stream of thought that has a tremendous impact on how ethical knowledge is shaped and textured by local culture, shared anecdotes, and personal and group-gendered interests.[32]

[31] Ali, K. (2016). *Sexual Ethics and Islam: Feminist Reflections on Qur'an, Hadith, and Jurisprudence*. Oneworld Publications; Expanded, Revised edition, London.
[32] Mattson, I. (2018). Gender and Sexuality in Islamic Bioethics. *Islamic Bioethics: Current Issues and Challenges*. Vol 2: 57–83.

Dr. Mattson continues to explain how a male scholar's presumptions about human nature can impact his legal conclusions, even to the point of discouraging women to enjoy sex. For example, Ibn Qayyim al-Jawziyya, a 14th-century prominent Hanbali legal scholar, wrote a book titled *Prophetic Medicine* that remains widely circulated and translated, and is often accepted as religious guidance despite its implications for gender norms. A passage from the book asserts that a "woman is passive by both nature and by law," concluding that "[i]f she should be the active partner, she contravenes the demands of nature and the law."[33] This biased presumption about women's desire illustrates how important it is to remember that all the rules of Muslim behavior articulated by the *fiqh* scholars are fallible human interpretations of scripture and Islamic tradition, and will likely reflect the invisible presumptions of those scholars. That is one of the reasons there are so many different schools of Islamic law. On any one given issue, there are usually many different interpretations.

Moving Toward a Values-Aligned, Healthy Sexual Relationships Framework

At HEART, we take seriously the reality that Muslims find Islam to be a helpful framework for decision-making, and often center in their thinking the goal of pleasing God. This includes sexual relationships.

Like many faith traditions, Islamic rules of behavior pertaining to sex consist of boundaries and guidelines, including abstaining from sex until marriage.[34] But the act of sex itself is not deemed a shameful thing in Islam. The Quran, Hadith, and the Prophet's life have numerous examples of the merits of sex as an act of love and mercy between married partners, and even deem it an act of worship. Moreover, sex is not treated merely as a mechanism of procreation. Instead, it is considered a vehicle to achieving physical, emotional, and spiritual gratification between partners. For example, the *sunnah* encourages foreplay and romantic creativity, and the *fiqh* scholars—even the classical ones living in patriarchal times—gave a woman's orgasm the same importance as a man's.[35]

Taking all this to heart, we believe that there is a strong Islamic tradition that values sex as a positive, pleasurable, and sacred experience for both partners. We researched and evaluated many things as we wrote this book, but there are several key ideas that we kept in mind as our guiding compass. They are:

• Islam promotes a framework of sex within marriage that includes mutual pleasure between partners.

• The expectation to abstain until marriage is for everyone, not only women and girls.

• The Prophet's life has countless examples of healthy, thriving sexual unions that are rooted in compassion, mutual respect, love, and justice.

• Muslims are racially, ethnically, socioeconomically, spiritually, and geographically diverse; they are also diverse with respect to gender identity, sexual orientation, and religious practice.

[33] Mattson, I. (2018). Gender and Sexuality in Islamic Bioethics. *Islamic Bioethics: Current Issues and Challenges.* Vol 2: 57–83.
[34] Ali, K. (2016). Sexual Ethics and Islam: Feminist Reflections on Qur'an, Hadith, and Jurisprudence. Oneworld Publications; Expanded, Revised edition, London.
[35] Ghazzālī, & Farah, M. (1995). *Marriage and Sexuality in Islam: A Translation of Al- Ghazali's Book on the Etiquette of Marriage from the Ihya'.* UMI Books on Demand.

- Having questions about your body and sex is natural and nothing to be ashamed of.

- Sex cannot be limited to one conversation; rather healthy dialogue around sex and relationships should happen over a lifespan.

- Decisions related to sexual health such as cancer screenings (i.e. pap smears or mammograms), abstinence, contraception options, and sexual trauma (i.e. assault or rape) can change over an individual's lifetime.[36]

- There is not one single action, with the exception of *shirk* (associating God with another), sexual orientation, or gender identity that determines whether one is Muslim or not; that is something known only to God.[37]

- Most topics in *fiqh* have many more than one *fiqh* opinion. With at least four *Sunni* and three *Shia* schools of thought, the world of *sharia* has always been characterized by diversity of thought.

- The rules of *fiqh* have never been static; they have evolved over time, elegantly responding to cultural, social, and political contexts and societal changes of Muslim societies. Advancements in reproductive fertility technology, for example, have prompted new *fiqh* doctrinal rules to respond to Muslim needs.

Self-Determination During the Time of the Prophet

The life and experiences of the Prophet Muhammad (peace be upon him) have clear examples of marital partnerships that were grounded in mutual love, pleasure, compassion, justice, and self-determination. We all know that the Prophet's first wife, Khadijah, may God be pleased with her, was the one to propose marriage to the Prophet to marry her, not the other way around. Less known, however, is that this tradition of women offering themselves to the Prophet (and also repudiating him) happened multiple times throughout his adulthood. Fatima Mernissi explains in *Beyond the Veil* that this decision for women to "initiate a sexual union seems to have been a casual gesture made by the woman herself, without reference to her father or male relatives" was fairly common.[38] According to Mernissi, this practice, known as *hiba* (the act by which a woman gives herself to a man) was outlawed after the Prophet died.

Moreover, there were situations where the Prophet (peace be upon him) contracted a marriage that remained unconsummated and ultimately repudiated by the woman by pronouncing a formula three times; in the event that this happened, the Prophet (peace be upon him), honored it, and asked that the woman return back to her tribe.[39] There are many speculations of why those women changed their minds and pronounced the end of the union. Mernissi continues to explain:

> What we are interested in is the fact that in the Prophet's time there was a customary formula by which a woman could dismiss her husband... If a woman could dismiss her husband at will, then she possessed substantial independence and self-determination.[40]

---

[36] Safety Card for Muslim Youth on Healthy Relationships. Developed by HEART, Advocates for Youth and Futures Without Violence, available at https://hearttogrow.org/resources/beyond-halal-and-haram-muslims-sex-and-relationships-safety-card/.
[37] Ibid.
[38] Mernissi, Fatima. (1975). *Beyond the Veil: Male-Female Dynamics in Modern Muslim Society.* Schenkman Pub. Co.
[39] Ibid.
[40] Ibid.

Also, it is notable to mention that the Prophet (peace be upon him) honored their agency and personhood to determine what they wanted for themselves. He did not get angry or aggressive, nor did he take revenge for their rejection of him. This demonstrates clearly that the problems of toxic masculinity, male attitudes of entitlement to womens' bodies, and expectations for their obedience that are at the root of gender inequities and violence against women are not from the example of our Prophet (peace be upon him) or the Islamic tradition.

The RIDHA Framework

HEART has developed the RIDHA framework as a useful decision-making tool to identify healthy (sexual) relationships that are rooted in choice, consent, pleasure, communication, and spiritual well-being. To create this framework, we drew upon these core Islamic values: *rahma* (compassion), *'ilm* (knowledge), *karamah* (dignity), *hurma* (sacred inviolability), *adalah* (equity and fairness), and *'aqd* (commitment) to promote healthy, thriving partnerships. We believe these Islamic values can form the foundation of healthy, ethical, and mutually fulfilling relationships. Indeed, many Quranic verses and Prophetic *hadith* emphasize these values as central to ethical human interaction. We hope that this framework will inspire an approach to decision-making that will help guide you in your intimate relationships.

HEART's framework for healthy sexual relationships is inspired by the Islamic concept of *ridha*, also known as "fullness of choice."[41] In a paper published by KARAMAH: Muslim Women Lawyers for Human Rights, Azizah al-Hibri and Ghada Ghazal write:

> When the Prophet (peace be upon him) married Safiyyah (may God be pleased with her), she declined to engage in sexual relations on her wedding night. The Prophet did not force himself on her, nor did he admonish her or even question her about the reason for her refusal. Most interestingly, he did not tell her that angels would curse her till morning. Instead, he let her be. He treated her with courteousness, gentleness, and affection. This *sunnah* of the Prophet deserves to be the controlling precedent in marital sexual relations since it honors a core Islamic concept, namely that of *ridha*, defined by some jurists as the 'fullness of choice'.[42]

According to the Arabic dictionary, the word *ridha* has many meanings. They include: to be satisfied, be content; to consent, agree; to approve, accept, sanction; to be pleased; to wish, desire; and to permit. In other words, the word depicts varying types of consent. In the sexual context of the story in the *sunnah* mentioned by al-Hibri and Ghazal, to have *ridha* means that you not only give permission or agree to something, but you also feel fully satisfied and pleased.[43]

We believe that centering the concept of *ridha*—fullness of choice—is the best way to honor a Muslim's right to fully consent and be in control of their sexual health decision-making.

[41] Our gratitude to Dr Azizah Al Hibri and Ghada Ghazal for introducing this concept to us in their "Angels Cursing Hadith" paper. We are also grateful to Dr. Kecia Ali for her invitation to imagine a sexual ethics framework grounded in Islamic values in her book Sexual Ethics in Islam and Dr. Juliane Hammer, Dr. Asifa Quraishi-Landes, and Dr. Zahra Ayubi for pushing us to challenge current discourse on sexuality.

[42] al-Hibri, A, and Ghazal, G. (2018). *Debunking The Myth: Angels Cursing Hadith*. Karamah Muslim Women Lawyers for Human Rights. Retrieved from https://karamah.org/debunking-the-myth-angels-cursing-hadith/.

[43] Ibid.

Ridha is reminiscent of the self-determination that women practiced during Prophetic times. The spirit of this self-determination to some degree remains in today's Islamic marriage contract—which usually has the the woman offering herself to the groom—and yet, the reality is that Muslim women rarely experience this self-determination in most daily experiences. It is with this spirit of self-determination in mind, that *ridha* is the core principle of our framework for healthy sexual relationships.

To make the details of this framework easy to remember, we have created this acronym for the Arabic word *ridha*:

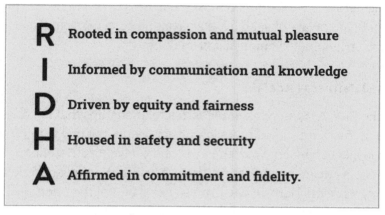

R Rooted in compassion and mutual pleasure

I Informed by communication and knowledge

D Driven by equity and fairness

H Housed in safety and security

A Affirmed in commitment and fidelity.

R Rooted in Compassion (*Rahma*) and Mutual Pleasure

The first principle in our RIDHA framework is that healthy, thriving (sexual) relationships are rooted in compassion and mutual pleasure. The Quran and *sunnah* offer numerous descriptions of what a healthy, thriving partnership can look like. The Quran emphasizes the notions of love and mercy between partners, and creates a "tranquil link between the human pair, man and woman:"[44]

> And Among His signs are that He created for your spouses from among yourselves, that you rest in them. And He made affection and mercy among you. Truly, in that are certainly signs for a folk who reflect. (30:21)[45]

> It is He who created you from a single soul. And out of it made its spouse that he rest in her. And when he laid over her, she carried a light burden and moved about with it. But when she was weighed down, they both called to God their Lord saying: If You would give us one accord with morality, we will certainly be the ones who are thankful. (7:189)[46]

The first of these two verses expresses that, as amina wadud explains in *Quran and Woman*, "man is intended as comfort to woman; woman is intended as a comfort to man."[47] In Islam, it is clear that companionship and sex is not solely to produce children, but rather to provide physical, spiritual, and emotional intimacy and gratification. Thus, it is *not* surprising that the Prophet often spoke of the importance of foreplay and sexually satisfying both partners in the hadith "Let none of you come upon his wife like an animal, and let there be an emissary between them." He was asked, "What is this emissary, O Messenger of God?" He said, "The kiss and [sweet] words."[48]

---

[44] wadud, amina. (1999). *Quran and Woman: Rereading the Sacred Text from a Woman's Perspective*. Oxford University Press.
[45] Bakhtiar, L. (2007). *The Sublime Quran: English Translation*. Kazi Publications.
[46] Ibid.
[47] wadud, a. (1999). *Quran and Woman: Rereading the Sacred Text from a Woman's Perspective*. Oxford University Press. New York.
[48] Ghazzāli, & Farah, M. (1995). *Marriage and sexuality in Islam: A Translation of al- Ghazali's Book on the Etiquette of Marriage from the Ihya'*. UMI Books on Demand.

I Informed by Communication and Knowledge ('Ilm)

One of the key elements of our RIDHA framework is that a healthy relationship is informed by communication and knowledge. Being able to have a healthy sexual relationship begins with understanding yourself, and becoming comfortable with asking questions and seeking knowledge about your body. Also, it means being informed about a lot of topics that come with sex, including contraception, pregnancy, sexually transmitted infections (STIs), and your own spiritual priorities and guidelines. Once you are armed with this knowledge, there are numerous conversations you can have with your (future) partner/spouse that can help communicate boundaries and desires, foster trust and connection, and ensure that all consent is full and informed. Moreover, communication is key for being aware of each other's past (and current) sexual history and experiences, and any other details that may be helpful to your decision-making.

D Driven by Equity and Fairness ('Adalah)

The next component of the RIDHA framework emphasizes relationships that are driven by equity and fairness. The Quran says many things about many groups of people, but one very remarkable feature of the Quran is that it established clear rights for women in the oppressively patriarchal society of sixth-century pagan Arabia. As Asma Barlas explains in her paper titled "Muslim Women and Sexual Oppression: Reading Liberation from the Quran," women's rights have always been a part of the tradition and scripture of Islam. She points out that a lot of Muslim behavior today is due to "cultural practices that may have nothing to do with Islam."[49]

Barlas asserts that the Quran offers a "radically egalitarian view of the equal worth and dignity of women that remains unparalleled, even in modern thought... and does not distinguish between the moral-ethical behavior and the potential of women and men."[50] For example, the Quran states several times that all human beings, regardless of race, gender, ability, or other identity, are created equal before the eyes of God:

> We held the Children of Adam in esteem... And we gave them advantage over many of whomever We created with excellence (17:70).[51]

> O humanity Be Godfearing of your Lord Who created you from a single soul and, from it, created its spouse and from them both disseminated many men and women (4:1).[52]

> "Truly, we created you from a male and female and made you into peoples and types that you recognize one another. Truly, the most generous of you with God is the most devout (49:13).[53]

Keeping all this in mind is a good reminder that the idea of women's rights is not inherently or solely a product of the West or white feminism. In fact, Barlas asserts that she "find(s) such a project to be intrinsic to the Quran's teachings, which is why [she] remain[s] skeptical of relying on Western feminisms and secularism for theorizing women's rights in Muslim societies."[54] There may be some that may argue that the Quran grants men superiority over women, specifically in verse 4:34 that states that "men are the maintainers of women [on

---

[49] Barlas, Asma (2001) Muslim Women and Sexual Oppression: Reading Liberation from the Quran, *Macalester International.* Vol. 10(15):118. Available at: http://digitalcommons.macalester.edu/macintl/vol10/iss1/15.

[50] Ibid.

[51] Bakhtiar, L. (2007). *The Sublime Quran: English Translation.* Kazi Publications.

[52] Ibid.

[53] Ibid.

[54] Barlas, A (2001). Muslim Women and Sexual Oppression: Reading Liberation from the Quran, *Macalester International.* Vol. 10(15):118. Available at: http://digitalcommons.macalester.edu/macintl/vol10/iss1/15.

the basis of] what Allah has [preferred] some of them over others...."[55] Feminist scholars such as Azizah al-Hibri have rejected the idea that this grants men control over women stating "only under extreme conditions (for example insanity) does the Muslim woman lose the right to self-determination...Yet men have used this passage to exercise absolute authority over women. They also use it to argue for the male's divinely ordained and inherent superiority."[56]

For this reason, it's critical to increase awareness about the importance of non-hierarchical interactions between spouses. At the root of inequalities and inequities usually lies an -ism (racism, sexism, classism, etc.)—an internalized, often subconscious, belief that one is better than another because of a specific identity. While these beliefs of being "better than" are sometimes explicitly communicated, most of the time they are implicit and subconscious. Some scholars have argued that this attitude is contrary to good Islamic character, and in fact, antithetical to Quranic teachings about all people being equal human beings before God.[57] Even as we all have different roles or positional authority in our lives and society, we are told to evaluate each other solely on the grounds of piety and service to God. This can be an important reminder to practice healthy mutual respect and understanding of each other's needs in a way that both partners feel whole and fulfilled.

H Housed in Safety and Security (*Hurma*)

A relationship cannot be healthy or thriving if it is not housed in safety and security, the next critical element of our framework. The Quran describes "believing men and women as each other's *awliya*," or mutual protectors, taking care of one another.[58] It also characterizes spouses as "garments" for each other.[59] Evoking the feeling of safety, security, and intimacy that clothing provides on our skin, this image points to the closeness and intimacy of spouses. It also reminds us that we should feel safe with our spouses.

All of this connects to the concept of *hurma*, or sacred inviolability—the idea that every person has a layer of protection surrounding them.[60] Literally, *hurma* means "the thing which is unlawful to violate...and it was previously used by various Islamic law schools for expressing the precise meaning for the intended meaning of 'bodily integrity.'"[61] As Dr. Ingrid Mattson explains, it is a core Islamic concept that everyone has physical limits that should not be transgressed. In other words, everyone has boundaries.[62] Even more than that, every person has a set of boundaries that are personal and specific to them.

The Quran bestows human dignity on the children of Adam,[63] and outlines restrictions and practices to protect bodily integrity.[64] This dignity is granted to the body even after death, as there are special instructions on how to care for even a dead corpse, and defacing a dead body is forbidden by Islamic law.[65] As such, the human body is regarded as an *amanah*, or trust, from God, and each individual is tasked to care for and respect their own body, and also respect the integrity of the bodies of those around them. This includes not

[55] Quran 4:34.

[56] al-Hibri, A. (1982). A Study of Islamic Herstory: Or How Did We Ever Get into this Mess? *Women and Islam: Women's Studies International Forum Magazines*, 5.

[57] al-Hibri, A. (2003). An Islamic Perspective on Domestic Violence. *Fordham International Law Journal*, 27(1), 195.

[58] Barlas, A. (2001). Muslim Women and Sexual Oppression: Reading Liberation from the Quran. *Macalester International:* Vol. 10, Article 15. (pp.118) Available at: http://digitalcommons.macalester.edu/macintl/vol10/iss1/15.

[59] Quran 2:187.

[60] Our gratitude to Dr. Ingrid Mattson for introducing us to this concept, and for her work to eradicate sexual misconduct and spiritual abuse among leadership through the Hurma Porject, hurmaproject.com.

[61] Alahmad, G., and Dekkers, W. (2012). Bodily Integrity and Male Circumcision. *Journal of the Islamic Medical Association of North America*, 44(1).

[62] Mattson, I. (2021). *Spiritual Abuse and the Hurma Project*. Muslim Network TV. Available at: https://www.facebook.com/MuslimNetworkTV/videos/451356129512697/.

[63] Quran 17:70.

[64] Alahmad, G., & Dekkers, W. (2012). Bodily Integrity and Male Circumcision. *Journal of the Islamic Medical Association of North America*, 44(1).

[65] Ibid.

harming oneself or another using emotional, physical, or spiritual violence. A relationship that includes any form of violence, coercion, or abuse is not a safe relationship and ultimately violates the Islamic tradition's calls to honor the human body and integrity.

A Affirmed in Commitment and Fidelity (*Aqd*)

The final component of our RIDHA framework for healthy sexual relationships is grounded in commitment and fidelity. References in *hadith* indicate that sex can be a deeply spiritual and sacred experience as the Prophet shared that "having intercourse with one's wife is charity."[66] In other words, the reward is great. They especially emphasize how rooting intimacy in a marriage can enhance this aspect of sex because marriage has several securities built-in for spouses. As we'll see in more detail later in the section on marriage in Chapter 5, a Muslim marriage begins with a contract (*'aqd*)—an eyes-wide-open agreement covering all sorts of life details - like the amount of *mahr*, financial planning, childcare, caretaking homelife, and so on.

That being said, commitment can take many forms beyond marriage, such as a long-term commitment to another person short of marriage, or to yourself, your religion, your boundaries, and your values regarding sex. Whether you make a commitment to God, your marriage, yourself, your partner, or some combination thereof, it is important to have an awareness of what commitment means to you before engaging in sexual activity.

Fidelity is the notion of being faithful to one's partner. Infidelity is a violation of the commitment made between partners. Therefore, an affair or other arrangement that brings another partner into a relationship without the first partner's knowledge is both a betrayal of the couple's mutual commitment as well breaking the important "H" seal of safety and "I" principle of open, honest communication in the relationship.

As you go through this book, we invite you to try on the RIDHA framework for yourself. Throughout this book, we have provided questions to help you reflect and practice what it feels like to think about healthy relationships in this spiritually-guided way. We will apply this RIDHA framework more deeply in Chapter 5, the chapter about healthy relationships.

On the next page is a short but detailed summary of the RIDHA Framework for you to keep on hand.

---

[66] Omari, H. K., & Chamwama, E. K. (2019). *Comprehensive Sex Education in Kenya: Islamic Perspective.* 2nd Annual International Conference Machakos University, Kenya. Machakos University; Al-Sheha, A. R., & Dabas, M. S. (2001). Islamic Perspective of Sex. Islamic Propagation Office; Hoel, N., & Shaikh, S. D. (2013). Sex as Ibadah: Religion, Gender, and Subjectivity among South African Muslim Women. *Journal of Feminist Studies in Religion*, 29(1): 69-91.

R *Rahma* — Rooted in compassion (*rahma*) and mutual pleasure. The Quran speaks of how God has created people in pairs, putting love and compassion between them, so that they may find tranquility in each other.[67] This means that intimate relationships, and the physical, spiritual, and emotional intimacy and gratification people find in them, are a divine gift—a mercy (*rahma*)—to be cherished and nourished.

I *'ilm* — Informed by communication and knowledge (*'ilm*). Open, honest dialogue and seeking knowledge (*'ilm*) is key between partners to uphold informed consent, build trust, facilitate an ongoing connection and communicate boundaries, needs and desires.

D *aDalah* — Driven by equity and fairness (*'adalah*). All people are created equal and have integrity before God. A relationship which reflects this equality in shared power and privilege by both partners will help create a healthy partnership rooted in fairness (*'adalah*).

H *Hurma* — Housed in safety and security (*hurma*). A relationship should provide each partner with a sense of safety and security (*hurma*). Any threat, or actual acts, of any kind of violence, abuse, or coercion is in conflict with the Islamic ideal of love and mercy between partners.

A *'Aqd* — Affirmed in commitment (*'aqd*) and fidelity. Sexual intimacy in Islam is preceded by a clear agreement (*'aqd*) between the partners, thus affirming their commitment to each other and honoring the reality of sex as a sacred, spiritual, and mutually beneficial experience.

---

[67] Quran 30:21.

Chapter 1 Key Resources

This list is not comprehensive, and for full citations please see the works-cited at the end of the book.

Fiqh and Sharia

- "Advancing America Toward Justice" by Dr. Asifa Quraishi-Landes. (video) The speech is available on youtube on the MPAC national channel.
- "Five myths about Sharia."(article) By Asifa Quraishi-Landes. *The Washington Post*.
- "Legislating Morality and Other Illusions about Islamic Government" (article) by S. Z. M. Siddiqui, &, Asifa Quraishi-Landes In *Locating the Sharī'a*.

Feminism, Islam, Muslims in America

- *Against White Feminism: Notes on Disruption.* By Rafia Zakaria (book).
- *Beyond the Veil: Male-Female Dynamics in Modern Muslim Society* by Fatima Mernissi (book).
- "Gender and Sexuality in Islamic Bioethics." by Dr. Ingrid Mattson. *Islamic Bioethics: Current Issues and Challenges*. Vol 2. (article).
- "An Islamic Perspective on Domestic Violence." By Azizah al-Hibri (article).
- *Muslim American Women on Campus: Undergraduate Social Life and Identity.* By Shabana Mir. (book).
- "Muslim Women and Sexual Oppression: Reading Liberation from the Quran" by Asma Barlas (article).
- *Quran and Woman: Rereading the Sacred Text from a Woman's Perspective.* By amina wadud. (book).

Islam and Sex

- *Sexual Ethics and Islam: Feminist Reflections on Quran, Hadith, and Jurisprudence* by Kecia Ali; Updated second edition (2016). (book)
- *Birth Control and Abortion in Islam* by Muhammad Ibn Adam Al-Kawthari. (book)
- *Sex and Society in Islam* by Basim F. Musallam. (book)
- *A Taste of Honey: Sexuality and Erotology in Islam* by Habeeb Akande. (book)
- Please check out the Muslim Women's League website at **www.mwlusa.org**.

Chapter 2: Sex Ed 101

L. KETHU

In This Chapter	Quick Snapshot
This chapter will cover the basics of sex education—it's a 101 course on your anatomy, sex, reproduction and pregnancy, contraception, and sexually transmitted infections.	

> **REFLECTION**
>
> How did you learn about sex? What do you wish you knew about sex earlier?
>
> _____
>
> _____
>
> _____
>
> _____
>
> _____
>
> _____
>
> _____
>
> _____
>
> _____
>
> _____
>
> _____
>
> _____
>
> _____
>
> _____
>
> _____
>
> _____

What is Sex?

This simple question and variations of it were asked throughout #TheFirstTime survey. Many shared that they had questions because they had not attended formal sex education class. Others shared that they still had questions about their anatomy despite having taken such classes. We also read that while some folks understood the textbook explanation of sex, the mechanics still felt unfamiliar. This finding, while unsurprising given how varied our communities' experiences are with sex education, was critical in setting the tone for moving forward with this book; we knew developing a shared foundation of language and knowledge would be the necessary first step.

This is why, before we talk about sex and healthy sexual relationships, it's important that we cover the basics *before* sexual activity; particularly, **what is sex? What anatomy is involved in sex? How do pregnancy, contraception, and sexually transmitted infections (STIs) work?**

Anatomy

 REFLECTION

What's in a name? Despite the fact that anatomical parts have proper names, it is often the experience of many families to not refer to these parts with their proper names. Instead, families may make up code names or dance around the words (baby in tummy instead of uterus). This can cause confusion, instill shame around one's body, and more importantly, it may make it difficult, especially for children, to communicate to a doctor if something is wrong.

Use this space to reflect on how your family spoke about anatomy. Were there special words for it? How did it make you feel? Has it impacted the way you talk about your body now? What words are commonly used to talk about anatomy and body parts in your native language?

In order to feel comfortable with the idea of sex, it's important to take a step back to get acquainted with the reproductive organs, which are the main body parts involved in sex.

The next page shows illustrations of the male and female reproductive organs. It is important to note that reproductive organs may determine one's biological sex, but they do not determine the gender individuals identify with.[68]

In short, all people have a **bladder**, **urethra**, and **anus**. The bladder captures urine, which is released through the opening called the urethra. The anus is the opening from which the body releases feces.

Some of the anatomy specific to cisgender women and people with vaginas include the uterus, ovary, fallopian tube, and clitoris. The **ovaries** produce eggs, which travel through the fallopian tubes to reach the **uterus**. If it is not fertilized, the egg is released along with the uterine lining through the **vagina**. The **clitoris**, which is a sensitive organ capable of an erection, is located at the end of the vulva and its sole function is sexual pleasure.

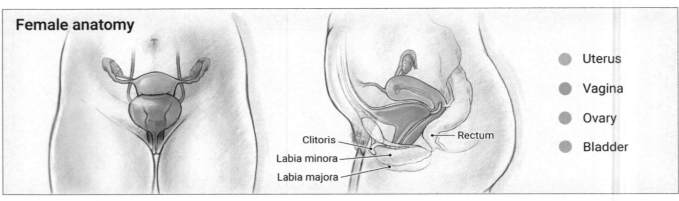

Female anatomy

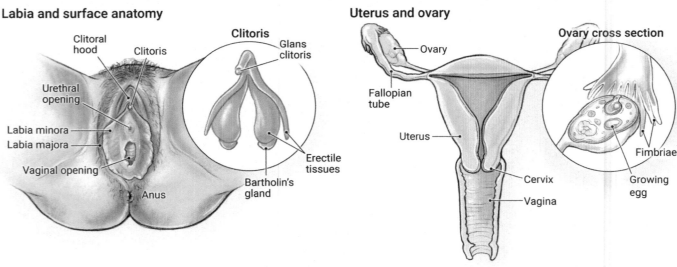

Labia and surface anatomy

Uterus and ovary

[68] Check out our glossary for definitions on gender, sex, gender identity, etc.

38

Some of the notable anatomy specific to men and people with penises are the **testicles (testes)** and the **scrotum**. The scrotum is a pouch that contains the testicles or testes, which are the organs that produce sperm. During ejaculation, the sperm is released through the urethra.

There are some great resources through which you can learn about the reproductive system in greater detail. Our favorite resources include:

- Planned Parenthood
- Scarlateen
- National Coalition for Sexual Health

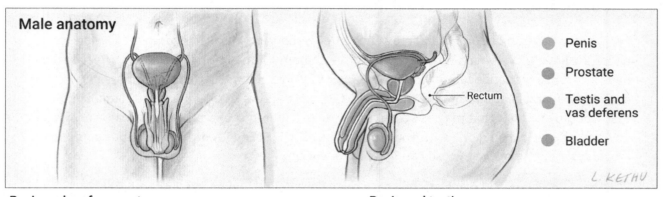

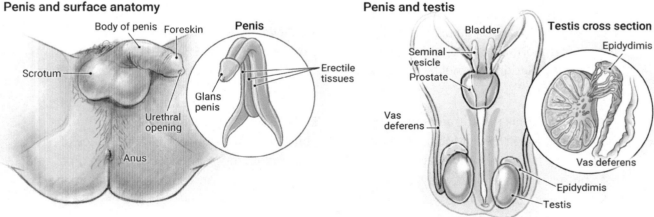

Terms to Know

- Sex is a label that's usually first given by a doctor based upon the genes, hormones, and body parts (like genitals) you're born with. It goes on your birth certificate and describes your body as female or male.

- Gender is how society thinks we should look, think, and act as girls and women and boys and men. Each culture has beliefs and informal roles about how people should act based on their gender. For example, many cultures expect and encourage men to be more aggressive than women.

- Gender identity is how you feel inside and how you show your gender through clothing, behavior, and personal appearance. It's a feeling that begins early in life.

Female Genital Mutilation (FGM) refers to cutting or removal of some parts or all of the outer parts of the female genitalia for non-medical reasons. There are 4 different types of FGM.[69]

- **Type 1** is known as the clitoridectomy, which is the partial or total removal of the clitoris.
- **Type 2**, excision, refers to the removal of the clitoris and inner labia, and in some cases the outer labia is removed as well.
- **Type 3** is known as infibulation. This is when the vaginal opening is sealed, leaving little room for menstruation. Type 3 can also include a clitoridectomy or excision.
- **Type 4** refers to any harmful procedure to the genitalia that includes pricking, piercing, cutting, or burning.

People who have undergone (FGM) may encounter feelings of physical incompleteness due to no longer having every part of their reproductive anatomy. It may be more difficult to feel desire, have sex, and experience full sexual pleasure, but this does not mean that it is impossible.[70] When dealing with and healing from the trauma of FGM, it is important to connect with organizations that work to end FGM that may be able to refer you to a therapist and other resources that can help you make sense of being one with your body again. The U.S. End FGM/C Network has compiled resources, ranging from advocacy and law to education.[71]

FGM predates Islam and can be traced back to ancient Egyptian customs and traditions, and some cultural communities believe that it can reduce a woman's sexual appetite and limit the possibility of having sex before marriage. While the practice is often misappropriated with Islam, it is important to note that FGM is not a religious requirement. It is actually in violation of Islamic principles and cannot be justified under any circumstances, the range of legal positions notwithstanding.[72]

Specifically, FGM is in contradiction with Islam's "Do No Harm" principle, and also contradicts *hadiths* from the Prophet Muhammad (peace be upon him) that highlight the importance of pleasure and intimacy between partners. It is also a direct infringement of women and girls' basic human rights as defined by the UN Charter of Human Rights, including their right to life. FGM has severe health and psychological complications for women and girls and can lead to severe complications including infertility, urinary tract infections, menstrual problems, sexual dysfunction, still birth, complications during labor, and psychological trauma such as PTSD, anxiety, and depression.

---

[69] World Health Organization. *Types of female genital mutilation.* Available at: https://www.who.int/teams/sexual-and-reproductive-health-and-research-(srh)/areas-of-work/female-genital-mutilation/types-of-female-genital-mutilation.

[70] Akande, H. (2018). *Kunyaza: The Secret to Female Pleasure.* Rabaah Publishers. pg 63.

[71] U.S. End FGM/C Network. (2021). *Resources.* Available at: https://endfgmnetwork.org/resources/.

[72] Al-Awa, M. S. *FGM in the Context of Islam.* UNFPA Egypt. Available at: https://egypt.unfpa.org/sites/default/files/pub-pdf/d9174a63-2960-459b-9f78-b33ad795445e.pdf; Fatwas against FGM. Stop FGM Middle East. Available at: http://www.stopfgmmideast.org/fatwas-against-fgm/; Muslim Women's League. (1995). *An Islamic Perspective on Violence against Women.* Available at: https://www.mwlusa.org/topics/violence&harrassment/violence.html; Akande, H. (2015). *A Taste of Honey: Sexuality and Erotology in Islam.* Rabaah Publishers. pg 83.

HEART

REFLECTION

How did your family approach the topic of sex (or not)? What about your community? Your school? Your faith?

 TRY IT OUT

When you are safe and alone in the privacy of your own room, take a mirror and familiarize yourself with your anatomy. What do you notice? While the media often portrays ideals around our body parts, keep in mind that every body is different, and these parts can come in all different shapes and sizes.

Types of Sex

Sex is an act between consenting individuals. This means that the people involved have agreed to everything that is happening and have the freedom to stop whenever they want. People choose to have sex for many reasons, including but not limited to, fulfilling a tenet of marriage, expressing their love and desire for someone, attaining physical gratification, or starting a family.

There are many types of sexual activity. Perhaps the most commonly described type is vaginal intercourse, that is, the insertion of a penis (or another object) into a vagina. Aside from vaginal intercourse, there are other types of sexual activity, for example:

Kissing (a.k.a. making out): When a set of lips is pressed against another person's lips or other body parts.

Oral Sex (a.k.a. eating out, giving a blow job, going down): When one person's mouth is used to stimulate another person's genitals.

Anal Sex: When a penis (or alternatively, a sex toy or fingers) is inserted into the anus.

Manual Sex:
- When a person stimulates their own genitals, sometimes using visual or auditory aid (masturbation).
- When a person stimulates someone else's genitals, sometimes using a visual or auditory aid (digital sex).

Virtual Sex: When sexual arousal, stimulation, or climax is achieved by sending or receiving sexually explicit message via digital communication (examples of virtual sex can include cybersex, sexting, phone sex).

- **Cybersex:** Sending someone a sexually suggestive text message or photograph via the Internet, such as instant relay chat services, roleplay games, webcams, or email.

- **Sexting:** Sending a sexually suggestive text message or photograph to someone's mobile phone via text messaging or mobile application (i.e. Snapchat, Instagram, or WhatsApp).

- **Phone sex:** Discussing and engaging in sexual activity through self pleasure while on the phone with another person.

These various types of sex can result in **orgasm**. An orgasm is when one feels a climaxing of sexual excitement and can result in powerful pleasure sensations, involuntary muscle spasming, and/or a discharge of genital fluid, such as semen or vaginal secretions. While every sexual experience *can* result in orgasm, **it is not always the case**. There is no shortage of literature on sexual pleasure and orgasms and how to achieve them, and we hope to provide you with our favorite resources throughout the book.

While sex is a natural and pleasurable part of life, it can also have numerous unexpected physical, emotional, social, and spiritual consequences. Specifically, sex may result in becoming pregnant, contracting a sexually transmitted infection (STI), or shifting dynamics within romantic relationships. In communities that are resistant to talking about sex openly, it may take time to unlearn the idea that sex is an act that is shameful, even within marriage. Due to this, access to comprehensive, medically accurate, and culturally-sensitive sexual health information and resources can help make you feel more equipped to make informed decisions as well as address any consequences that may result.

REFLECTION

Do you know how to have sex? How did you get this information and from whom?

Mechanics of Penetrative Sex

Despite having access to sexual health information, often the mechanics of sex are hard to wrap one's brain around until actually experiencing it. While nothing can replace lived experience, we have tried our best to name some of the key aspects of sex below.

How the body gets 'ready' for sex (intercourse)

Most of the time, couples don't jump straight to sex. There are activities leading up to it, which are called **foreplay**. Foreplay can include but is not limited to: kissing, touching one another's genitals, sharing fantasies, using sex toys, etc.[73] Foreplay can add to sexual excitement and increase lubrication to help with sexual intercourse.

As such, this can result in increased **vaginal lubrication** for cisgender women, or those with a vagina. During sexual arousal, the amount of normal vaginal lubrication increases to help reduce any friction or irritation.[74] Vaginal lubrication can also result from **clitoral stimulation**, which is the process of stimulating the clitoris through touch or using a toy. The clitoris is responsible for sexual pleasure when stimulated.

For men, or those with a penis, this can look like an **erection**. An erection is when blood flows to the penis faster than it flows out, and makes the spongy tissue in the penis swell (making it hard).[75]

Having sex (vaginal intercourse):

When individuals reach a point during foreplay where both are at heightened stimulation (erected penis and clitoral stimulation), this usually leads to the penis (or a sex toy) penetrating the vagina during intercourse. This can ultimately result in ejaculation from the penis. **Ejaculation** is when a sticky liquid substance (ejacualte/cum/semen) shoots out of the penis when it gets hard and is sexually aroused, leading to an orgasm. Women can also achieve orgasm through penetrative sex, though this is not always the case. Moreover, women can also ejaculate through clitoral stimulation. That said, sexual intercourse also may not result in an orgasm for either person, nor is it always the goal.[76]

In Your Own Words   #THEFIRSTTIME SURVEY RESPONDENT

"Really, [I'd like more information on] the basics of having sex, for an adult. Most things out there are geared at teens. Some basic medical advice—like knowing what a yeast infection is, etc. (Had my first a couple months after marriage, and the best theory was that sometimes new activities can trigger it). What is normal/not normal--could help some who accidentally contracts an STI etc. Also, common issues people may have, and solutions to them (ie, painful sex, knowing when to penetrate, etc.) Oh! and maybe a simple checklist of things to have on hand when having sex (didn't know it would be that messy lol!)."

---

[73] WebMD Editorial Reviewers. (2021). *What is foreplay?* Available at: https://www.webmd.com/sex/what-is-foreplay.
[74] Villnes, Z. (2019). What to Know About Vaginal Lubrication. *Medical News Today.* Available at: https://www.medicalnewstoday.com/articles/326450#_noHeaderPrefixedContent.
[75] Planned Parenthood. *What's the Deal with Erections, Ejaculations, and Wet Dreams?* Available at: https://www.plannedparenthood.org/learn/teens/puberty/whats-deal-erections-ejaculation-and-wet-dreams.
[76] Ibid.

Reproduction and Pregnancy

In 2017, HEART partnered with OB-GYNs at the University of Illinois at Chicago to learn more about the health of self-identified Muslim women ages 18-45 in the United States. We asked them about their reproductive health knowledge, their attitudes, and their behaviors around sexual and reproductive health and garnered over 730 responses from women across the country. Findings from this study affirmed some of the themes that emerged in #TheFirstTime survey. These findings include evidence that more than half of Muslim women don't understand what happens during the reproductive cycle, or the most effective form of birth control. In addition, more than a third of participants did not have accurate knowledge about how sexually transmitted infections (STIs) are transmitted.[77]

 DID YOU KNOW?

While many resources focus on traditional penile-vaginal sex as leading to pregnancy, there are other ways to get pregnant that don't require traditional penis and vaginal sex. Some people choose to get pregnant through sperm donors, while others may need assistance getting pregnant using reproductive assisted technology like in vitro fertilization (IVF).[78]

The Menstrual Cycle, Ovulation, and Pregnancy

The menstrual cycle is the duration between one period to the next; the average cycle is 28 days, but regular cycles can range from 21-40 days. This does not include people who have endometriosis,[79] polycystic ovary syndrome (PCOS),[80] or other reproductive health issues whose cycles may vary. The menstrual cycle is controlled by hormones, and it is during this time that the uterus prepares for a potential pregnancy. In the first half of the cycle, an egg grows and is released from one of the ovaries. It then travels up one of the fallopian tubes in a process known as ovulation. Ovulation typically occurs between the twelfth and fourteenth day of the menstrual cycle. In the fallopian tubes, the egg waits for potential sperm. Meanwhile, the uterus creates a tissue lining within itself where the egg and sperm will potentially attach. A person cannot get pregnant without the presence of sperm. If no sperm penetrates the egg, the unfertilized egg and the uterine lining are shed, resulting in a **menstrual period**. After this period, the cycle begins again by releasing another egg and rebuilding the uterine lining.

Pregnancy can occur anytime during a menstrual cycle; however, a person is most fertile during their ovulation period, specifically when the egg has already been released into the fallopian tube. If sperm enters the vagina during ovulation, it will seek out the egg in order to fertilize it. Once the sperm enters the reproductive tract, it can survive for up to 5 days and has the potential to fertilize an egg that has yet to be released. After fertilization, the egg, fused with the sperm, is now called a **zygote**. The cells begin to multiply, and the zygote travels to the uterus. About eight to ten days later, the zygote embeds in the uterine

[77] Safdar, A. (2017). *Sexual Health Knowledge and Practices of Muslim American Women.* Blog post. Available at: https://hearttogrow.org/sexual-health-knowledge-and-practices-of-muslim-american-women/.

[78] American Pregnancy Association. (2021). *In Vitro Fertilization.* Available at: https://americanpregnancy.org/getting-pregnant/infertility/in-vitro-fertilization/.

[79] Office on Women's Health. *Endometriosis.* Available at: https://www.womenshealth.gov/a-z-topics/endometriosis.

[80] Office on Women's Health. *PCOS.* Available at: https://www.womenshealth.gov/a-z-topics/polycystic-ovary-syndrome.

wall. The zygote is now referred to as an **embryo**, and menstruation will cease for the duration of the pregnancy.

A full-term pregnancy lasts 40 weeks, and the weeks are grouped into three trimesters. Check out the Baby Center and Chapter 4 later in this book.

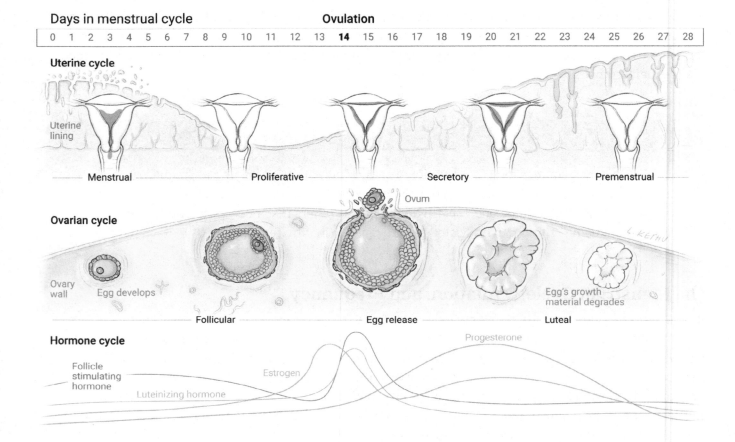

Contraception

Contraception, also known as birth control or family planning, is a means of preventing pregnancy, either temporarily or permanently, and can also protect one from contracting a sexually transmitted infection (STI).

REFLECTION

What do you know about contraception?

What are some attitudes and beliefs in your faith community or cultural tradition about contraception?

What methods of contraception have you heard about?

Is there a mechanism or system for sharing information in your community regarding contraception?

What factors are important to you as you decide on what contraception is best for you?

While there is a difference of opinion and a wide range of rulings on contraception, most Islamic scholars would agree that contraception or family planning is not in conflict with Islamic guidelines.[81] Yet, misinformation that contraception is impermissible because it interferes with God's will or that it can cause fertility issues in the future can be one of the reasons why the idea of contraceptive use is sometimes frowned upon in faith communities. Contraception is a useful solution for those who want to prevent pregnancy or sexually transmitted infections (STIs).

There are many forms of contraceptives, and they all work in different ways to prevent pregnancy. This includes:

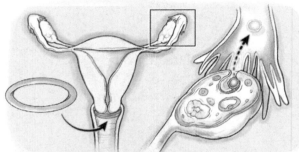

Prevent ovulation so no egg is released into the fallopian tube (i.e. Pill, Patch, Ring, Shot)

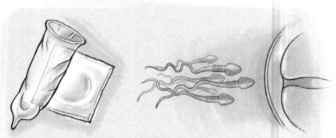

Prevent the sperm from being emitted into the vagina (barrier methods such as condoms, dental dams, gloves)

Decrease the sperm's motility to reach the egg (IUD [hormonal and non-hormonal], spermicide, sponge, cervical cap, diaphragm)

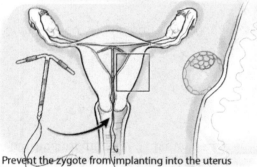

Prevent the zygote from implanting into the uterus (IUD [hormonal and non-hormonal)

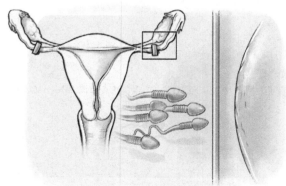

Permanently cut off the travel routes of the egg and sperm (sterilization, Essure, tubal ligation, vasectomy)

[81] Roudi-Fahimi F. (2004). *Islam and Family Planning*. Population Reference Bureau. Available at: https://www.prb.org/wp-content/uploads/2004/09/IslamFamilyPlanning.pdf

TRY IT OUT

Bedsider.org is a website that offers an in-depth analysis on contraceptive options, their cost, availability, and side effects. It even allows you to compare methods. Check it out to determine what birth control methods would be best for you as a way to prepare yourself to speak to your healthcare provider.

DID YOU KNOW?

Doctors may prescribe oral contraception for other, non-pregnancy prevention medical reasons as well. Oral contraception can be used to manage reproductive health issues such as irregular periods, endometriosis, and polycystic ovary syndrome. It can also be used to manage acne.

In Your Own Words #THEFIRSTTIME SURVEY RESPONDENT

What advice would you give to your friend who is going to have sex for the first time?

"Have they thought about birth control and talked about it with their partner? I would tell her to be sure that she's not being pressured into doing something she doesn't want to or in a place she is uncomfortable in. I would advise her to be sure to have a conversation with the partner about the experience before and after to understand what the expectations are and to have a honest conversation about likes and dislikes, and levels of comfort. I would tell her to be herself, and that anxiety is natural but to enjoy the process."

Types of Contraception

H Hormonal contraceptive
N Non-hormonal contraceptive
X No STI protection
Y Protects against STIs

There are temporary and permanent methods of contraception. All contraceptive methods prevent pregnancy from occurring with varying degrees of effectiveness. Not all contraceptive methods, however, protect against sexually transmitted infections (STIs). As such, it may be helpful to use more than one method of contraception if you want to protect yourself from both pregnancy and STIs. We have provided a review of the various types of contraception below.[82]

ORAL CONTRACEPTIVE (BIRTH CONTROL PILL) **H** **X**

91-99% Effective

How it works: Protects against pregnancy by preventing ovulation. The pill contains the estrogen and/or progesterone hormones.

Usage: Must be taken daily at a specified time.

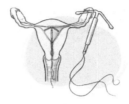

HORMONAL INTRAUTERINE DEVICE (IUD) **H** **X**

99% Effective

How it works: Prevents fertilization by thickening the cervical mucus, blocking and trapping sperm.

Usage: To be used for 3-5 years. Can be used discreetly.

PATCH **H** **X**

91-99% Effective

How it works: Prevents pregnancy by stopping ovulation. This patch is worn on part of the body (upper arm, buttocks, abdomen, or back).

Usage: Must be changed weekly.

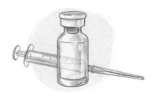

INJECTION **H** **X**

94-99% Effective

How it works: Protects against pregnancy by preventing ovulation.

Usage: You must get a shot every 3 months. Can be used discreetly.

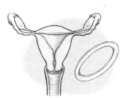

VAGINAL RING **H** **X**

91-99% Effective

How it works: The vaginal ring is inserted into the vagina and releases hormones to prevent ovulation from occuring.

Usage: Must be changed every 3 weeks.

ARM IMPLANT **H** **X**

99% Effective

How it works: Prevents fertilization by thickening the cervical mucus, blocking and trapping sperm, and blocking the ovaries from releasing an egg.

Usage: To be used for up to 3 years. Can be used discreetly.

---

[82] Check out HEART's video on birth control choices: https://www.youtube.com/watch?v=aLknFhVO7b4. Another great resource is Planned Parenthood, which also offers in-depth information on various types of birth control and it is available at: "Birth Control," https://www.plannedparenthood.org/learn/birth-control.

FEMALE CONDOM

79-95% Effective

How it works: Made from latex, and inserted into the vaginal canal to prevent semen from entering the womb.

Usage: To be used each time you have sex.

MALE CONDOM

85-98% Effective

How it works: A thin barrier, usually made from latex, worn over the penis as a barrier between the penis and the vagina (or mouth) to prevent semen from entering the body.

Usage: To be used each time you have sex. Scarleteen has an excellent user manual.[16]

DIAPHRAGM

94% Effective

How it works: A dome-shaped cup that fits over the opening to the cervix to serve as a barrier between the vagina and the penis.

Usage: To be used each time you have sex.

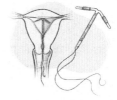

COPPER INTRAUTERINE DEVICE (IUD)

99.9% Effective

How it works: Inserted into the uterus, and uses copper to repel sperm. It is effective for up to ten years.

Usage: To be used for up to 10 years. Can be used discreetly. Can be expensive.

SPERMICIDE

70-80% Effective

How it works: A substance that kills sperm cells before they can touch the egg. Must be inserted vaginally before sex.

Usage: To be used each time you have sex.

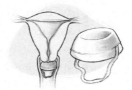

CONTRACEPTIVE SPONGE

88% Effective

How it works: Inserted vaginally, and stops the sperm from passing through the cervix and entering the uterus.

Usage: To be used each time you have sex.

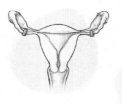
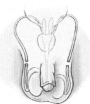

PERMANENT STERILIZATION   Over 99% Effective

How it works: A procedure that involves cutting, burning, or removing the fallopian tubes. This procedure is not reversible. A vasectomy, which can be reversible, is a procedure that blocks semen from reaching sperm being ejaculated.

Usage: One-time procedure

83 Corinna, Heather. (2019). Condom Basics: A User's Manual. *Scarleteen*. Available at: https://www.scarleteen.com/article/sexual_health/condom_basics_a_users_manual.

Fertility Awareness

Outside of hormonal and non-hormonal birth control options, there are also behavioral methods of birth control such as abstinence and fertility awareness. Abstinence refers to the choice to not engage in any sexual activity and is 100% effective in preventing STIs and pregnancy. Fertility awareness refers to natural family planning methods that work by observing and keeping track of your body's different fertility indicators throughout your menstrual cycle.

These methods include tracking your cycle in addition to tracking your ovulation, body temperature, cervix placement, and cervical mucus consistency.[84] Natural family planning also involves "pulling out" or the rhythm method. This method works to varying degrees, but at most, it is 76-88% effective at preventing pregnancy; and further, it does not prevent STIs.

POINT OF INTEREST

While not a reliable method of birth control, breastfeeding can disrupt your cycle and delay ovulation. This means it is possible that you may not get pregnant while breastfeeding. Because this method is not a guaranteed method of birth control, if you do not want to get pregnant again, be sure to have another more reliable method of contraception ready.

When you know your fertile window, you will be able to determine when to have protected or unprotected sex, or no sex at all depending on whether or not you're trying to plan or avoid pregnancy. It takes about 3-6 menstrual cycles or longer with daily recording keeping to recognize your fertility indicators, but keep in mind that factors such as stress, illness, travel, breastfeeding, and other events may disrupt your cycle. These methods can make you more aware of your fertility and can help recognize abnormal vaginal secretions and how to plan for or avoid pregnancy. It does not involve using chemicals, hormones or devices, and there are no physical side effects. Fertility awareness methods are more effective when used in conjunction with each other.

THE BASAL BODY TEMPERATURE (BBT) METHOD

STI Protection: No
Usage: Daily

Basal body temperature (BBT) must be taken every morning before getting out of bed using a thermometer that is specifically designed for that.

Each daily temperature reading should be recorded to check for changes in temperature during ovulation. When ovulation just occurs, the BBT may increase slightly (about 1/2 degree F or 0.3 C). If one is avoiding pregnancy, it is important to abstain from unprotected sex or use alternative forms of contraception for 3 days after the temperature rise.

If one plans on getting pregnant, these 3 days are the most ideal to have sex.

---

[84] There are also apps, such as Natural Cycles (which has been FDA approved), that help you track your period and ovulation that in turn can notify you when you can and cannot have unprotected sex to either get/not get pregnant. Please note that in a post Roe V Wade world, that the use of apps may collect your data and therefore be a safety concern. With these types of apps, one must also be aware that being able to monitor your cycle requires lots of practice and persistent accounting of your cycle to check patterns, as no app will be perfect.

THE CERVICAL MUCUS METHOD

STI Protection: No
Usage: Daily

The color, amount, and texture of the cervical mucus change depending on one's menstrual cycle stage, especially during ovulation.

Cervical mucus must be looked at and felt daily in order to be tracked accurately.

When the egg begins to ripen, there is an increase in mucus creation, and the mucus is usually white, yellow, or cloudy, and sticky.

Mucus secreted right before ovulation and is clear and very slippery; this is when one is most likely to get pregnant.

THE CALENDAR METHOD

STI Protection: No
Usage: Daily

The calendar method predicts fertile days through tracking one's menstrual cycle lengths. In order to utilize the calendar method as birth control, one must track their menstrual cycle for at least 6 straight cycles. The calendar method will be inaccurate if your cycles are all shorter than 27 days.

In order to predict fertile days during one's current menstrual cycle, identify the shortest cycle recorded. From there, subtract 18 days from the total days in that cycle. The first day marked will be the first fertile day. This means that if a person's shortest cycle is 28 days, the first fertile day will be Day 10.

In order to predict the last fertile day of one's cycle, identify the longest cycle recorded and subtract 11 from that number. If one's longest cycle is 32 days, then the last fertile day is Day 21.

The calendar method predicts safe and unsafe days for sexual activity, but cannot necessarily predict when one is fertile.

THE STANDARD DAYS METHOD

STI Protection: No
Usage: Daily

The standard days method is similar to the calendar method, but can only be used if a person's cycle is 26-32 days in length.

With this method, one cannot have unprotected sex during day 8 through day 19 of a their cycle.

Sexually Transmitted Infections (STIs)

Sexually transmitted infections, also known as STIs, are infections transmitted through sexual contact and are caused by bacteria, viruses, or parasites.[85] Unlike pregnancy, STIs can be passed on from sexual activity that involves the mouth, anus, vagina, or penis. STIs are generally spread through sexual activity that brings a person in contact with bodily fluids from a person who has an STI. They may also be spread when one person's genitals come into contact with another person's skin or mucous membranes. These membranes are mucous-secreting glands, and it includes those lining the mouth, nasal passages, vagina, and urethra (in both men and women). These membranes are mostly involved in absorption and secretion. *Simply touching or interacting with a person with an STI infection won't give you the infection, neither will sharing eating utensils, holding hands, or using public toilets.* However, your chances of getting an STI are increased if you are sexually active (especially without barrier protection such as a condom), if you have more than one sexual partner, if you have a sexual partner who has or has had multiple sexual partners, or through needle sharing during injection drug use. It is important to note that not everyone with an STI displays symptoms of illness.

Here are other methods through which STIs can be spread:

- direct contact with open sores;
- a mother to her baby before or during birth, or during breastfeeding;
- through semen, blood, or vaginal secretions.

STIs that are transmitted via childbirth and can cause harm to a fetus, such as infant blindness deafness, heart defects, miscarriage, or even death.

Who can get STIs?

People of all genders and sexual orientations can contract STIs. Although there are many myths and stigmas associated with contracting, preventing, and treating an STI, it is true that people with female reproductive systems are more susceptible to contracting STIs due to the anatomy of this reproductive system.[86] They are also more likely to be asymptomatic when they have STIs. This doesn't mean that only people with female reproductive organs are at risk; all genders can contract and spread STIs. If you are sexually active, the best way to protect yourself from STIs is to use condoms or dental dams[87] and learn the facts about different types of STIs. Before engaging in sexual activity, ask your partner(s) about the last time they got tested and which STIs they got tested for. Not all medical visits will screen for all STIs. Ask for a comprehensive STI testing exam if you are not sure, and talk to your health care provider and partner about STI testing.[88]

[85] Familydoctor.org editorial staff. (2019). *Sexually Transmitted Infections (STIs)*. Available at: https://familydoctor.org/condition/sexually-transmitted-infections-stis/.
[86] Asha, A. (2020). *Women And STIs*. American Sexual Health Association. Available at:http://old.ashasexualhealth.org/sexual-health/womens-health/women-and-stis/.
[87] a piece of latex or similar material used for protection against direct mouth to genital or mouth to anal contact during oral sex.
[88] HEART. (2020). *HEART to HEART STIs*. [video] Available at: https://www.youtube.com/watch?v=KFELpk1wsd8&feature=youtu.be.

Types of STIs

There are many types of STIs, which we will introduce you to on the next few pages. Please note that this is still just an overview, and a great resource to learn more in detail is Planned Parenthood and the Centers for Disease Control and Prevention.[89] STI definitions can also vary from country to country so it is also important to look at local resources depending on where you reside.

There are three main categories of STIs: bacterial, viral, and parasitic. **Parasitic STIs**, although uncomfortable, rarely have long term effects and are easiest to treat. **Bacterial STIs** may or may not be symptomatic, are typically easy to treat, usually with antibiotics. If left untreated, a person may experience moderate to severe long term effects, such as infertility, pelvic inflammatory disease, and painful sex. The final category of STIs are **viral STIs**, which are more serious infections and have higher risk for negative health outcomes. Currently, while many viral STIs can be managed or controlled, most still do not have a cure.

BACTERIAL VAGINOSIS   BACTERIAL INFECTION

Type of infection:
Bacterial

Management:
Antibiotics, though BV may go away without treatment

Symptoms
Unusual discharge, pain, itching or burning in or outside the vagina, burning when urinating, strong odor, especially after sex

More Information
Researchers are unsure of the cause of BV and how it is linked to sex, but women who are sexually active have a higher chance of getting it.

CHLAMYDIA   BACTERIAL INFECTION

Type of infection:
Bacterial

Management:
Antibiotics

Symptoms
Women: Painful urination, abnormal/unusual discharge, bleeding between periods, painful periods, abdominal pain and fever, burning or itching in and around the vagina, painful sex

Men: Abnormal/unusual discharge, painful urination, pain and swelling around testicles, burning and itching around opening of the penis

More Information
Chlamydia is asymtomatic in 70% of girls and women and 50% of boys and men.

If left untreated:

Women: Can cause pelvic inflammatory disease, which can damage the fallopian tubes; may also cause infertility and increase risk of ectopic pregnancy and lead to premature births.

Men: Can cause an infection of the urethra and/or testes, can also cause an inflammation of the rectum.

[89] Planned Parenthood. *STDs.* Available at: https://www.plannedparenthood.org/learn/stds-hiv-safer-sex; Centers for Disease Control and Prevention. *STD Prevention Success Stories from Around the Country.* Available at: https://www.cdc.gov/std/default.htm.

Sexually Transmitted Infections

GONORRHEA `BACTERIAL INFECTION`

Type of infection:
Bacterial

Management:
Antibiotics

Symptoms
Women: Unusual discharge, painful urination, bleeding between periods

Men: Unusual discharge, painful urination, testicular pain

More Information
Gonorrhea is asymptomatic in up to 80% of women and 10-15% of men.

Complications are similar to chlamydia.

PELVIC INFLAMMATORY DISEASE (PID) `BACTERIAL INFECTION`

Type of infection:
Bacterial

Management:
Antibiotics

Symptoms
Abdominal pain, fever, painful sex, unusual discharge or bad odor from the vagina, bleeding between periods. PID does not affect men or people with male reproductive organs because it is an infection of the fallopian tubes and uterus

More Information
The likelihood of getting PID increases if you have an untreated STI, have multiple sex partners, or have a partner who has multiple sex partners.

SYPHILIS `BACTERIAL INFECTION`

Type of infection:
Bacterial

Management:
Antibiotics

Symptoms
Symptoms are divided into different stages: primary (sores), secondary (skin rash and fever), latent (no symptoms), and tertiary (severe medical problems such as blindness, difficulty walking, cardiovascular problems, even death)

More Information
Can spread to the brain and nervous system during any of the stages.

GENITAL HERPES `VIRAL INFECTION`

Management:
Treatment is available to remove sores, but there is no cure for the infection.

Symptoms
Painful sores on the genital region (and mouth if transmitted through oral sex)

More Information
Also makes one more susceptible to HIV.

You can get genital herpes from your sex partner even if they don't have a visible sore.

H.I.V.   `VIRAL INFECTION`

Management:
Though incurable, treatment is available to inhibit the virus and many HIV patients live extremely fulfilling and long lives.

Symptoms
There are 3 stages of HIV, Stage 1 is 2-4 weeks post infection and yields flu-like symptoms. Stage 2 is the latency period and has no symptoms. Stage 3 is when the infection progresses to AIDS and includes rapid weight loss, tiredness, mouth sores, genitals and anus, memory loss and depression.

More Information
HIV destroys a key element in one's immune system, CD4 cells, which fight infections. With a decrease in CD4 cells, one's immune system is compromised and at great risk for many infections. When an HIV-infected person reaches a CD4 count that is extremely low, they have progressed to AIDS.

GENITAL WARTS   `VIRAL INFECTION`

Management:
Treatment is available to remove warts, but there is no cure for the infection.

Symptoms
Warts found on the genital region

More Information
Caused by the human papilloma virus (HPV). While there are over 100 types of of HPV, we know that Types 6 and 11 cause most genital warts. Gardasil is a vaccine that reduces the incidence of cervical cancer by preventing a woman from contracting the HPV infection (specifically types 6, 11, 16, and 18), and this vaccine is most effective when given at ages 11-12.

HEPATITIS B   `VIRAL INFECTION`

Management:
Treatment of hepatitis depends on how long one has been infected. If one seeks treatment within the first few days, emergency treatment can stop the infection.

If infected for a short period (under 6 months), one may only need treatment to relieve symptoms as the body fights off the infection. If it's been over 6 months (chronic hepatitis), then the only treatment available is to manage the virus in order to lessen liver damage.

Symptoms
Flu-like symptoms, loss of appetite, jaundice (yellowing of eyes and skin), stomach pain, diarrhea

More Information
Hepatitis can also be passed through injection drug use. Chronic hepatitis has been linked to liver cancer as well.

TRICHOMONIASIS   `PARASITIC INFECTION`

Management:
Antibiotics

Symptoms
Women: Discolored and unusual smelling vaginal discharge, painful urination, and vaginal bleeding

Men: Itching or irritation inside the penis; burning after urination or ejaculation; Discharge from the penis

More Information
Can cause genital inflammation that makes it easier for one to get infected with or pass the HIV virus.

PUBIC LICE (CRABS) | PARASITIC INFECTION |

Management:
Insecticide cream

Symptoms
Intense itching in pubic area

More Information
It may take several weeks after the infection before pubic lice appear.

 **TRY IT OUT**

Being exposed to STIs can be a scary experience, and it is always comforting to have the necessary information ahead of time to be prepared for a time you or a friend might need it. Check out gettested.cdc.gov to get familiar with local testing sites.

Now that we've discussed the biology of sex, anatomy, birth control, and STIs, the next chapter will provide a more in-depth discussion of consent and the emotional, relational, and spiritual aspects of sex.

Chapter 2 Key Resources

This list is not comprehensive, and for full citations please see the works-cited at the end of the book.

Sex

- Planned Parenthood (website) **www.plannedparenthood.com.**
- Scarlateen (website) **www.scarlateen.com.**
- National Coalition for Sexual Health (website) **www.nationalcoalitionforsexualhealth.org.**

Anatomy

- *Our Bodies, Ourselves* by Boston Women's Health Collective.
- Planned Parenthood (website) www.plannedparenthood.org. More information on anatomy can be found under the health and wellness and sexual and reproductive anatomy tabs.
- Scarlateen (website) at www.scarleteen.com Recommended articles include:
  - "With Pleasure: A View of Whole Sexual Anatomy for Every Body" by Heather Corinna.
  - "Innies & Outies: The Penis, Testes and More" by Hanne Blank and Heather Corinna.
  - "Innies & Outies: The Vagina, Clitoris, Uterus and More" by Heather Corinna.

Female Genital Mutilation (FGM)

- End FGM/C US Network (website) **https://endfgmnetwork.org/resources.** Contains a list of websites, organizations, and articles about FGM.
- UN Populations Fund (website) **www.unfpa.org.** Check out the FGM FAQs page for more information on FGM.
- Sahiyo (website), **https://sahiyo.com/.**

Menstrual Cycle

- Scarlateen website at **www.scarleteen.com.**
  - Recommended article: "Quickies: Periods and the Menstrual Cycle" by Sam Wall and Heather Corinna.

Pregnancy:

- Planned Parenthood (website) **https://www.plannedparenthood.org/learn/pregnancy.** More information can be found under the "learn" tab.
- Baby Center (website) **www.babycenter.com.**
- Scarlateen (website) **www.scarleteen.com.** Recommended articles include:
  - "Human Reproduction: A Seafarer's Guide" by Heather Corinna with Isabella Rotman.

Contraception

- Bedsider (website) **https://www.bedsider.org/methods**. Includes a comprehensive resource on contraceptive methods.
- Planned Parenthood (website) **https://www.plannedparenthood.org/learn/birth-control**. More information can be found under the learn and birth control tabs.
- HEART's YouTube video on birth control FAQ. Search "HEART to Heart: Birth Control FAQs" on YouTube.
- Scarlateen (website) **www.scarleteen.com**. Recommended articles include: "Condom Basics: A User's Manual" by Heather Corinna.

Fertility Awareness

- National Health Services UK (website) **www.nhs.uk**. More information on natural family planning can be found under the Health A-Z tab, under "your contraception guide."
- American College of Obstetricians and Gynecologists (website) **www.acog.org/womens-health**. More information on fertility awareness can be found under the "Fertility Awareness-Based Methods of Family Planning FAQ."

Sexually Transmitted Infections (STIs)

- Centers for Disease Control and Prevention (website) **https://www.cdc.gov/std/default.htm**.
- Visit the Planned Parenthood (website) **https://www.plannedparenthood.org/learn/stds-hiv-safer-sex**.
- Centers for Disease Control and Prevention **https://gettested.cdc.gov/** for more information on STI screening.
- Planned Parenthood (website) **https://www.plannedparenthood.org/online-tools/should-i-get-tested** for more information on STI screening.
- HEART's YouTube video on STIs. Search "HEART to Heart STIs on YouTube for the video.
- RAHMA (website) **https://haverahma.org/**. RAHMA's mission is to reach all HIV+ Muslims in America.

Chapter 3: What to Expect

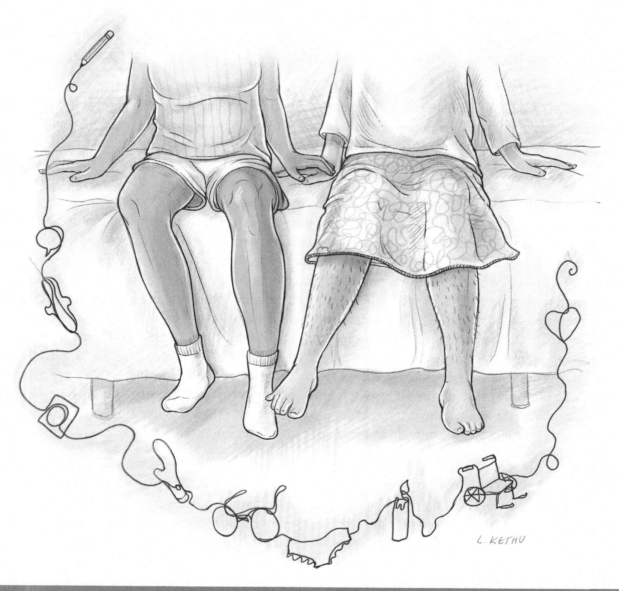

L. KETHU

In This Chapter	**Quick Snapshot**

You may be reading this book well before the first time you have sex, as you prepare for your first time, or after you've already had sex. That's perfectly ok. It's good to be informed and prepared for whatever stage of life you are in. This information will give you tools to make communication, consent, faith, and pleasure the center of your future sexual activity.

Beginning with Abstinence

We begin this chapter with a discussion on abstinence because everyone begins being in a state of abstinence, until they are not. Whenever you choose to have sex (or not), this decision should be an active, empowered, informed one, and not a result of fear or pressure. This section reclaims sexual decision-making as a *tool of empowerment*—both for those who choose to abstain as well for those who engage in sexual activity.

This is unusual for a book dedicated to the topic of sex. On the one hand, white feminism and sex positive frameworks have traditionally excluded abstinence due to the idea that it is unaligned with sexual freedom and have even portrayed faith guidelines for sex as oppressive. On the other hand, mainstream religious-based writings on sex tend to emphasize abstinence at the expense of complex questions about sexual health and sexual pleasure. In this book, we aim to chart a middle course. We want to talk openly about sex, and that includes all the issues surrounding abstinence and being sexually active. Although it is true that sometimes religious communities misuse abstinence (and contraception and family planning) as a way to overly control sexuality, and often place an undue burden of responsibility on women, this is not the only personal narrative. There are many Muslims as well as followers of other religions who actively commit to abstinence as an empowered choice and turn to their faith to inform their decision-making. Many Muslims consider the Islamic guidelines around abstinence and sexuality to be personally beneficial (and not oppressive), and, in fact, centrally important to their spiritual well-being. These Muslims are often eager to learn how to better incorporate these values throughout their lives. The decision to practice abstinence can involve daily decision-making and active work to avoid temptation and find the right balance in one's life. There are countless stories of individuals who practice abstinence. Some of these individuals are actively delaying sexual activity until after they are married, for the sake of their faith, and exploring romantic relationships and companionship, but still striving to maintain their physical boundaries, while others are returning to abstinence after being sexually active, for the sake of their faith.

We are also mindful that calls for abstinence might not be experienced the same way by all people, and the very topic itself can lead to struggle and frustration. As growing numbers of Muslims remain single for longer (either by choice or circumstance), decision-making around sex becomes increasingly and understandably complex. Most Muslim leaders today are hesitant to speak about the many nuances of the different realities of American Muslim lives, especially as these realities impact our sexual lives.

? DID YOU KNOW?

There are many Muslims who identify as Lesbian, Gay, Bisexual, Trans, Queer/Questioning+ who have questions, concerns, needs and, like others, are vulnerable in many ways. Excluding them from conversations pertaining to sex and sexuality is a disservice to them, and can make them more vulnerable to uninformed decision-making and intimate partner violence. Moreover, the discourse on same-sex intimacy is more complicated than it appears. As Dr. Julianne Hammer explains:

> It is tempting to conclude Muslims are divided into two categories: those who reject homosexuality and LGBTQI+ Muslims and those who identify as LGBTQI+ and their allies. The actual landscape is significantly more complicated and it is the recognition of the complexity of these configurations that allows for the possibility of multiple and responsible critique.[90]

Despite this complexity, currently the dominant understanding in Muslim communities is that same-sex relationships are not recognized in Islam, but this is being challenged by emerging scholarship. As such, calls for abstinence for a queer person could feel like a demand that they spend their entire lives without sexual fulfillment. No matter where your own personal beliefs land on this issue, deciding whether or not to be sexually intimate is an important exercise for all people, regardless of identity and orientation. The personal reflection exercise on page 68, along with the resources at the end of this book can be helpful for queer Muslims looking to ground themselves in their own beliefs for decision-making. Some academics have written about sexuality in Islam, including the topic of same-sex intimacy, and we have included several titles below. Full citations are available at the end of this book in the Works Cited section.

- Alhaj, Maher. (2021). *Halal this way: Towards a Viable Queering in Sunni Islam*. Available at https://www.halalthisway.org.

- Ali, Kecia. (2016). *Sexual Ethics and Islam: Feminist Reflections on Quran, Hadith, and Jurisprudence*. Oneworld Publications; Expanded, Revised edition.

- Hammer, Juliane. (2020). "Queer Love, Abrahamic Morality, and (the limits of) American Muslim Marriage." *Theology & Sexuality* 27(1): 20-43.

- Jahangir, Junaid and Abdullatif, Hussein. (2016). *Islamic law and Muslim Same-Sex Unions*. Lexington Books.

- Kugle, Scott. (2010) *Homosexuality in Islam: Critical Reflections on Gay, Lesbian, and Transgender Muslims*. Oxford: Oneworld Publications.

- wadud, amina. (2022). *Queer Islamic Studies and Theology*. Available at: https://qist1.com/.

- Shahar, Zaynab. (2022). "LGBTQ Muslim Marriage Praxis and Queer Ethics of Relation." in Ali, Kecia, ed. Tying the Knot: A Feminist/Womanist Guide to Marriage in America. Boston: OpenBU. https://hdl.handle.net/2144/44079.

---

[90] Hammer, Juliane. (2020). Queer Love, Abrahamic Morailty, and (the Limits of) American Muslim Marriage. *Theology & Sexuality 27*(1): 20-43.

It is long overdue for Muslims to have accessible information about how to make informed and spiritually-grounded decisions about their sexual health. This book offers some help in that direction. If and when you do decide to have sex, being able to consider how your values and beliefs about sex can facilitate informed decision-making rooted in choice, consent, pleasure, communication and one's spiritual well-being. Different readers will, of course, understand and apply the information in this book differently. That is as it should be—it is a natural result of the diversity of God's creation.

REFLECTION

What messages did you receive growing up about virginity? What were these informed by? How did these messages differ by gender?

POINT OF INTEREST

While the first time having sex may be a significant milestone in our societies, that is not always the case. Virginity, although a well-known term, is a social construct and not a medical term. In order to deconstruct some of the myths surrounding the concept of virginity, here are some key points:

- What we refer to as virginity has historically been understood as a person who has not yet had penetrative or penile-vaginal sex, though this is changing.

- Not everyone engages in penetrative sex, and there are many ways to partake in sexual activity that are not captured within this current heteronormative definiton of virginity.

- Sexual activity may mean different things for different people, and how it is defined may differ from person to person as they explore what sex means to them.

- Although there is a common misconception that the intactness of a hymen determines virginity, this is not true.[91]

- The hymen is not anatomically identical for everyone, and it is possible for someone to be born with little or no hymen.

- Using a tampon or having a pelvic exam before becoming sexually active does not compromise a person's virginity.

- There is absolutely no way to know—even by looking at the hymen—whether or not a person has had sexual intercourse.

- While bleeding is common due to the stretching and tearing of the hymen, **not everyone bleeds**. This does not mean that something is wrong or that a person lied about being a virgin; it simply is an acknowledgement that everyone's body reacts differently to first-time sex.

It is important to note that the Islamic emphasis on virginity is for all genders, not just women. Even more important, according to Islam, virginity does not have to be a crucial attribute of an eligible candidate for marriage. There are countless examples from Islamic history that show there are no barriers for non-virgins to marry, remarry, or be considered of less worth. In most cases, those barriers are a legacy of colonialism and patriarchy.

---

[91] Center for Young Women's Health. (2021). *Types of Hymens.* Retrieved from: https://youngwomenshealth.org/2013/07/10/hymens/; Muslim Women's League. (1995). *Sex and Sexuality in Islam.* Available at: https://www.mwlusa.org/topics/sexuality/sexuality.html.

In Your Own Words

"I am getting married in a few months and I am increasingly getting anxious about my first time. Our wedding is arranged and although since our engagement we have formed a strong bond, I still feel like I am missing that strong physical attraction that I always fantasized about. This also may be the case because we both live in different cities and have only spent limited time physically together. I know relationships take time to build but do you think it is normal to not have sex on your wedding night (or the first few nights) if you are not totally comfortable? Also, how would you even commence lovemaking? What type of foreplay would be best? How would you make sure you are doing your best to please your spouse?"

UNDERSTANDING YOUR VALUES

Beginning With Yourself

In an ideal world, sexual health decision-making begins well before the heat of the moment. It can be helpful to begin with a strong understanding and awareness of the self, even without any specific partner/spouse in mind. This includes idenfitying your own values about sex, awareness of your personal and spiritual boundaries, and what you will need to feel ready for this next step in a relationship. As we mentioned earlier, many different values, beliefs, and life experiences can inform decision-making. Some are grounded in religion and an expression of faith, while others come from culture, self-determination, family expectations, peer pressure, media messaging, and so on. Whether you decide to have sex or not, these decisions can be complicated, and can evolve over time. For this reason, it is useful to do a self-reflection about your expectations and belief systems about all these topics, even before you meet your future partner/spouse, as a way of beginning the conversation with yourself.

Through the following reflection exercise, consider the conditions that you might want to meet before engaging in sexual activity. For example, one person may want to be married before they engage in sexual activity, whereas another may want to ensure that desire, consent, contraception, and commitment are present. Or, perhaps in the initial stages of your sexual relationship, you prefer contraception to be present, while later on, this may be more negotiable, such as if you are actively trying to conceive. Learning to effectively communicate with yourself about your expectations, values, and boundaries can lay a great foundation for communicating with your (future) partner about sex. For example, couples do not always agree about when or if they want to have children, so talking about that before you start or stop using contraception can go a long way toward preserving a relationship and family life.

Undertaking this self-reflection exercise provides an opportunity for you to deeply think about what you need in order to feel fully engaged, safe, and empowered in a sexual relationship. It can also serve as a great conversation starter with your partner as you set expectations and boundaries. It is a tool you can use throughout your sexual journey, even to help you decide when *not* to have sex.

REFLECTION

Am I ready for sex? What do I need to feel comfortable?

People choose to have sex for a variety of reasons. This can be a means of fulfilling a tenet of marriage, expressing love and desire for a partner, a step to starting a family, or a way to satisfy a physical need. Below you will see a list of words/phrases. Choose the conditions from the list below that resonate most with you when thinking about this question: What needs to be present for me to feel comfortable with sexual activity? Remember that this list is by no means exhaustive; if there are words that are not on the list, please add them. As you choose these words, also think about the following questions:

1. What words/phrases best describes my ideal sexual relationship?
2. What conditions are important to how I understand my cultural and religious values regarding sex?
3. What conditions must absolutely be present for me to have a successful sexual relationship?
4. Are these conditions non-negotiable? Under what circumstances might they change?
5. What do I want for a spiritually elevating relationship?

Love	Compassion	Kindness	Generosity	Selflessness
Desire	Modesty	Responsibility	Curiosity	Fidelity
Consent	Patience	Marriage	Commitment	Desire to Conceive
Positivity	Enthusiasm	Trust	Open	Contraception
Spiritual	Respect	Boundaries	Loyalty	Self-Control
Being Present	Privacy	Spirituality	Gentleness	Free of Violence
Physical Safety	Emotional Safety	Romance	Attraction	Acceptance & Vulnerability
Health Insurance	Understanding of Anatomy	Financial Stability	Alignment with Partner's Values	Knowledge of Partner's Sexual History
Pleasure	Free of Shame	Responsibility	STI Testing with Partner	Access to Healthcare

The words/phrases you have chosen will help guide you when making decisions about engaging in sexual activity. It is important to know that these conditions may evolve or change as you grow, mature, or get more experience. Remember to revisit this exercise every so often as you continue to navigate the world of sex and relationships. What other conditions or items can be added to this list?

TRY IT OUT
Keeping Your Commitment to Abstinence

The reflection exercise on decision-making is also a way to reclaim abstinence as a tool of personal agency and empowerment: choosing not to have sex is an active decision and should be seen as a form of sexual liberation, not sexual oppression. Many people wait until they are married to have sex, or recommit to abstinence after divorce or a death of a spouse, and they view that decision as an active choice. The modern era has delayed the average age of marriage as compared to earlier times, which means that waiting to have sex until marriage means waiting longer than our ancestors did, and that can be challenging and quite difficult, especially in a society that is hypersexualized. It's important to acknowledge that committing to abstinence at 15 may be easier to follow through on than committing to abstinence if one is 25 or 30. Moreover, it is a different layer of challenge if one has already enjoyed sexual activity in a previous marriage or relationship and now is unexpectedly having to live a life of abstinence. Nevertheless, there are things you can do to help you keep your commitment at any age:

- Renew your commitment to abstinence whenever YOU need to. This may be yearly, monthly, or daily; you are in charge. It can be easier to commit to something for a concrete amount of time, rather than an uncertain duration of time. This is your agency and your autonomy, so remember to be flexible with your needs.

- Surround yourself with people who respect your decision to wait and who can check in with you and offer a safe space to process frustrations.

- Find an accountability partner (or several!) that you can call specifically on days you are feeling weak or vulnerable to help remind you of your commitment and talk you through your decision.

- Use *dhikr* and other forms of remembrance of God to ground yourself in your commitment.

- Consider the following question: what boundaries do you need/want to communicate to remain committed to abstinence (e.g. meeting only in public spaces)?

UNDERSTANDING YOUR VALUES

Sex and Spiritual Guilt

Sometimes a person may decide to have sex, and then regret it later, because they may feel they compromised on their values. This feeling might be further exacerbated by spiritual guilt for those who choose to have sex but are not married. Decisions around sex, especially within the constraints of religious binaries of "good" or "bad" and "heaven" or "hell," can cause major internal psychological battles. When a person makes decisions that are deemed sinful, they may punish themselves doubly. First, by believing they are beyond salvation, and second, through feeling like they deserve any consequence or misfortune that comes into their lives. This attitude can sometimes lead to unhealthy decision-making. Unhealthy decision-making after sex can look like a person forcing themselves to be with or marry the person they had sex with, despite knowing that person may not be good for them or that they are abusive. It is important to make informed decisions for one's future, no matter what is in their past—and leaving the rest to God. In doing this, it can be helpful to remember spiritual practices that bring a person closer to divine insight, such as prayer and meditation, and reminding ourselves that God is the Most Forgiving and the Most Merciful.

As we've stated before, worship is personal, but one way you can honor God is through honoring yourself, and not despair or feel like you are beyond redemption. Being merciful and gracious towards yourself can simply be the act of acknowledging that your actions may have been a mistake, but understanding that you can still move forward. It means recognizing that there is always an opportunity to nurture your spiritual health as long as you are willing to try and seek guidance from God. Our mistakes don't define us. What is important is how we choose to live despite them.

It is important to note that sex outside of marriage for unmarried single people is a very different thing than adultery or deceptive second marriages. While having sex outside the religious boundaries of marriage as a single person can be a source of individual spiritual guilt, cheating on a partner/spouse with a secondary secret relationship violates the RIDHA framework by harming the "H" safety and "I" communication between the partners, and we will discuss this more thoroughly in Chapter 5. The core sense of trust, essential for healthy and transparent communication, has been breached as well as the real possibility that the relationship may be over. In addition to the spiritual repentance that an unfaithful partner may want to engage in, the kind of repair that is necessary after infidelity can be a painful and difficult journey involving multiple people. Cheating also causes more than spiritual and relationship harm. It also puts one's partner/spouse and children vulnerable to physical harm from an STI.

REFLECTION

When you say yes to sex, where is that "yes" coming from? What feelings come up when you do say yes/give consent? How do you feel or think after you have said yes? Do you have moments with thoughts that question that yes? Is saying yes aligned with your emotional state and your values?

Have you ever regretted consenting? If so, why? What would you do differently?

REFLECTION

If you have had sexual experiences in the past, take a moment to reflect on those circumstances, and whether your decision-making was coming from a passive stance or an empowered, informed one:

What were the circumstances?

_____
_____
_____
_____

What ideas or notions about sex did you have, and were they changed by that experience? If so, how?

_____
_____
_____
_____

If there is anything you could change in future experiences, as informed by past experiences, that would center you in your own comfort, pleasure, and boundaries, what would it be?

_____
_____
_____
_____

In what ways did you practice the RIDHA framework? How could you better implement the framework in future experiences?

_____
_____
_____
_____

The First Time *Expectation vs. Reality*

First-time sex doesn't always happen the way it does on TV or the movies, or even the way you planned, and that's okay. In fact, it's likely that it will be very different from what you expect. First-time sex can be awkward, and it can even be uncomfortable or painful. There might be weird moments as you get to know your partner along with some embarrassing exchanges of bodily fluids, smells, or noises. It's clumsy, yet fascinating. What it also is—or what it can be—is an early page in writing your agency and defining what your sexual needs are. The good news is what might be awkward for you will likely also be awkward for your partner/spouse. Even if your partner has more sexual experience than you or vice versa, it will still be important for both of you to be honest with your expectations prior to sex and your feelings during sex. If you have more sexual experience than your current partner, you might want to volunteer information when appropriate and also give your partner space to explore their desires. Regardless of whether one partner is more experienced than the other, it will still be your first time with each other.

Moreover, sex may not happen the first time you try, especially if it is the first time for both of you. Although there are different ways to have sex, vaginal penetrative sex especially may require several attempts and a lot of patience before it fully occurs. There is no right or wrong, and it may not be the right moment for either of you. It is worth having a conversation with your (future) partner/spouse about your expectations for your first time to avoid unexpected misunderstandings, disappointment, or hurt.

 POINT OF INTEREST

It is possible that a conversation about sex on your wedding night can cause tension. Wedding night sex has been the focus of attention in many Muslim cultures, and it has, at times, been accompanied by uncomfortable and invasive family traditions. Before you know it, the very private and personal decision to have sex or not on the wedding night becomes everybody's business and loses its sacred intimacy. Moreover, partners or others may attempt to use Islamic evidence from *hadith* to guilt one into having sex. While these family dynamics and cultural traditions can be hard to break, the justifications for these ideas are often misconstrued and misinformed. Cultural practices such as showing family members bloody sheets after the wedding night to prove the bride was a virgin, or providing proof of the consummation of marriage are often framed as Islamic and religious—despite the scientific inaccuracies presumed by these practices. In reality, these practices are invasive and go against Islamic principles of privacy during intimate moments between partners. Most importantly, these practices are based on scientifically incorrect information: the notion that first-time sex results in bleeding and the absence of blood means the bride is not a virgin. These situations can be hard to navigate and are best resolved by communicating with your future/potential spouse, as these practices can shape the foundation of your marriage. It is also important that both you and your partner speak with your families together, before getting married, to explain why this practice makes you uncomfortable and is not something you will be carrying forward.

REFLECTION

Whether you have or have not had sex, what were/are some of what others shared with you about sex? How did this or could this inform your first time? Were these messages gendered? How has that set of expectations for you? How do you think that has set expectations for your partner?

What fears or anxieties do you have about sex? What hopes and dreams do you have about sex?

#THEFIRSTTIME SURVEY RESPONDENT

In Your Own Words

"Consider NOT having sex on your wedding night. The first night is a great time to RELAX after a long day of celebrations. Fatigue and stress are not conducive to enjoyable sex, so the first night is probably not the best time to experience having intercourse with your new partner for the first time. The first day, or perhaps the first few days are excellent opportunities to practice foreplay, and to get to know each other's bodies and sensitivities. For example, one person may be appalled by a certain behavior that the other finds enjoyable. It's also great to talk about what each partner's image of good sex is. And, if you're not the talkative type, just allow yourselves to gradually touch one another and enjoy the sensual experience of bodies touching. It is very common for women to experience tightness and pain the first few times. Sex is a learning experience for both partners. Do not under any condition feel compelled to 'tolerate' the discomfort so as not to disturb your partner's 'pleasure.' Allow your body to gradually acclimate to the experience, and allow your partner to slowly learn the ways to treat you gently so that the experience does not cause you discomfort. Lubrication can be very helpful in easing some of the discomfort, but the best solution is good foreplay, and waiting for your mid-cycle when your libido is at its peak. If discomfort continues, as it does for many people, there is no shame in seeing a doctor for possible treatments."

Consent

Safe and healthy sex doesn't only mean protection from infections and unintended pregnancy; it also means safety on an emotional and physical level. Sexual desire varies from person to person. While one person may find certain sexual positions or acts pleasurable, another person may feel apprehensive, uncomfortable, repulsed, or scared by them. It is important to discuss this openly with your partner/ spouse to prevent any coercion toward sexual activity. It is also crucial to respect boundaries for when one partner/spouse does not want to have sex, and center consent as a critical part of the experience. Open communication is imperative to make you and your partner feel safe and satisfied, and this includes having complete information about other current sexual partners. In other words, if one partner is cheating on another partner, or is secretly married to two different people without one partner's knowledge, it is no longer a consensual relationship, because they don't have full knowledge of each others' sexual activity.

Consent is the explicit—verbal and nonverbal—confirmation to engage in a specific sexual activity. Consent lies on a spectrum, and it is always evolving. It also happens across one's lifespan. This means that a person must be able to give consent or retract consent when in any situation related to sexual activity, physical touch and/or intimacy. **Sex without consent is sexual assault.** Informed affirmative consent must be given regardless of the relationship. This means that sexual assault can and does occur both within and outside of a marriage. The focus is not the relationship itself, and more about the autonomy an individual has over their body. More specifically, consent is:

- an informed, specific, and conscious decision,
- voluntary, without force, coercion, or intimidation,
- ongoing throughout sexual activity and can be revoked at any time,
- not just about agreeing to a particular sexual activity, but also includes boundaries that you set within sexual activity (i.e. using contraception or kissing but no sex, etc.),
- something to be obtained from your current partner if you wish to enter a relationship with someone else who is not your current partner.[92]

If you do consent to having sex, you and your partner/spouse may want to consider coming up with a "safe word." A safe word is a word that you both can agree on that will signal to your partner that you do not want to continue or that you need them to slow down. Words like "no" or "stop" are not the best words to use, as those words commonly come up even in pleasurable sexual experiences. You can revisit doing that activity again when you feel comfortable, proceed to another activity, or end the encounter completely. Coming up with and utilizing safe words is a way to respect the boundaries and desires of your partner.

Sex involves responsibility toward your partner—to honor the other person's desires, boundaries, and integrity as a fully consenting partner. If your partner is not comfortable with a certain sexual act or does not want to participate, it is your responsibility to honor and respect that. If you do not, it can have serious legal, physical, and emotional implications, which will be discussed in more detail in Chapter 5. Similarly, if you are in a situation where you have refused being sexually intimate, but the other person forces you anyway, you have the option of seeking help from a trained professional or law enforcement. Being sexually violated will never be your fault, and you can refer to Chapter 5 to learn more about your options.

---

[92] We are aware that there are interpretations of religious law that permit a husband to take on another wife without seeking consent. While these interpretations may exist, we believe they can cause more harm than good as they can still be emotionally, physically, mentally, and spiritually harmful to the people involved.

Preparing for Sex

If and when you do decide to have sex with your (future) partner/spouse, there may be some conversations you might want to have and items you might want to gather or buy to help you prepare. Below, we discuss some of these options; you don't have to follow all or any of them—just feel free to adopt whatever works best for you.

COMMUNICATE

It is helpful speak with your (future) partner/spouse at length about your boundaries and desires before having sex. Discuss what experiences you are okay with and what you would rather wait to try. Communication is a form of sexual preparation and foreplay. By talking about your wants, needs, and desires, you can have a better idea of the expectations that you and your partner have for each other. This may be difficult for first-timers or those with little sexual experience, especially if you do not have any experience with self pleasure. Do what feels right for you, and keep communicating as your sexual relationship progresses. Don't be afraid to say no if you don't feel comfortable yet trying new things; and don't be afraid to speak up if you change your mind later. Sexual preferences and desires change with experience; what may have been painful or uncomfortable in the beginning may start to feel pleasurable as you become more sexually experienced.

Moreover, consider your various contraceptive options and decide on what will best suit you and your partner's needs. If you are using condoms or other contraception, make sure you have plenty easily accessible. It is also possible that you and your partner/spouse may not want to use contraception at all, or may be trying for a baby right away.

 REFLECTION

Ask your partner: What were you told as a child about your body? About desire? Share with your (future) partner your hang-ups, the things that hold you back, and the things you fantasize about.

_____

_____

_____

_____

_____

_____

_____

_____

_____

DID YOU KNOW?

The right to enjoy sex and gain pleasure is one granted to all people, regardless of gender. Despite the fact that cultural messaging in some communities may discourage women from experiencing pleasure from sex, there are many traditional Muslim scholars who believe that the right to orgasm is a God-given right for all people.[93]

A reputable resource to learn more about pleasure in Islam is The Village Auntie who can be found on social media @TheVillageAuntie. She teaches women about the right to sexual pleasure drawing upon East African traditions. One of these traditions is the practice of Kunyaza, which centers female pleasure and facilitates male ejaculation. You can learn more about this practice in the book by Habeeb Akande, titled *Kunyaza: The Secret to Female Pleasure.* Another useful resource is @thehalalsexpert, who also regularly hosts webinars and courses on sexual pleasure, focusing on techniques to pleasure your partner, including but not limited to, foreplay, oral sex, and more.

 **TRY IT OUT**
Exploring Your Contraceptive Options

While there are tons of resources available about contraception, there are two people in particular with whom you may want to speak regarding your choice of contraception:

A Healthcare Provider

Your healthcare provider will be able to provide you with accurate information about the effectiveness of various types of contraception and how to use each one correctly. Different types of contraceptives require different types of care, and almost all can come with side effects. Talk to your doctor about which method will work best for you and your body. Note that some contraception is available over the counter, such as condoms, but some will require a prescription or an office visit. Doctor-patient confidentiality also ensures that they are not allowed to disclose any of your medical information to anyone—even to your family—without your consent. If you are concerned that your healthcare provider might disclose your health information to your family or anyone else, consider finding a different provider. Of course, finding the right healthcare provider and the right contraceptive method can be difficult depending on your health insurance coverage and what you can afford. This is something we will cover in Chapter Four (Keeping Up with Your Sexual Health) of this book, including a sample list of questions to ask your provider.

---

[93] Akande, H. (2015). *A Taste of Honey: Sexuality and Erotology in Islam.* Rabaah Publishers. pg 300.

Your Partner or Spouse

If you feel safe doing so, it is helpful to discuss contraceptive use openly with your partner, so that everyone is aware of contraceptive options and has similar expectations about preventing pregnancy and sexually transmitted infections (STIs). Having a conversation with your partner about contraception should ideally be done before engaging in sexual activity. Both parties can determine who should primarily be responsible for contraceptive use, taking into account each person's health needs, and what is most feasible. While all relationships require some compromise, it is still important to clearly communicate your health, needs, and desires. You may also find it helpful to speak with a trusted healthcare provider to facilitate an informed conversation before discussing your options with your significant other. Remember to prioritize both parties' comfort and safety while engaging in safe and responsible practices.

Finally, we know that it is common for Muslims to feel inclined to seek the opinion of an Islamic scholar or spiritual guide, to inquire whether a particular contraceptive method has religious implications. For example, some contraceptives work at different times during the menstrual cycle, before or after an egg is fertilized. While Islam does encourage family planning, there are a number of different opinions on these various methods, depending on which school of thought you choose to follow and who is interpreting it. Advice from religious scholars can vary greatly from scholar to scholar. It is also important to realize that not all religious scholars are equally trained, and thus not all advise people in an informed way. In other words, many may not have accurate medical information or accurate understanding of how each type of contraceptive works. As a consequence, this can result in more harm and misinformation. If you are interested in information about the range of classical Islamic scholarship on the topic, we recommend BF Musallam's *Sex and Society in Islam: Birth Control before the Ninetheeth Century*.[94]

TRY IT OUT
Breaking the Ice

Just like your first conversations with your healthcare provider about sex, these first few conversations with your partner might feel unfamiliar. If you feel too nervous talking to them verbally, try other modes of communication that may be just as clear and direct, but perhaps a little less intimidating; for example:

- **Write to them.** An email or a letter can help you clear your own thoughts as well by seeing what you have said or not said, and it can also be an untapped source of intimacy. Writing and reading affectionate and understanding words can bring people closer together as well as help avoid interruptions before a thought is completed and likely misunderstood. You can also text or instant message your partner what you would like to discuss about sex and boundaries if you do not feel comfortable talking to them directly or feel anxious.

- **Take advantage of technology.** You can try watching educational videos on consent or visit informational websites on contraception such as bedsider.org to break the ice to an important conversation.

Remember, the best way to know your partner's sexual needs is to ask them.

---

[94] While this book does a good job of explaining the historical *fiqh* opinions on birth control and abortion, it also cites scholars who used patriarchal and misogynistic justifications for deeming birth control and abortion permissible. This is a limitation of this book and can make reading this book quite challenging. We recommend you read this with the proper care and attention that you need for yourself.

These conversations can definitely be awkward, and it's natural to be nervous about talking to your partner about certain aspects of sex that may include details on specific sexual acts, logistics, or frequency. Couples who are not physically intimate before marriage may find these to be challenging conversations since it is primarily based on speculation rather than life experience. As such, conversations with your partner do not have to be about the specific logistics or mechanics of sex—as that evolves over time with your relationship and life stage. Rather, consider the decision-making reflection exercise mentioned on page 68 as a way to start talking about expectations.

ASKING YOUR PARTNER ABOUT THEIR SEXUAL HISTORY

It is important to speak to each other about your sexual history: both of you should know whether there is a possibility of either of you being exposed to STIs. You don't necessarily need to ask details as your partner may still want to protect the intimacy and privacy of those relationships. Even if both parties have never had any sexual experiences, getting tested regularly for STIs is good practice. Athough the chances are minimal, STI's like HIV and Hepatitis can be passed through unsterilized needle usage, and from sharing razors and other non-sexual acts where there is a potential for blood transmission.[95]

Unfortunately, there is still a stigma associated with STIs, which makes it difficult to have a conversation with your partner about getting tested. Asking a partner to get tested doesn't mean you don't trust them or that you think they're cheating on you. It is simply a way to take control of your health, and theirs, too. Ideally, you would want to get tested or talk about getting tested before any sexual intercourse happens. This may feel unnecessary especially if you know your partner well. It may be that you've remained abstinent your entire life and believe your partner has waited until marriage as well. Even if you make the assumption that they don't have any STIs, remember, most STIs are asymptomatic, so you will not know unless you both get tested.

---

[95] Refer to Chapter Two for more information on STIs.

TRY IT OUT
Getting to Know Your Partner

Learning about your partner's sexual health should be part of getting to know them. In an ideal world, asking questions about their health should be as simple and straightforward as asking your partner about their favorite color or favorite food. Although these questions are necessary questions to ask in every relationship that could be sexual, people may struggle with phrasing these questions in ways that don't sound judgmental or nosy. Here are some suggestions on how to ask your partner about their sexual health and STI status.

You can start this conversation with a phrase such as "I find you attractive/I love you/we are getting married soon, and I know we will eventually have sex. Before we can do that, I think it's important that we both learn about each other's beliefs about sex and sexual health practices." Conversation starters can include:

Beliefs and Boundaries
- How do you define the words "intimacy" and "sex?" Physically, emotionally, and spiritually?
- What is your love language?[96]
- What does consent mean to you? What does it look like to you?
- What do you need to feel safe to engage in sexual activity?
- What are your boundaries with sex (if any)?
- Are you already sexually active? If not, do you plan on waiting until marriage?
- Are there aspects of intimacy or sex you are uncomfortable with? What topics do you need more information about or need more time to think about? Where can you get that information?
- What are your beliefs about contraception?
- I prefer using condoms (or some other birth control) when having sex until we decide to get pregnant and/or we're more comfortable with each other. What about you?
- Do you want to have children? If so, when? How many?

Sexual Health History
- If have had sex before, what do your current sexual practices look like?
- Are you currently having sex with anyone else? Are you using protection or birth control in that sexual relationship?
- Is there any negative or traumatic experience with sex that you'd like to talk about?
- Who do you believe should be the person primarily responsible for contraception when we do decide to have sex?
- Is there anything I need to know about your past sexual history?
- Have you ever gotten tested for STIs? When was the last time you got tested?
- Would you be willing to get tested together?

If your partner does not know their sexual health status or has not been tested, you can bring it up in different ways. If you're nervous that they may perceive your request the wrong way, suggest getting tested together. You may even plan a date around it and make it a fun activity. If you've been tested recently, bring it up with your partner, and explain to them how the process went, how simple it was, etc. This may ease their worries if this will be the first time they are getting tested.

---

[96] More information about the 5 love languages available at: https://www.5lovelanguages.com/.

Expectations for your first time

- What are your expectations for our first time?
- Are you okay with taking things slow so we can figure out what we like and dislike?
- If I feel discomfort, this is my safe word [insert safe word], please make sure you stop immediately
- This is my first time having sex, and it would be nice to spend some time after sex cuddling or [insert what might bring you comfort and ease].
- This is my first time having sex, and I have a lot of anxiety around it being painful. Is it ok if I changed my mind and asked you to stop or take it slower?

What other questions would you want to ask your partner before starting a sexual relationship with them? As this section emphasizes, communication is a key component of a healthy and satisfying sexual relationship. Sometimes communicating about what you want and don't want sexually means thinking back to earlier experiences in your life and sharing these with your partner as an act of emotional and physical intimacy. Communication can also be key to learning and knowing how to please your partner. If you discover that your desires do not directly align with your partner's, offer other kinds of sexual intimacy and closeness. Remember—and this deserves repeating: **sex doesn't always have to mean vaginal penetration.** Keep the door to this conversation open over the course of a relationship. It is a good habit to regularly check in with each other on how your shared sex life is going. You and your partner's sex drives will vary over a lifetime, and someone's past behavior does not determine their sexual interest over time.

Shop for Helpful Products

There are a few things you may want to have on hand. Even if you've been sexually active for a long time, it might be helpful to have some of these (maybe new to you) items on hand to enhance your sexual experiences.

Lubricant can be especially helpful for all genitalia and condoms. First-time jitters can cause vaginal dryness. Using lubricant liberally in the vaginal area and directly on a penis or sex toy can help ease penetration. For penetrative sex, adding some lubricant inside of a condom or rubbing some on the outside of the condom or sex toy can greatly assist in lessening friction and decrease the likelihood of the condom breaking. Alternatively, arousal can also produce vaginal or penile fluids; this is simply the body's natural way of lubricating. Some people become even wetter in anticipation of sex, and during ejaculation, the penis releases semen. Either bodily response is completely normal, so the use of lubricant entirely depends on the individual and the occasion. In fact, the same body may produce vaginal fluids during one encounter and not during another.

When choosing a lubricant, look for water-based lubricants; oil-based lubricants can make latex condoms degrade faster. Easily available and reliable brands include KY and Astroglide, both of which can usually be found in drugstores and grocery stores as well as through online vendors. SLiquid is also a great brand that has been around for a long time.

Condoms can be found in an assortment of sizes, texture, lubrications, and yes, even flavors. Feel free to experiment with your partner to determine which brand fits the both of you best. However, be aware of potential latex allergies or other irritants that may be present in different brands.

Optional Extras: There are also plenty of items that may be a fun addition to sex, but are in no way mandatory. *Candles* and *lingerie* (for people of all genders!) can help set the mood and increase anticipation and arousal, while *massage oils* and *sex toys* can introduce various new angles to intimacy.

If you feel embarrassed buying these items at a drugstore in person, fret not. Everything is available online. In fact, you'll probably find a better variety online than in the store. You can go directly to a drugstore website, Amazon.com, or do a general Google search to see what options are out there. We do recommend reading reviews if you are new at purchasing particular items as others' experiences may give you at least a general sense of how effective any given product might be. As such, shopping online offers the benefit of discretion with the delivery of items right to your doorstep; at the same time, this may not be a perfect solution either as it can also cause some discomfort. For those who are new to websites selling sex toys, lingerie, and other products, the imagery and photos can feel graphic and perhaps cause embarrassment too.

In addition to the purchases you may need to make especially for sex, there are a few other household items that may be helpful to have when you have sex:

- **Towels:** You may want to lay down a large towel to catch any secretions, sweat, blood, or ejaculate as well as have a few smaller towels within reach for cleanup afterwards.

- **Tissues:** A box of tissues is also handy to have within arm's reach, especially if you don't want to use your towels for cleanup.

- **Panty Liner:** Ejaculate can linger inside a person and drip throughout the day if a condom is not used. Wearing a thin feminine napkin or panty liner after intercouse can help.

POINT OF INTEREST

People experience first-time penetrative sex in different ways: some may find it pleasureable, while others may find it painful, or both. There is a misconception that pain and bleeding happen the first time a penis, finger, or sex toy goes into a vagina; however, this is not the case for everyone. Further, penetrative sex may not even happen on the first try. The amount of hymenal tissue one has can determine whether there is pain or bleeding during intercourse, as the hymen stretches during this period. Hymenal tissue is not identical, and people with more hymenal tissue are more likely to experience pain and bleeding.[97]

If pain and bleeding continues after first-time penetrative sex, try stretching your hymen tissue slowly over time. For example, you can use your fingers or dilators that come in various sizes. If the pain is consistent and recurring, you may need to talk with a doctor and/or visit a local health center for more information.

There may be cases where you might need a small procedure to open your hymen. These can include possibly having a:

- **Septate hymen:** which is an extra band of tissue that is blocking the opening to the vagina.
- **Imperforate hymen:** which is where the hymen covers the whole opening to the vagina.
- **Microperforate hymen:** which is a thin membrane covering almost the entire vagina, with a small hole in the middle, making it very difficult for menstrual blood to flow.

---

[97] Planned Parenthood. *What Happens When You Lose Your Virginity?* Available at: https://www.plannedparenthood.org/learn/teens/sex/virginity/what-happens-first-time-you-have-sex.

Setting Expectations for Your First Time

Sex May Not

- **Happen the first time** you try it, or on your wedding night.
- **Be pleasurable the first time.** It may be an uncomfortable or painful experience at first.
- **Result in bleeding** from a stretched or torn hymen.
- **Make you feel suddenly closer** to your partner or strengthen your relationship.

Sex Should

- **Get better with time.** The more you have sex and try things out, the better you'll get at it. If it doesn't, you may want to consult your doctor to rule out any health issues such as vaginismus or other pelvic pain issues.
- **Require keeping up with your sexual health.** Decisions on contraception, preventing pregnancy, and STIs will be part of your regular care for your body as you become sexually active.
- **Evolve over time.** As you grow to better understand your body and your needs, the kind of sex you may have enjoyed in your 20's may not be the sexual activity you will want to have in your 40's. Your partner's needs will also evolve, so it is important to continue to have open conversations about how your needs have changed and how to maintain a sexual connection throughout.
- **Not make you feel embarrassed** and inadequate if you are unable to have sex and are in constant pain.
- **Always be consensual.** Read Chapter Five to learn more about consent and your options, should you experience sex that is not consensual.

Sex Can Be Complicated

- For folks who have experience trauma from sexual violence because they may have different and varying relationships with sex. There may be an increased or decreased interest in having sex.[98]

Having sex for the first time is a big decision and can cause a myriad of feelings. Remember that you don't have to have sex if you are not ready, even if your partner/spouse is expecting it or it is your wedding night. It is also possible to decline sex without contraception. Even in the heat of the moment, if something does not feel right to you or your partner/spouse is not willing to use a condom and that is a prerequisite for you, it is important to communicate that boundary. With the appropriate planning, you can reduce any feelings of anxiety or uncertainty that may come up. We hope this section has offered a beginning to that preparation and some tools as you consider this next step in your life.[99]

---

[98] Mills, B, and Turnbull, G. (2004). Broken Hearts and Mending Bodies: the Impact of Trauma on Intimacy. *Sexual and Relationship Therapy*. (19): 3. Available at: https://www.recoveryonpurpose.com/upload/Broken%20Hearts%20and%20Mending%20Bodies%20The%20Impact%20of%20Trauma%20on%20Intimacy.pdf.

[99] For an even more in-depth list of questions to consider, this Scarlateen checklist is great: https://www.scarleteen.com/article/relationships/ready_or_not_the_scarleteen_sex_readiness_checklist.

Sex as an Act of Worship

#THEFIRSTTIME SURVEY RESPONDENT

In Your Own Words

"I wish there was someone I could call, without judgment, and say 'Hey, what does it mean when this happens?' Now, there is the internet, but years ago there were no answers to embarrassing questions. The problem with the internet is that the answers are not always right or reputable and none of their advice is based on fiqh/Quran/sunnah. I never knew what was ok Islamically because no Muslim teachers ever talked about sex."

In Islam, sex within marriage is considered to be an act of worship, as you are fulfilling the mutual right to sexual pleasure of your spouse.[100] For this reason, there are numerous spiritual acts that you and your partner can engage in before having sex. First, you can pray two optional *raka'* of prayer together. You can also recite the *dua* (supplication) before intercourse to bless the act and any children that may result from the encounter.[101]

Another suggested activity is for each person to spend a moment of quiet reflection prior to initiating sexual activity. For example, one could reflect on the path of how they were brought to meet and eventually marry or commit to their partner, shared moments of intimacy in the past, and the spiritual and emotional message they hope to convey to their spouse during intercourse. Mindfulness activities such as deep breathing and visualizing colors, feelings, and sensations related to shared emotions and spiritual space can be helpful in feeling grounded in the moment and bringing forward one's intentions.

 DID YOU KNOW?

The Quran states that vaginal intercourse during menstrual periods is not permissible. Other forms of intimacy such as kissing, caressing, and foreplay during menstruation are allowed and encouraged.[102]

---

[100] Learn Islam. *Intimacy in Islam.* Available at: https://learn-islam.org/class3-intimacy-in-islam.
[101] To find the full dua, please see here: http://duas.com/dua/332/dua-before-sexual-intercourse.
[102] Sahih Muslim. Touching a menstruating woman above the izar. Book 3, Hadith Number 2.

Sex with Disabilities

There are a plethora of Quranic verses and hadiths that celebrate diversity in Islam. They serve to continuously remind us that disability is not a sin nor a punishment from God and that people with disabilities are equal members of society. As we continue to strive for justice and a more equal world, it is important to remember the unique challenges that people with disabilities face when it comes to sex.

There are running stereotypes that people with intellectual and physical disabilities are either hyper-sexual or asexual. These negative stereotypes continue to be perpetuated, even in sex positive spaces, as most sex education material only caters to able-bodied people. These stereotypes can be harmful on much greater scales, given historical eugenicist contexts where people with disabilities have been forcefully sterilized and deemed too unfit to reproduce.[103]

Disability justice movements continue to advocate for fulfilling sex lives that recognize and celebrate diversity in bodies. This has led to innovations in sex toys that cater to people with different disabilities. These toys can differ in shape, size, ease of use, accessibility, and other factors and help in ensuring that people with disabilities, like all people, enjoy happy, healthy sex.[104]

In Muslim communities that discourage premarital sex and masturbation, it can be even more difficult for unmarried people with disabilities to receive the sexual pleasure they desire. There is a need for nuanced views around sex and disability in Islam that acknowledges these struggles and offers practical solutions beyond the advice to be patient. If you or your partner have a disability, the *Ultimate Guide to Sex and Disability: For All of Us Who Live with Disabilities, Chronic Pain, and Illness* by Cory Silverberg and Miriam Kaufman is an important resource to check out on sex and disability.

There are many options for people who have a disability and want to have sex or understand their sexuality. Not only do disabled people have fulfilling, happy, and healthy sex lives, writing and work on disabled sex offers a lot to non-disabled people. Disability justice challenges dominant, heteropatriarchal, and hierarchal approaches to sex. By disrupting power, disability justice opens up new possibilities for sex, sexuality, and relationships, especially regarding communication, mutual pleasure, and sex as fluid. Non-disabled sex isn't necessarily the norm, nor is it the "better" way to have sex (surprise: there is no one way to have sex!). Be sure to check the resource box at the end of this chapter to learn about resources that explore sex and disabilites in depth.

---

[103] ABC Law Centers. (2018). *Involuntary Sterilization of Disabled Americans: An Historical Overview.* Available at: https://www.abclawcenters.com/blog/2018/11/06/involuntary-sterilization-of-disabled-americans-an-historical-overview/.
[104] Disability Horizons. (2019). 8 accessible sex toys and aids for anyone with a disability. *Disability Horizons.* Available at: https://disabilityhorizons.com/2019/02/8-accessible-sex-toys-and-sex-aids-for-anyone-with-a-disability/.

POINT OF INTEREST

Individuals with different disabilities may be at a higher risk for sexual violence as they may face unique challenges that make them vulnerable, especially if much of the power lies with their caretaker or someone who is more able bodied. Moreover, it may be harder for a disabled person to identify abuse due to lack of awareness or because they are being groomed to believe that kind of treatment is part of their care. Some things to consider if you or someone you know has a disability and may be susceptible to violence:

- The disabled person may lose access to communication; for example, their abuser may take their phone or laptop away. Further, if they have been sexually assaulted or abused, they may find it difficult to access services to file a report and are less likely to be believed.
- Depending on the type of disability, the person may rely on someone regularly for assistance and this may create a situation where the disabled person is coerced, manipulated, and/or harmed.
- Consent may look different if certain disabilities require the caretaker to make decisions. For example, certain cognitive disabilities may result in a person not being able to consent.[105]

Places to get help if you suspect someone is in danger of being harmed:

- Consent Laws by state: https://apps.rainn.org/policy/?_ga=2.113411022.898739024.1635203779-1307391086.1635203779
- Deaf Abused Women's Network (DAWN): https://deafdawn.org/
- CAVNET: http://cavnet.blogspot.com/
- National Disability Rights Network: https://www.ndrn.org/

---

[105] RAINN. *Sexual Abuse of People with Disabilities.* Available at:https://www.rainn.org/articles/sexual-abuse-people-disabilities.

Asexuality

An asexual person does not experience sexual attraction or sexual desire. Being asexual does not mean that you are not attracted to your partner. Rather, it means that you may find them attractive in other ways such as aesthetically pleasing, just not sexually. Further, asexuality is a spectrum that includes demisexuality and grey-asexuality. Those that are on this spectrum choose to engage in sex for many reasons that may or may not be related to sexual attraction. If you are asexual, it does not mean your relationship is doomed. With open communication about expectations, couples with asexual members have been able to find a balance between meeting the needs of both partners. This is a good reminder that while healthy sex can have positive implications for a relationship long-term, a long-lasting relationship is not solely based on sex. Sex is only one aspect of an intimate relationship; there are many more to enjoy.[106]

Terms to Know

DEMISEXUALITY

Demisexuality is a type of sexuality or sexual orientation. Demisexuals need to feel a strong emotional bond or connection with their partners first to feel sexual attraction.[107]

GREY-ASEXUALITY[108]

Grey-Asexuality, also known as gray-a, gray-ace, or grey-ace. Often a term to describe people who identify as asexual, but don't fit into the main types of asexuality, included below:

- **Sex-Repulsed:** Someone who is repulsed by or completely disinterested in the idea of sex.
- **Sex-Neutral:** Someone who isn't repulsed by sex, but also doesn't actively seek it out. These people may still have sex, such as when they might be in a relationship and want to please their partner.
- **Sex-Positive:** Someone who identifies as asexual, in other words, they don't feel sexual attraction to others, but will still have sex for pleasure.

---

[106] A helpful site to learn more about asexuality is The Asexuality Archive at http://www.asexualityarchive.com/http://www.asexualityarchive.com/.
[107] Fletcher, J. (2021). Demisexuality: What to Know. *Medical News Today*. Retrieved from: https://www.medicalnewstoday.com/articles/327506.
[108] WebMD Editorial Contributors. (2021). *What Is Gray Sexuality?* WebMD. Retrieved from:L https://www.webmd.com/sex/what-is-graysexuality.

Roadblocks to Sex and Intimacy

What are some possible factors that can cause one partner to no longer be interested in having sex or being intimate?

_____

_____

_____

_____

_____

_____

_____

_____

_____

No matter how much one prepares for sex, sometimes the body and mind do not cooperate. While it is important to remember that it may take a few attempts to have penetrative sex, an individual's overall sexual experience should become more natural, less painful, and more pleasurable over time. If some time passes from when you become sexually active, and you or your partner are still experiencing difficulty or pain with sex, there may be a few things happening that can have long-term implications for the relationship. This include experiencing sexual dysfunction, the impacts of sexual trauma and health issues, struggling with sexual orientation, and sex after major life changes.

Sexual Dysfunction

There are several types of sexual dysfunction that can impact both men and women. These conditions can lead to a lot of physical pain, making penetrative sex either extremely difficult, or impossible, in addition to the emotional distress and tension between partners.[109] While a number of these may sound similar in how they present, it is important to ultimately seek the advice from a medical professional for the true diagnosis. The good news is most of these are treatable with medication and therapy.

VAGINISMUS

Roadblock: Vaginismus is an involuntary tightness of the vagina during attempted intercourse because of uncontrollable contractions of the pelvic floor muscles. As a result, vaginal penetration may be painful or even impossible. This can often be the cause of unconsummated relationships. Women who have never had pain-free intercourse may be suffering from primary vaginismus. Vaginismus that develops later in life, triggered by a medical condition, traumatic event, childbirth, surgery, or other life change is known as secondary vaginismus.

Symptoms: Burning or stinging with tightness during sex, difficult or impossible penetration, ongoing sexual discomfort or pain triggered by an event, difficulty inserting tampons or undergoing a pelvic/gynecological exam, and/or avoidance of sex due to pain and /or failure of penetration. Individuals with vaginismus have made statements such as "It's like hitting a brick wall;" "I don't have a hole;" and "It's a panic attack of the vagina."

Solution: Vaginismus is considered one of the most treatable sexual disorders. Many studies have shown treatment success rates approaching nearly 100%. Successful vaginismus treatment does not require drugs, surgery, hypnosis, or any other complex invasive technique. Effective treatment approaches combine pelvic floor physical therapy, dilator insertion training, pain elimination techniques, transition steps, and exercises designed to help women identify, express, and resolve any contributing emotional components. In addition, therapy options such as sex therapy and talk therapy can also help your partner understand the medical condition.[110]

ERECTILE DYSFUNCTION

Roadblock: Erectile dysfunction (ED)[111] is the inability to get or keep an erection firm enough to have sexual intercourse. It can also be called impotence. For those experiencing erectile dysfunction, it can lead to lower confidence and feelings of inadequacy. Partners should be understanding and patient. The causes for ED may include medications, stress, a medical disorder, or a lack of sexual interest.

Symptoms: Difficulty getting an erection or keeping an erection, and/or reduced sexual desire.[112]

Solution: Many treatment options are available, including medications such as Viagra. Talk to your doctor for more information.

---

[109] Muslim Women's League. (2001). *Female Sexual Dysfunction*. Pamphlet. Available at: https://www.mwlusa.org/topics/health/fsd.pdf
[110] To learn more about vaginismus, please visit the website vaginismus.com.
[111] To learn more about erectile dysfunction, see: https://www.healthline.com/health/erectile-dysfunction.
[112] Mayo Clinic Staff. (2022). *Erectile Dysfunction*. MayoClinic.org. Available at: https://www.mayoclinic.org/diseases-conditions/erectile-dysfunction/symptoms-causes/syc-20355776.

VULVODYNIA

Roadblock: Chronic pain and/or discomfort around the opening of the vulva (vagina) that can potentially last for months to years. The cause for vulvodynia is unknown. Further, the pain associated with vulvodynia can be burning or irritation that can be very uncomfortable, especially if you sit for long periods of time or have sex.

Symptoms: Burning, soreness, stinging, rawness, painful intercourse (dyspareunia), throbbing, and/or itching. The pain can be either constant or occasional, and may only occur when the sensitive area is touched

Solution: Treatments focus on relieving the symptoms and you may need a combination of the different treatment options. Treatment options include medications, biofeedback therapy, local anesthetics, nerve blocks, pelvic floor therapy, and/or surgery.[113] Please consult a medical professional for further information.

DYSPAREUNIA

Roadblock: A persistent or recurrent genital pain that occurs just before, during, or after intercourse. The cause of dyspareunia can differ depending on emotional factors, and/or pain that can occur either at entry or with deep thrusting.

Symptoms: Pain at sexual entry, pain with every penetration including putting in a tampon, deep pain during thrusting, burning or aching pain, throbbing pain, lasting hours after intercourse.[114]

Solution: Depending on the pain, the treatment options can vary and may include medication, desensitization therapy, counseling, or sex therapy. Please consult a medical professional for further information.

CULTURAL AND PSYCHOLOGICAL

Roadblock: Some Muslims, especially women, do not feel comfortable showing their desire for sex. They may have been taught that desiring sex is inappropriate or shameful, and so they wait for their partners to make the first move and fear showing any sort of enjoyment during sex. Some women have been taught that passivity and, to some degree, unfamiliarity about their own sexuality is a way to prove their virtue and innocence. This can be an unintended consequence in cultures that prize virginity and sexual purity. Often, this value is communicated to young women and men through shame. Many Muslims have shared about the challenges of being told something was *haram* or forbidden for so long and then have to come to terms with the expectation that they will suddenly be able to embrace their sexual selves after marriage.

Solution: If you think this is true in your situation, the first step is simply to be kinder to yourself. Many times, mental pressure is what makes people stumble the most. Be understanding of your acculturation and acknowledge the reasons why you may not be comfortable engaging in sex, even if it is now religiously permissible for you to do so. You are not a machine; you are human, and humans do not have easy on/off switches. Take your time to get comfortable with your own body's desires as well as your partner's.

[113] Mayo Clinic Staff. (2020). *Vulvodynia.* MayoClinic.org. Retrieved from:.https://www.mayoclinic.org/diseases-conditions/vulvodynia/diagnosis-treatment/drc-20353427.
[114] Mayo Clinic Staff. (2022). *Painful intercourse (dyspareunia)—Symptoms and causes.* Mayo Clinic. Retrieved from: https://www.mayoclinic.org/diseases-conditions/painful-intercourse/symptoms-causes/syc-20375967.

SEXUAL TRAUMA

Roadblock: Sexual trauma can result from sexual harassment, sexual assault, threat of harm if you do not perform a sexual act, inappropriate touching, rape, sexual coercion, or being pressured to perform or engage in sexual activity. Future sexual activity can trigger past sexual trauma, and a victim may experience difficulty in engaging in intimacy. Traumatic stress can extend beyond intimate encounters.

Solution: Individuals suffering from sexual trauma have the option to seek individual therapy. Couples psychotherapy or sex therapy can also be beneficial to helping your partner understand what you're going through and improving your communication. Be patient with yourself and/or your partner.

Finding Your Path

It is not uncommon to find individuals struggling with their sexual orientation who still commit to a heterosexual partnership, especially in faith communities that do not welcome LGBTQ+ relationships. As such, many times LGBTQ folks may pursue heterosexual relationships or marriages because they either are struggling to reconcile their sexual orientation with their faith, or they feel pressure from their families to get married and start a family.[115] Further, there are scenarios where someone may feel there is no choice but to marry someone out of obligation, as it is directly related to their safety.

#THEFIRSTTIME SURVEY RESPONDENT

In Your Own Words

"I am queer, but I am thinking of getting married to a distant male relative to get my parents off my back and to move out of a violent home. I can't help worrying if he will be able to tell that I'm not attracted to him. It sounds crude, but all I have to do is spread my legs, right? I wouldn't want to be labelled as 'gay' as it would hurt my family too much. I am also thinking of using birth control discreetly."

Regardless of the reason for pursuing such a relationship, if one of the partners is struggling with their sexuality, it can have a lasting impact on sexual intimacy. The struggling individual may not feel any sexual attraction to their partner and therefore will not want to or be able to have sex. They may also fall into depression for being stuck in a sex-less marriage, or they may pursue a secret same-sex relationship. It is also possible that this struggle can create unhealthy dynamics, particularly if the struggling partner is in denial about their sexuality. Instead of addressing the root cause of the sexual tension, the struggling partner may lash out at their partner and blame them for being the reason they don't want to have sex. This can further cause distress, low self esteem, and increased conflict between both partners.

It may be helpful to access support groups and find a space to speak to the struggles of either being queer in a straight marriage, or being straight in a marriage with someone queer. Support groups and therapy (if one is able to afford and access this) can be great ways to process, understand, and feel a connectedness to a community when your own family or marriage cannot cultivate that space.

[115] Shahar, Z. (2022). LGBTQ Muslim Marriage Praxis and Queer Ethics of Relation. in Ali, Kecia, ed. *Tying the Knot: A Feminist/Womanist Guide to Marriage in America.* Boston: OpenBU. https://hdl.handle.net/2144/44079.

DID YOU KNOW?

Coming out to one's family or loved ones can be complicated in faith communities and is often not as simple as it seems. In fact, the idea of "coming out" does not consider that coming out to one's family can sometimes be a matter of safety.[116] For example, it can compromise one's physical or emotional safety with their family or friends. Other times, the news can cause great distress to loved ones, and as such having to carry the weight of that burden, or it can result in one no longer being welcome in the family. As such, the decision to disclose can have numerous short-term and long-term impacts on the individual struggling, as well as their friends and family.

There is no "right way" or "one way" to "come out," and when we reject the notions of an experience that is a western concept, then we can see the nuance of the diverse ways queer Muslims can find joy and compassion in who they are and how they wish to exist. This also means there are several different ways queer Muslims can choose to share their queer identity, or not. Not choosing to share one's queer identity does not make one less queer.

Further, a more inclusive tool/language that can serve as a guide for queer folks to understand and navigate queerness is "coming in/letting in" instead of coming out.[117] This tool allows queer people to have more agency over their identity and has four functions according to therapist Gina Ali:

1. The personal agency to choose who you let in, when, and how. This is getting your power back.
2. The ability to create boundaries between your romantic and/or sexual partner and your family.
3. Reframe and prioritize privacy about love, sex, and intimacy.
4. Allows sexuality and gender to be fluid, and removes the expectation to "come out" or "confess" to be able to exist as you are.[118]

Support groups can be a great way to cultivate a sense of belonging not only for queer Muslims, but also for parents/caregivers of queer Muslims. Refer to the resources at the end of this chapter to learn more.

[116] Lang, N. (2020). How Do You Celebrate Coming Out Day When You Can't Be Out? them. Available at: https://www.them.us/story/coming-out-day-2020-fawzia-mirza-interview?fbclid=IwAR3fGuhayKHFM6Os-4H12SJb5h2ufUvfxuIMt2AMLaptkeWezdv-BiR4agw.
[117] Espinoza, R. (2016). "'Coming Out' or 'Letting In'? Recasting the LGBT Narrative." HuffPost. Available at: https://www.huffpost.com/entry/coming-out-or-letting-in_b_4070273.
[118] therapist Gina Ali, who is a Queer non binary Muslim therapist, organizer, and PhD student in Canada. See https://www.instagram.com/p/CP1W7DdAV6m/?.

Health Concerns

Depression or stress can absolutely have an impact on one's libido (sex drive) and sexual desire. If this is indeed the case, it may be helpful to discuss this issue with a healthcare provider who can come up with ways to help reduce stress or alleviate depression. Certain medications can also reduce libido, especially antidepressants, so this is also important to keep in mind. Your healthcare provider can help you find the balance between a better mental health state and managing your sex drive.

Life's Stressors

Life is stressful. Finances, work, housing, children, and family can all take its toll, and this stress can manifest in many ways such as disrupting one's libido and sexual desire. In some partnerships, one person may have a full-time job and still be tasked with running the household and childcare, which can cause extreme fatigue and limit time for pleasure. If this sounds familiar in your relationship, ensuring an equitable and balanced household when it comes to chores and childcare may be a way to help your partner feel less stressed. This will also ensure that they have more time on their hands to take care of themselves. Remember, it is also important to take time for yourselves as a couple outside of children and other expectations, even if it is an hour a week. Helping one another in the house and spending time together can build on intimacy and other connections that lead to sexual desire.

REFLECTION

What are some ways you can make time for intimacy in your partnership?

Sex After Life Changes

Life changes can also impact one's physical experience of sex and one's perceptions of their bodies. These changes, such as pregnancy, childbirth, menopause, or illnesses such as cancer, and other chronic conditions can disrupt sexual activity and desire. This can manifest as a lack of desire or fear of intimacy and can be a crossroads for a person to rediscover, reevaluate, redefine and reconnect with their sexual selves.

Menopause, particularly because of fluctuating hormones, is a life change that may cause a decreased sex drive, decreased sensitivity, and decreased arousal due to hormonal changes. These are often exacerbated by health concerns as menopausal people experience issues such as anxiety, depression, stress, sleep disturbances and much more.

Pregnancy and child birth can also lead to physical and hormonal changes that impact how a person may view their body and sex life. They may no longer find themselves attractive, or may just not be open to having sex. Outside of pregnancy, the process of delivering a child can be traumatic to the female sexual organs and healing can be a timely process. Doctors often recommend a 6-week waiting period after delivery before having sex, but this duration recommendation is not one-size-fits-all, and some wait much longer before resuming sexual activity.

While menopause, pregnancy, and childbirth can be part of a person's expected reproductive health journey, other life experiences that can impact one's relationship with sex, such as illness. Being diagnosed with cancer, or chronic illness such as pelvic pain or multiple scleorsis can change your sex life. Depending on the type of illness one has been diagnosed with, living through, or has survived, treatments can cause low libido, or can be invasive enough to remove a sex organ, which is an unquantifiable loss. In these cases, it is hard to feel like a sexual being, let alone be in the mood to have sex.

It may take time to feel like you want to have sex again, and this new sex may feel different from the old sex, but you are also a different person now. Different is not bad. It just means that you now have a new opportunity to explore and come to terms with what your new normal is. Take your time to make sense of this new normal. All these life changes can lead to vaginal dryness or other forms of reduced sexual function. Don't be afraid to explore other forms of intimacy. Try introducing lubricants, sex toys and other types of sexual play as you navigate intimacy again.

Remember you are not alone. Explain to your partner what you are going through and communicate what this next stage of sex and intimacy will look like for both of you. It may also be helpful to find community in a support group.

 **TRY IT OUT**

If you are experiencing sexual tension or roadblocks to intimacy with your partner and are unsure of what the root cause may be, here are a few things you can try to navigate the situation:

1. If your partner seems stressed or more tired than usual, offer ways to help relieve their stress.

2. If you are experiencing pain, see a medical professional to rule out any pelvic pain or sexual dysfunction you may have to address.

3. If you feel safe, consider having an open conversation with your partner about why their desire may not be there.

4. Explore the possibility of seeing a trained professional together. A couples counselor or a sex therapist can offer objective mediation to help navigate the sexual tension you might be feeling.

5. If you have recently experienced a life change, such as recently having had a baby or been diagnosed with an illness: have compassion with yourself, and consider seeking support from support groups or group therapy.

Chapter 3 Key Resources

This list is not comprehensive, and for full citations please see the works-cited at the end of the book

LGBTQ Muslims

- *Homosexuality in Islam: Critical Reflection on Gay, Lesbian, and Transgender Muslims* (book) and *Living Out Islam: Voices of Gay, Lesbian, and Transgender Muslims* (book) by Scott Kugle. Available online at Amazon.
- Visit the Muslim Alliance for Sexual and Gender Diversity (MAGSD) website at **http://www.muslimalliance. org/**.
- "Same-Sex Sexual Activity and Lesbian and Bisexual Women" (article) by Kecia Ali for The Feminist Sexual Ethics Project. Available online at: **https://www.brandeis.edu/projects/fse/muslim/same-sex.html.**
- Visit the Advocates for Youth website at **www.advocatesforyouth.org**. Check out the "I'm Muslim and I Might not be Straight" resource and "I'm Muslim and My Gender Doesn't Fit Me" resource under the "For activists and Health Information" tabs.
- "Queer Love, Abrahamic Morality, and (the limits of) American Muslim Marriage" (article) written By Julianne Hammer. Published in the *Journal of Theology and Sexuality* 2020. Available online.
- Visit the Masjid Al Rabia website at https://masjidalrabia.org. Masjid al-Rabia is a mosque and Islamic community center in Chicago that centers spiritual care for marginalized Muslims
- Visit the Queer Crescent website at www.queercrescent.org.
- Alhaj, Maher. (2021). Halal this way: Towards a Viable Queering in Sunni Islam, available at https://www. halalthisway.org.
- *LGBTQ Muslim Marriage Praxis and Queer Ethics of Relation.* (article) written by Zaynab Shahar. Published in Ali, Kecia, ed. *Tying the Knot: A Feminist/Womanist Guide to Marriage in America.* Boston: OpenBU. https://hdl.handle.net/2144/44079.

Duaa for Sexual Intercourse

- Please visit **www.duas.com** for a collection of duas. The dua for sexual intercourse can be found by searching "children" in the search box.

Sex with Disabilities

- Visit the Scarlateen website at **www.scarleteen.com**. More information on sex with disabilities can be found on the sex with disabilities page. Recommended reading includes the "Ultimate Guide to Sex and Disability: For All of Us Who Live with Disabilities, Chronic Pain, and Illness" article which can be found at www. scarleteen.com/article/disability.
- *Ultimate Guide to Sex and Disability: For All of Us Who Live with Disabilities, Chronic Pain, and Illness* (book) by Cory Silverberg and Miriam Kaufman.
- *PleasureABLE: Sexual Device Manual For Persons With Disabilities* by Kate Naphtali, Edith MacHattie & Stacy Elliott: 2009 available at: http://www.dhrn.ca/files/sexualhealthmanual lowres 2010 0208.pdf.
- *Sex & Disability* (book) by Robert McRuer.
- *Sex, Sexuality, and the Autism Spectrum* (book) by Wendy Lawson and Glenys Jones.
- Come as You Are (website) http://www.comeasyouare.com/sex-and-disability.html.

Sexual Dysfunction

- Hope and Her Vaginismus (website) **www.vaginismus.com** for more information on Vaginismus.
- Planned Parenthood (website) **www.plannedparenthood.com**. More information on sexual dysfunction can be found under the "learn", "sex and pleasure", and "sexual dysfunction" tabs.
- Scarleteen (website) at **www.scarleteen.com**. Recommended articles include- "Getting to Know Your "New Normal": Tips for Sex When You Have Pelvic Pain" by Nicole Guappone.

Chapter 4: Keeping Up With Your Sexual Health

L. KETHU

In This Chapter

This chapter will explore what it means to maintain your sexual health. From keeping up to date with life saving preventative care to understanding your body and health after you become sexually active, learn about all the ways you can ensure you are keeping up with your sexual health.

Quick Snapshot

Prevention Before Intervention

REFLECTION

At what age did you first visit a healthcare professional for your sexual and reproductive health? What are some cultural or religious messages you received from your family about pelvic exams?

Whether or not you are sexually active, keeping up with your sexual and reproductive health is critical and even lifesaving. From addressing common health issues such as urinary tract infections and yeast infections to preventative screenings for cancers to navigating pregnancy, fertility, or STIs, there are a range of medical professionals that can make this journey more accessible. Having the right provider and knowing what questions to ask can make all the difference in helping you feel informed and in control of your reproductive health.

The American College of Obstetricians and Gynecologists (ACOG) recommends that cisgender women and people with vaginas start seeing a women's health care provider between the ages of 13 and 15.[119] Examples of a women's health care provider are pediatricians specializing in adolescents, certified nurse midwives (CNMs), physician assistants (PAs), women's health nurse practitioners (WHNPs), and obstetrician/gynecologists (OB/GYNs). These trained professionals can ensure that people are receiving accurate sexual and reproductive health education. It also opens the lines of communication for a person to ask medical professionals about their body.

DID YOU KNOW?

Gynecological visits are critical for cisgender women, non-binary people with vaginas, and trans men who need to keep up with their reproductive health. For trans men, these visits can be doubly uncomfortable and bring up feelings of dysphoria and trauma. However, these visits can be lifesaving, identify common health issues early on, and prevent cancer or other chronic illness.[120]

---

[119] American College of Obstetricians and Gynecologists. (2020). The Initial Reproductive Health Visit: ACOG Committee Opinion. Number 811. *Obstetrics and Gynecology*, 136(4), e70-e80.

[120] For more information on how trans men can ensure their reproductive health needs are being met, check out https://web.archive.org/web/20170424225956/http://checkitoutguys.ca/.

TYPES OF HEALTHCARE PROVIDERS TO VISIT FOR
YOUR SEXUAL AND REPRODUCTIVE HEALTH:

Family Medicine Doctor

A family doctor is a doctor who provides comprehensive care for every family member regardless of their age. These doctors are trained in all aspects of primary care medicine.

Nurse Practitioner

Nurse practitioners are primary caregivers who are well-trained to deliver quality care for patients. OB/GYN nurse practitioners focus specifically on healthcare for cisgender women and people with a uterus.

Obstetrician/Gynecologist

An OB/GYN is a doctor who specializes in reproductive health for cisgender women and people with a uterus. Obstetricians work with pregnant people and deliver babies, while gynecologists treat a wide range of issues when it comes to the female reproductive system such as STIs. OB/GYNs specialize in both obstetrics and gynecology.

Urologist

A urologist is a doctor who specializes in diagnosis and treatments of the urinary tract for all genders. In addition to this, urologists also treat all issues related to the male reproductive tract.

Midwife

A midwife is a trained healthcare professional who provides care for pregnant people and newborns during labor and birth.

Health Educator

Health educators who specialize in sexual and reproductive health are workers tasked with educating people on their sexual health. They work in different settings such as clinics, hospitals, communities, and schools.

Pharmacist

Pharmacists are often able to provide expertise on birth control options and how to access emergency birth control.

Mental Health Professional

Mental health professionals can address mental roadblocks and traumas that may lead to sexual health issues.

Physical Therapist

Physical therapists who specialize in pelvic pain can help provide therapy and exercises to address painful sex or difficulties with vaginal intercourse.

Sexologist

Sexologists are therapists who specialize in sex. This means that they offer resources, education, and counseling to patients in order to help them lead healthier and more fulfilling sex lives.

Doula

Doulas are people trained to offer support during health experiences such as pregnancy, delivery, abortion, etc.

CONSIDERATIONS FOR PEOPLE WHO DON'T HAVE INSURANCE

In countries like the United States, healthcare is a privilege, not a right. It is difficult to access appropriate healthcare treatment regardless of your insurance coverage, but this is often exacerbated when you are uninsured or underinsured. This means people may have to pay exorbitant out-of-pocket costs to see a provider and, consequently, people may delay utilizing preventative health care measures, which can lead to poorer health outcomes in the future.

Fortunately, there are several options available for accessing free or low-cost healthcare, depending on your location and income:

Community clinics can often be accessed at no cost or at very low costs, depending on the service being utilized. They often provide preventative care, routine care, and primary care.

Government funded programs such as your local public health department or Planned Parenthood also offer low-cost access to healthcare. The amount you pay is determined by a sliding-scale, which means that what you pay depends on your current income.

University or teaching hospitals are able to provide free or reduced healthcare if they have a charity care program or if you have a chronic illness and are seeking long-term care.

Charity or non-profit hospitals also provide care for people who cannot afford treatment.

Walk-in clinics and urgent care centers are available for patients who are not insured and are a way to pay cash to see healthcare providers. These options may be cheaper than seeing a healthcare provider directly.

University-affiliated student health clinics are available for registered students and services are included in tuition fees, so do not cost anything additional to access. These clinics offer a full range of services and also include mental health services and access to ongoing therapy.

POINT OF INTEREST

Did you know you could get medical care without it being revealed on your insurance?

It may be important to you to seek a certain service or test and not have it reported on your insurance, especially if you are on your parent's or partner's health insurance. There are ways to get the care that you need, while still protecting that health information. Here are some tips:

1. If you are a student, consider your student health center at your college or university. These clinics are available to registered students, do not require additional insurance information, and are paid for via tuition and student health fees.

2. Title X clinics are federally funded clinics that provide individuals with comprehensive family planning and preventative health services.

3. Talk to your healthcare provider about what your options are for billing. Sometimes they can bill in a way that protects health information on statements.

 TRY IT OUT

Outside of locating a cheap provider, there are other ways that may cut costs when seeking healthcare. These include:

- Find out whether you are eligible for Medicare and Medicaid, and how to apply in order to access free or low-cost healthcare.
- Double-checking and itemizing your medical bills. It is possible for hospitals to make mistakes or overcharge for procedures, and asking for an itemized bill allows you to understand exactly what you were charged for. Requesting for an itemized bill may also give you the opportunity to negotiate hospital bills.
- Depending on your provider, you may be able to request a payment plan in order to reduce the potential upfront costs.
- Request generic medications and utilize prescription saving websites and applications such as GoodRx to reduce the amount you have to pay for prescription medication.

The First Visit

It is important that people of all genders visit their healthcare providers for sexual health exams. This ensures a long and healthy sexual life and an overall better quality of life.

Urological and genital examinations are performed for people with male reproductive organs in order to identify, treat, and ensure the overall health of the penis, testes and prostate. During these exams, doctors are also able to perform breast exams to rule out male breast cancer. They will also test for STIs through either taking a blood sample or a urine sample.

Your provider will initially do a visual exam of the sexual organs, as well as gently touching the areas around them to feel for abnormalities. They may also ask you to turn your head and cough during the exam so they can have a better feel of the organs. Though not common for young men, your provider may also conduct a rectal exam. They will ask questions about your sexual health history to have a better understanding of your sexual health behaviors.

Gynecological exams are performed to examine female reproductive organs. The first annual gynecological exam is not recommended unless a person has had sex, feels like there is something wrong with their sexual organs, or is 21 years of age. This visit will involve an examination of several body parts. First, the health care provider will examine the breasts for any lumps or abnormalities. Next, they will do a pelvic exam. This involves the doctor examining the genital area from the outside and may involve a tool called a speculum to examine the inside. A speculum helps healthcare providers have a better look at the inside of the vagina and cervix. They may also use one or two fingers to palpate the reproductive organs and to determine the size and shape of the uterus. Lastly, they may do a pap smear, also known as a pap test. The American College of Obstetricians and Gynecologists recommends a pap smear beginning at age 21, and then typically every three years if the initial results are normal.[121] If the results are abnormal, you may be requested to have a pap smear every six months to a year. A pap smear involves gently swabbing the cervix with a small brush or spatula. These cells from the swab will check for any cervical abnormalities. An abnormal pap smear can indicate several possibilities:

- An infection or an inflammation of the cervix
- Potential HPV exposure
- Early detection for cervical cancer
- Recent sexual activity. You are advised to not have sex less than 24 hours before a pelvic exam.

One particular STI of concern is human papilloma virus (HPV). Most HPVs are low risk, meaning that they only can cause skin warts. For example, HPV types 6 and 11 cause 90% of all genital warts. However, some strains of HPV are high-risk and can lead to cancer. HPV types 16 and 18 are responsible for most HPV-caused cancers, and there are other less common cancerous strains.[122]

---

[121] You can learn more about pap smears and what to expect at the visit here: https://www.youtube.com/watch?v=50BEEDBJqR4.
[122] World Health Organization. (2022). *Cervical Cancer*. Available at: https://www.who.int/news-room/fact-sheets/detail/human-papillomavirus-(hpv)-and-cervical-cancer.

Currently, HPV vaccines protect against several types of HPV, including types 16 and 18, which cause the greatest risk for contracting cervical cancer. However, the HPV vaccine will not prevent against all types of HPV, so it is advised to still use protection during sexual activity and get tested for STIs regularly. Moreover, condoms only reduce the risk of HPV as HPV is also transmitted via skin-to-skin contact.

Also, it is important to remember that cisgender men and people with penises can contract and spread HPV and that they are also eligible to get the HPV vaccine.[123] Most insurance companies will cover the HPV vaccine regardless of someone's sex, but please check with your insurance company to verify this. HPV is also visible in men and can lead to genital warts and cancer. However, unlike Pap testing with women, there is no HPV test for men other than visual examination of warts and visual presence of cancer (penile, testicular, etc.)

The Pap Smear/Virginity Myth

It is not uncommon in Muslim communities for elders or other family members to be uncomfortable with younger people visiting a gynecologist before they are married and/or sexually active. This is because they fear that the hymen may be compromised during the visit. The need to preserve the hymen is falsely conflated with a desire to preserve a person's virginity. In reality, these attitudes are often influenced by cultural beliefs that are misappropriated as being grounded in religion. Visiting a gynecologist before one is sexually active is neither wrong nor is it a sexual activity that compromises one's virginity.[124]

If you are not sexually active, and you are worried that the pelvic exam and pap smear might be painful, speak to your healthcare provider about these concerns so they may better ease you through the process. Depending on the circumstances, there are also some providers that may be open to considering delaying a pelvic exam until after you have had sex or using a smaller sized speculum.

 DID YOU KNOW?

Many modern medical advances should be credited to a Black woman named Henrietta Lacks.[125]

In 1951, a 30-year-old Henrietta Lacks visited The Johns Hopkins Hospital, where she would be diagnosed with cervical cancer. As she was being examined, a piece of her tumor was sampled and cultured without her or her family's consent. Over the past 70 years, most cells used to conduct scientific experiments such as polio vaccine testing, in vitro fertilization, and drug development for illnesses like herpes, appendicitis, influenza, and certain STIs can be traced back to those cells. HeLa cells, as they are known in medical research, are the backbone of a multi-billion-dollar research industry.

Lacks' family was unaware of their existence until 20 years later and have yet to receive any compensation, despite the overwhelming importance of these cells. To find out more, Lacks' story is told in a book titled *The Immortal Life of Henrietta Lacks.*

[123] Centers for Disease Control and Prevention. (2022). *HPV and Men—Fact Sheet.* Available at: https://www.cdc.gov/std/hpv/stdfact-hpv-and-men.htm.
[124] Muslim Women's League. (1995). *Sex and Sexuality.* Available at: https://www.mwlusa.org/topics/sexuality/sexuality.html.
[125] Skloot, R. (2010). *The Immortal Life of Henrietta Lacks.* Crown Publishing.

STI TESTING

A pap smear isn't the only way to test for STIs. STI testing may include:

- A urine test (chlamydia, gonorrhea)
- A cheek swab (HIV)
- A genital swab (chlamydia, gonorhhea, syphilis, trichomoniasis)
- A blood test (HIV, genital herpes, syphilis)
- A physical exam (trichomoniasis, warts)

Most STIs are asymptomatic, meaning they have no noticeable symptoms. Therefore, if one has had sex without protection or one's partner has an STI, testing is the only way to know for sure if they have an STI.

 DID YOU KNOW?

BREAST HEALTH

It is important to keep up with your breast health, no matter your age and gender. Breasts may look or feel different over time, so it is important to have an understanding of what is normal for you and what is not. Certain organizations like the American Cancer Society no longer recommend self breast exams due to the heightened fear and anxiety that accompany benign breast lumps. Routine annual mammograms are recommended for individuals after they turn 40. It is still important to look out for signs such as:

- Breast and/or nipple pain
- A change in breast size or shape
- Nipple discharge that is not breast milk
- Dimpling and irritation of the breast skin
- Redness or discoloration of the breast and/or nipple[126]

Although breast cancer development may be gene-, age-, or race-related, some environmental risk factors include:
- Diet and exercise
- Alcohol consumption
- Smoking
- Stress and anxiety

---

[126] Watch our video on self breast exams here: https://www.youtube.com/watch?v=j6NHVjHh4jw.

Preparing for your first gynecological visit and pelvic exam

Visiting a gynecologist for the first time may be a daunting experience, and getting a pelvic exam can be uncomfortable whether or not you've been sexually active. Regardless of where your discomfort with your first gynecological visit and pelvic exam stems from, here are some tips that may make the experience a lot less stressful:

Before the Appointment

- **Find the right healthcare provider.** Consider the characteristics you would like your provider to have. Learn about their education and training. Read patient reviews if they are available.
- **Prepare yourself for the appointment.** Make a list of health issues you want to raise with your provider and any questions you may have.
- **Share your concerns.** When you get to your appointment, let your healthcare provider know that this will be your first visit. They will be able to answer any questions you have before the exam.

During the Appointment

- **Communicate clearly.** Be clear with your symptoms, and do not be afraid to be assertive if your provider wants to dismiss them.
- **Ask for documentation.** If you ask for a service and your provider refuses it, make sure they document why it's been refused and add it to your charts.[127]
- **Ask questions.** Do not be afraid to ask questions during the examination. If you want to know about why the doctor is doing something or just learn more about the process, don't be shy. You are not wasting their time by asking them.
- **Ask for what you need.** Ask your provider to use a smaller speculum during the exam. This may reduce the amount of pain and discomfort you may feel, especially if you're not sexually active.
- **Ask for a lubricant.** If you are not allergic to lubricants, ask your provider to use a lubricant before inserting the speculum. This will ensure that the speculum slides in and out much easier.
- **Remember to breathe.**

---

[127] If you feel like your provider is not helpful, then do not be afraid to look for a new one. Your provider, at minimum, should take your concerns seriously and follow up on them.

REFLECTION

Before you make a list of questions you have for your doctor, consider the following prompts to help you. Are there any concerns you have about your reproductive health?

Are there any questions you have about sex, contraception, or pregnancy?

Have you experienced any form of trauma that may be helpful for your doctor to know before they examine you?

DID YOU KNOW?

Although there have been great strides in healthcare, science, and medicine, there are still limitations when it comes to women's health. Women, especially women of color, are under-diagnosed and under-treated, often leading to poorer health outcomes overall. Women of color, specifically Black women, bear the brunt of this discrimination as they are 3.3 times more likely to die from pregnancy or maternal-related incidences.[128] It is important to advocate for yourself when seeing a healthcare professional.[129]

 TRY IT OUT
Questions to Ask Your Healthcare Provider

When preparing for your visit to your healthcare provider, you may want to come up with a list of questions that will make your visit smoother. Here are a few that you can ask.

- What is normal when it comes to vaginal/penile discharge?
- What birth control is best for me?
- I have been feeling (insert symptom). Is this normal? Can I get tests for it?
- How do I know if I have an STI? How can I get tested for an STI?
- What should I do if sex is painful for me?
- Can certain medications I'm taking affect my sex drive?
- How can I start preparing to get pregnant?

[128] Neighmond, P. (2019). Why Racial Gaps in Maternal Mortality Persist. *NPR*. Retrieved from: https:// www.npr.org/sections/health-shots/2019/05/10/722143121/why-racial-gaps-in-maternal-mortality- persist?t=1586793409588.

[129] To learn more about health disparities in Black communities, check out the HEARTfelt Conversation series with Community Health Compass at https://www.youtube.com/watch?v=0JoemhgDM8U&feature=youtu.be. Also check out this amazing list of six organizations that support Black women's health: https://www.vogue.com/article/black-womens-health-support-organizations.

Sex: What Happens Next? Immediate and the Long Term

Preventative care aside, there are both immediate and longer-term considerations that may require keeping up with your sexual (and spiritual) health once you are sexually active. These include considering post-sex routines such as hygiene as well as addressing unexpected outcomes such as contraception failure or an unplanned pregnancy.

Hygiene

While routines after sex may differ—some may want to shower immediately, while others may choose to sleep or doze off—there are some recommendations that can be helpful with respect to hygiene, such as:

- For those having experienced vaginal penetrative intercourse, it is recommended to urinate and wash the vulva shortly afterward.[130] This practice can help reduce the occurrence of urinary tract infections and yeast infections, which sometimes happen more frequently once someone becomes sexually active. The vagina, which is an internal organ, is self-cleansing and does not need to be douched or cleaned with soapy and scented products.

- Islamically, it is required to take a head-to-toe shower (*ghusl*) in time for the next prayer. The rules for this ritual washing can differ depending on how you practice.[131]

 DID YOU KNOW?

Urinary tract infections (UTIs) and yeast infections can occur more frequently after becoming sexually active. UTIs and yeast infections have different causes and symptoms and thankfully they can both be easily diagnosed and treated.

A UTI occurs when bacteria gets into your urinary system. You don't have to have sex to get a UTI, but sexual activity can increase your risk. Yeast infections occur when too much fungus builds in a moist area of your skin, which, in this case, is the genital region. You can also develop a yeast infection without having sex. Peeing shortly after having sex can be an easy preventative measure against getting a UTI or a yeast infection.

You need a medical professional to diagnose a yeast infection or UTI, but there are symptoms that may help you differentiate between the two. Yeast infections often lead to swelling, pain, and itchiness in the genital area. People also tend to experience unusual discharge, although odorless, and pain when urinating and having sex. Symptoms of UTIs include pain and burning during urination and foul smelling and discolored (or bloody) urine. If you feel the continuous urge to

[130] Corinna, H. (2014). First Intercourse 101. *Scarlateen*. Retrieved from: https://www.scarleteen.com/article/ sexuality/first_intercourse_101.

[131] To learn more, check out @villageauntie on instagram for a tutorial on *ghusl*. Lindsey-Ali, Angelica. (2020) A Quick & Dirty Guide to Ghusl! Part 2 Retrieved from: https://www.instagram.com/tv/B8w00Vag5HP/?igshid=pir41zlfeqtd. https://www.instagram.com/tv/B8w00Vag5HP/?igshid=pir41zlfeqtd.

urinate even during your sleep, this could also be a sign of a UTI. Its symptoms can also consist of pain and pressure in the pelvic area, back, and lower abdomen. You may even start to vomit, feel nauseous, and have a fever and chills if you have a more serious urinary tract infection.

If you have any of these symptoms, it is recommended to visit your healthcare provider as soon as possible to prevent further complications.

Unexpected Outcomes

Becoming sexually active can also sometimes have unexpected outcomes. Perhaps by having sex, your relationship has changed for the better and you may feel closer to your partner after sharing that experience. It's possible that it may create awkwardness or distance, especially if one of you regrets having sex. Sex may also have certain consequences that may manifest in unexpected outcomes, such as:

BROKEN CONDOM

It is not uncommon for couples to experience a broken condom at least once during their sex life. If you do not want to risk pregnancy, emergency contraception is a safe and effective way to ensure that pregnancy does not result from that sexual encounter.[132] Depending on the state or country you live in, it is available over the counter at most drugstores without a prescription or proof of age.[133] It's important to note that it is effective when taken as soon as possible (up to 72 hours after sex). So, it may be a good idea to have it on hand in your medicine cabinet at home. Depending on the state in which you live, it is available over-the-counter in most drugstores without a prescription or proof of age (although in some states that may be required). If you have access to a pharmacist or medical professional, try to seek their advice as well if you are considering emergency contraception as an option. Certain emergency contraceptive options are not effective for people over a certain weight, so take this into account when deciding your options.[134] While emergency contraception has been regulated as being safe, as with any medication, every body may respond differently, and it is not meant to be used as a regular form of birth control. Typical side effects can include nausea, headache, dizziness, fatigue, breast tenderness, and irregular bleeding or menstrual cycles.

A copper IUD is 99.9% effective at preventing pregnancy when inserted within 5 days after unprotected sex. It needs to be inserted by a doctor or nurse, so make sure to make an appointment as soon as possible.[135]

UNPLANNED PREGNANCY

No matter how diligent couples are about contraception, there is *always* a risk of getting pregnant when engaging in penis-vagina sex. The only 100% effective birth control method is abstinence from any sexual activity that involves semen near the vagina. In fact, according to the Centers for Disease and

[132] Lavendar, N. (2019). Here's How Emergency Contraception Actually Works. *Self*. Retrieved from: https:// www.self.com/story/how-emergency-contraception-works.
[133] Guttmacher Institute. (N.d.). *Emergency Contraception*. Retrieved from: https://www.guttmacher.org/state-policy/ explore/emergency-contraception.
[134] Note that if you are on the pill, you can take multiple pills as emergency contraception, but this is not recommended for all pills and requires research on dosage and which pills to take. Speak with your healthcare provider before taking multiple pills.

Control, almost half of pregnancies are unplanned.[136]

After the initial shock of an unplanned pregnancy, people will likely feel a mix of emotions, which may range from worry and fear to excitement and joy. Unplanned pregnancies can still be in the "nice surprise category," depending on whether or not a person is ready to be a parent in their current stage in life. If that sounds like you, then congratulations! As you enter this new stage in life, you will experience so many emotions and changes, and there are numerous pregnancy and childbirth resources that offer a wealth of information.[137]

For others, unplanned pregnancies can cause much uncertainty, panic, fear, and anxiety. We live in a world where everyone has something to say about decision making around pregnancy, especially if the circumstances aren't aligned with cultural, social, and political norms. This is even greater for those from faith and cultural communities where pregnancies that occur outside of marriage are stigmatized, or for expectant parents who are above or below the socially acceptable "parenting age." If this sounds like you, take a moment and breathe. While it may seem like your options are limited, you will get through this. Deciding what to do can be very overwhelming, but there are people who can help. Your doctor, a trusted friend or adult, or your partner can be that source of support you might need to navigate this time. However, it's also possible you don't want anyone in your friends and family circle to know, and you want to keep this decision entirely private. That's fine, too, and there are still people who can help.

From the moment of the positive pregnancy test, the pregnant person is inundated with decision after decision. Choosing to parent or not to parent, what to eat and drink, which vitamins to take, whether to opt in or out of genetic testing become a new normal. This can further be complicated as the family and friends around you share unsolicited advice of what you should or should not be doing. The pressure of the responsibility can feel insurmountable; however, having the right support systems and access to critical information can help move you to more informed decision making that reduces self-doubt and guilt. Many health clinics, including Planned Parenthood and Exhale Pro Voice offer confidential counseling through their hotline, and their websites also have information as well if you want to remain completely anonymous.[138]

[135] Planned Parenthood. (N.d.). *How Do IUDs Work as Emergency Contraception?* Retrieved from: https://www.plannedparenthood.org/learn/morning-after-pill-emergency-contraception/how-do-iuds-work-emergency-contraception.

[136] To learn more about your options, see: https://www.cdc.gov/reproductivehealth/contraception/unintendedpregnancy/index.htm.

[137] A great resource to learn about your developing baby is WebMd's pregnancy week-by-week: https://www.webmd.com/baby/pregnancy-week-by-week/default.htm.

[138] Links to hotlines and different counseling services are available at the end of this chapter under Resources.

TRY IT OUT
Explore Your Options for an Unplanned Pregnancy

Whenever you are faced with an unplanned pregnancy, your options are:

Parenting: You always have the option to follow through with the pregnancy, give birth, and raise the child. This can disrupt any immediate plans you had for the future, such as school, work, finances, any other children you may already have, or may even have implications for your current relationship and social circles. It is an option that many people choose, and it is possible to successfully adjust to a new life with a baby.

Adoption: Another option that you have for an unplanned pregnancy is to continue with the pregnancy, but place your child with another family permanently. The adoption process varies from state to state, but a good resource to begin your research is Adoptive Families.[139] Many reproductive health clinics have outlined questions you can ask yourself, people that you can turn to help you make this decision, the locations for their clinics, and the timeline for when you have to make each decision.[140]

Abortion: This option is one that involves taking a medication (also known as medication abortion or the abortion pill) or undergoing a procedure that terminates the pregnancy (also known as a surgical abortion or in-clinic abortion).[141]

Remember, your pregnancy will continue to progress, even as you decide what to do. Be aware of this, as abortion restrictions vary state by state in terms of how far along you can have an abortion and what your insurance will cover. The same applies to different adoption agencies and their policies on setting up adoption paperwork. Moreover, often Muslims have questions about the spiritual implications of abortion and adoption, which will be discussed later in this chapter.

---

[139] To see adoption laws by state, see: https://www.adoptivefamilies.com/adoption-laws-by-state/.
[140] Planned Parenthood. (N.d.). *Pregnancy Options*. Retrieved from: https://www.plannedparenthood.org/learn/ pregnancy/pregnancy-options
[141] To learn more about abortion, see: https://www.plannedparenthood.org/learn/abortion.

CONTRACTING A SEXUALLY-TRANSMITTED INFECTION

Condoms, dental dams, and female condoms provide the greatest level of protection for most STIs after abstinence. If you think you are at risk of contracting an STI from your partner, do not have unprotected sex. For information on the various STIs, refer to the previous chapter in this book. As mentioned, many STIs do not exhibit symptoms at all, so if you are sexually active, it may be helpful for you and your partner to get tested for STIs periodically.

You can get tested for STIs at numerous places: the OB/GYN office, your college campus or local health clinic, and Planned Parenthood clinics. Often many city health departments also offer free STI testing.

 TRY IT OUT

How to tell your partner you have an STI

Here are a few tips that may help ease the process of telling your partner you have an STI:

Plan for the conversation: After getting tested and speaking to a health professional about the best route of treatment for you, decide on how and where you want to speak with your partner. This can be in person, via text or phone call, or through whatever medium you feel safest. Make sure this is done before having any sexual contact with your partner, including kissing if you have an infection that could be transmitted through kissing.

Be specific and answer questions: There's no easy way to have this conversation, but you do have to be specific when it comes to letting your partner know what STI you have. You may want to explain to them what that means, its course of treatment, and address any other questions your partner may have. If they have questions you can't answer, direct them to trusted resources such as a healthcare professional, trusted organizations, or well-researched books.

Ask questions about their sexual practices. If this diagnosis has caught you off guard, and you have not had any sexual contact with anyone other than your partner, then it may be important to consider whether it is possible that your partner has had sex with someone other than you. It is also possible that they acquired an STI from a previous partnership without knowing it.

Ask them to get tested. If your partner has never been tested, this may also be a good time for them to get tested.

Consider the future of your relationship. It is possible that your partner may not be as receptive to this information as you would hope. If they get upset, react negatively, or make you feel bad, then it may be helpful to distance yourself from them for a while. You may both also decide not to continue the relationship.

Find a support system. It is important to surround yourself with loving and supportive people as you get the necessary care you need for your specific condition.

Starting a Family

POINT OF INTEREST

There are multiple paths to starting a family.

We are all familiar with getting pregnant through penetrative vaginal sex as a way to start a family, but it is important to remember that all families are different. There is no singular way to experience parenthood/caregiving. Not everyone wants to or can have biological children, and even though the pressure to do so is strong in many Muslim communities, it's important to remember that Islam does not place religious value on one's parental status. Moreover, not everyone is in a relationship that allows for both partners to have a child biologically. As such, there are many paths to caregiving, ranging from formal adoption and fostering, assisted reproductive technology, to caring for a family member's child.

Families choose to adopt or foster children for various reasons. For some families, being a parent means raising your grandchild, niece, nephew, or any other family member. Sometimes fostering or adopting as a form of caregiving/parenthood is not always planned for, but it doesn't make it any less real. Every non-biological family is valid as long as love and care are involved. Non-biological parenting is not always an easy road, and a lot of families may lack community support for it. Parent Center Hub has a list of resources available that may be beneficial as you navigate parenting.[142]

Pregnancy

Pregnancy is not always unwanted or unplanned. In fact, pregnancy can be an option that people choose to actively pursue to fulfill their desire to start a family. If you do make the choice to have a child biologically, here is some information to consider as you plan a pregnancy.

Preconception

Having a safe and healthy pregnancy and post-pregnancy are the goals for parents-to-be. One of the ways to ensure a safe and healthy pregnancy is to prepare for preconception with care. Eating a nutritious diet and living an active lifestyle are great ways to prepare one's body for the changes during pregnancy.[143]

---

142 Center for Parent Information and Resources. (N.d.). *Resources Especially for Foster or Adoptive Families*. Retrieved from: https://www.parentcenterhub.org/fosteradoptive/.
143 A great resource on preparing to get pregnant: https://www.cdc.gov/preconception/planning.html.

 TRY IT OUT

If you and your partner are actively trying to conceive, here are a few ways you can increase your chances:

Have regular sex. Have sex every other day between day 10–20 of your cycle.[144]

Reduce stress. Stress, fatigue, illness can all disrupt your cycle and delay conception.

Track your cycle. There are plenty of methods and tools to help you track your cycle. These include:

- Ovulation predictor kit
- Saliva ferning kits
- Tracking basal body temperature
- Cervical mucus charting

L. KETHU

Maternal Nutrition

If a person intends on getting pregnant, it is important to consume adequate nutrition even before pregnancy. Healthy nutrition before pregnancy and throughout has been proven to yield positive long-term health effects, not just for the pregnant person, but also for the child.[145] Poor diet can lead to poorer health outcomes for one's baby. Pregnant people should make sure to eat a variety of foods to obtain all the necessary vitamins and minerals for both mother and child.

L. KETHU

So, why is a healthy diet so important before pregnancy? The most critical structural developments of the fetus occur within the first 100 days, including the development of the brain and spinal cord. Some people don't know that they are pregnant at this time, and if the mother has a folate deficiency, the fetus runs a higher risk of developing neural tube defects such as spina bifida or anencephaly. The CDC recommends taking folate supplements specifically for this reason.[146] If a person wants to get pregnant, it is also important that they stop smoking or drinking alcohol at this time, too.

For people who intend on getting pregnant, are pregnant, or just gave birth, it is important that their diet consists of foods with a good amount of vitamins and minerals with minimal or no processed food. A healthy pregnancy diet consists of consuming foods with high folic acid, iron, protein, omega-3s, calcium, fortified grains, and other vitamins and minerals. During the second and third trimesters of pregnancy, pregnant people need up to an extra 350–500 calories a day to house and feed a growing fetus. Fruits, vegetables, and dark leafy greens also contain adequate supplies of vitamins and minerals. Some other good foods to eat while pregnant include dairy products like Greek yogurt. High protein foods such as lean meats, eggs, and legumes, fortified grains. It is also important to take prenatal vitamins and drink a lot of water.

---

[144] This recommendation is based on a typical 28-day cycle. If your cycle is shorter or longer, then this timeline may be different. Get to know your cycle and patterns and speak with a healthcare provider to determine if it is different for you.

[145] Check out our video on maternal health nutrition here: https://hearttogrow.org/resources/heart-to-heart-maternal-health-nutrition/.

[146] Center for Disease Control and Prevention. (2021). *Folic Acid.* Available at: https://www.cdc.gov/ncbddd/folicacid/.

DID YOU KNOW?

Prenatal vitamins are one way to ensure that the body is receiving all the recommended daily nutrients needed for pregnancy. It takes about three to six months for the body to have adequate amounts of vitamins, so these should be taken well before conception. One particularly important vitamin is folic acid. Consuming 400 micrograms of folic acid daily at least one month before and during pregnancy will lower the chance of neural tube defects in the baby.

Depending on the state you live in, some government-funded health programs cover all aspects of prenatal care, including vitamins. It is also important to find out whether you are eligible for programs specifically focused on maternal nutrition such as Women, Infants, and Children (WIC), which could aid in ensuring that you have adequate nutrition. WIC distributes food, milk, and other supplies to pregnant people.

During Your Pregnancy

After a positive at-home pregnancy test, it is important to make an appointment with your doctor to confirm the pregnancy via a blood test or another urine test. This should usually take place between 6–8 weeks after your last period. In case of a pregnancy, an ultrasound will be performed to detect the heartbeat of the fetus and to ensure that it is healthy.

Throughout your pregnancy, your doctor will run tests to check on you and the fetus' health. This will include regularly taking blood to determine immune system function, nutritional level, and gestational diabetes.

Trimesters

Pregnancies are divided into three stages, or trimesters. The first trimester is the first 12 weeks of pregnancy; the second trimester is from week 13 to the end of week 26; the third trimester is from week 27 to the end of the pregnancy.

The first sign of pregnancy is often a missed menstrual period, which is an indication that fertilization and implantation have occurred. This occurs during the first trimester. The first trimester is also a vital time for fetal development when all major organs and systems are formed. Most miscarriages and birth defects tend to happen during the first trimester.

Some of the major developments happening during the first trimester include:

- The nervous system (brain and spinal cord) forms.
- The baby's heart forms and begins to beat.
- The arms and legs develop and begin to grow.
- The fingers and toes also begin to form.
- The external sex organs form and begin to show.
- The face begins to develop.

During this time, the pregnant person may start to feel symptoms such as fatigue and morning sickness. This is in part due to changes the body has to undergo to support the development of the fetus and placenta. Your body will also increase its blood supply in order to carry nutrients and oxygen to the fetus.

By the second trimester, the fetus has developed most of its vital organs and continues to grow in size and weight. Some of the major developments happening during the second trimester include:

- The musculoskeletal system forms.
- The skin forms.
- The taste buds form and the ability to suck and swallow develops.
- Footprints and fingerprints begin to form.
- Meconium develops in the baby's intestinal tract, resulting in the baby's first bowel movement.
- The sleep cycle is developed.
- The lungs are formed, but do not start to function.
- The ability to hear occurs.
- There is increased activity and movement.

Morning sickness tends to decrease at this time, and the pregnant person typically has higher energy levels and is more comfortable in this trimester. This is when most pregnant people start to show.

Development for both the fetus and pregnant person continue during the third trimester. Developmental milestones for the fetus include:

- The bones are formed.
- There are increased movements and kicking.
- There is increased body fat and storage of iron, calcium, and other vital minerals.
- The eyes can open and close.
- There is continued growth, making it harder for the baby to move around.

By the end of the third trimester (37+ weeks), the baby can function independently and is considered full term. At this time, the pregnant person may feel more discomfort and may struggle with shortness of breath, difficulty sleeping, and more frequent urination. Swelling around the face, fingers, and ankles is also normal to a certain extent as well as breast tenderness. If the swelling is sudden or extreme, it is important to see your doctor right away as this could be a sign of a more serious condition. As the pregnant person gets closer to their due date, the cervix starts to thin and soften in a process called effacement. This will help the cervix open during childbirth.

 DID YOU KNOW?

The sperm determines the baby's sex. All eggs carry the X chromosome, while sperm carry 50% X chromosomes and 50% Y chromosomes. If the sperm contributes a Y chromosome, the fetus will be XY and will be assigned male at birth; if the sperm contributes an X, the XX fetus will be assigned female at birth. On some occasions, a person can be born with a missing sex chromosome or an extra copy of a sex chromosome; this is known as a sex chromosomal abnormality.

DID YOU KNOW?

Zygote, Embryo, Fetus, Baby... What's the Difference?

We've all come across these terms at one point or another when describing what is inside the uterus of a pregnant person. The same way pregnancies are divided into trimesters, the growth of a baby is also divided into stages of development. Once an egg is fertilized by the sperm, that single cell is called a **zygote**. From conception, this zygote then becomes an **embryo**, which is the earliest stage of human development. The embryo stage lasts 8 weeks from conception, and from there, it becomes a **fetus** for the rest of the pregnancy. The fetus then becomes a **baby** once a pregnant person gives birth.

Labor and Childbirth

As you near the final stages of pregnancy, your body prepares for birth through a series of changes. Before labor begins, certain visible changes occur, such as the discharge of the mucus plug that seals the uterus during pregnancy as well as less visible ones like the softening of the cervix, which dislodges the mucus plug. It is almost impossible to predict what will happen during labor and delivery, so as important as it is to have a delivery plan, it is also very important to be gentle with yourself and be open to adapting the plan as necessary. The process of labor and childbirth can include unpredictable things like having bowel movements on the delivery table, being in a lot more pain than expected and opting for an epidural instead of a natural birth, and much more.

When does labor begin? Labor begins when contractions start, and the cervix begins to dilate. This is the stage when the amniotic sac releases its fluids, more commonly known as the water breaking. In the early stages of labor, the cervix is about 3–4 c.m. open. The cervix must be open 10 c.m. before a pregnant person is fully dilated and can push. This first stage of labor can be a few hours or a few days.

The second stage of labor is known as the pushing stage, which is when you feel the most pressure as your body actively works to deliver the baby. Once the head of the baby surfaces, your healthcare provider may ask you to push gently to prevent vaginal tearing. If complications arise during labor such as an abnormal fetal position or the baby's heart rate drops, then a doctor might schedule a C-section, a surgical procedure, to ensure the health and safety of both you and the baby. Once the baby has been delivered, the final stage of labor occurs, which is the delivering of the placenta.

POINT OF INTEREST

There are a few techniques that can ease vaginal delivery and prevent excessive tearing.

Perineal massage. A perineal massage involves gently stretching and massaging the perineum, which is the muscle and tissue that lies between the anus and the vulva. Pregnant people can learn this technique themselves, and do a regular perennial massage leading up to childbirth, or a healthcare provider can do it during the final stages of labor as the pregnant person pushes. Research shows this practice is associated with lower rates of tearing, including a lower likelihood of needing an episiotomy, which is an incision the healthcare provider can make during childbirth to ease delivery.[147]

Various birthing positions. There are certain birthing positions that can help facilitate less tearing, specifically finding a way to deliver in a more upright position, rather than laying flat.[148] If the pregnant person has not taken the epidural for pain management, then additional positions such as kneeling or squatting may also be possible.

Water births. Being in a warm tub of water, either for much of the labor or for the final stages of pushing can help reduce the likelihood of perineal tears.[149] Not all healthcare providers are open to this option or have the capacity to provide this, so be sure to talk with your doctor if this is important to you.

Talk with your doctor ahead of delivery to ensure you feel supported about your options for a smooth delivery. Being informed about all possibilities can be extremely helpful and minimize vaginal tearing and other complications that may make postpartum recovery more difficult.

It is important to prioritize healing and recovery after childbirth as your body has gone through a major change. At this time, your uterus will continue to contract to push out anything left, and you will often continue to experience pain and discomfort. You must rest as much as you can to give your body the chance to heal.

[147] Beckmann M.M., Stock O.M. (2013). Antenatal Perineal Massage for Reducing Perineal Trauma. *Cochrane Database of Systematic Reviews* (4).

[148] Rocha, B.D.D., Zamberlan, C., Pivetta, H.M.F., Santos, B.Z., & Antunes, B.S. (2020). Upright Positions in Childbirth and the Prevention of Perineal Lacerations: a Systematic Review and Meta-Analysis. *Revista da Escola de Enfermagem da U S P*, 54, e03610. PMID: 32935765.

[149] Sidebottom, A.C., Vacquier, M., Simon, K., Wunderlich, W., Fontaine, P., Dahlgren-Roemmich, D., ... & Saul, L. (2020). Maternal and Neonatal Outcomes in Hospital-Based Deliveries With Water Immersion. *Obstetrics and Gynecology*, 136(4), 707-15.

TRY IT OUT
Pain Management Techniques

Preparing for childbirth can be daunting, especially when thinking about pain management. There are a number of pain management options with the most common tool being the epidural, which is an anesthetic inserted into the space around the spinal nerves to alleviate pain and lasts a couple of hours. While the epidural is the most commonly used method, there are other options, including medication-free methods, to help manage pain. These include:

IV medication: Medication given intravenously (through the vein), such as narcotics including morphine, fentanyl, and butorphanol.

Regional anesthesia: Anesthesia injected in a specific area of the body to provide pain relief/numbing; can last up to a few hours; an epidural is a type of regional anesthesia.

Nitrous oxide: An inhaled anesthetic gas used for anxiety and pain relief known as "laughing gas." Does not numb or take away the pain, but rather makes you less aware of it. Wears off minutes after the gas is turned off.

Breathing: Controlled breathing can help manage pain during childbirth, and there are often classes pregnant people and their partners can take to learn helpful techniques.

Hypnobirthing: Hypnosis, or hypnobirthing, is a method to help the laboring person reduce anxiety and fear through the use of music, visualization, positive thinking, and words. Studies have not proven hypnosis to be more effective than other relaxation methods.

Bradley Method: Another medication-free technique, this method helps you prepare for childbirth by teaching the pregnant person and their partner relaxation methods and other pain management techniques.

There is no shortage of labor and childbirth classes and, depending on where you live, you might have a plethora of options. Due to the Covid-19 pandemic, many of these courses are now offered virtually, expanding opportunities to take classes in a different region. For example, Sistersong offers a Labor Intensive Training to help families prepare for birth during a pandemic.[150] Have a conversation with your healthcare provider and/or doula to help decide what is best for you.

---

[150] See: https://www.sistersong.net/bjprogramming.

Your Body After Birth

Your body undergoes significant physical and emotional changes after giving birth. Although many of these changes are normal, they are not discussed enough, leaving new and expectant parents feeling lost. Here are some changes that your body may undergo after birth:

- You may still feel vaginal and uterine pain as well as soreness for a few weeks after birth. This is especially true if you breastfeed, as nursing compels the uterus to contract with each feeding.

- Your stomach may not go back to how it was pre-pregnancy right after you give birth.

- Bleeding and discharge after pregnancy can last up to 6 weeks and can also be intermittent (for example, you may stop bleeding and think that postpartum bleeding has stopped, only to find that it starts again a few days or a week later). This discharge is known as lochia.

- The first bowel movement after delivery can be painful, it is recommended to eat plenty of fruits, vegetables, and whole grains, and drink lots of water. Your healthcare provider may also give you a stool softener to assist with this.

- It is important to keep track of blood loss and blood clots after delivery. If you feel like you're losing a lot of blood, please contact your healthcare provider immediately.

- Your body does not produce breast milk immediately. The first few days it produces colostrum, a substance that is rich with antibodies and nutrients. Breastmilk should come in within a week; sometimes, this is delayed if the baby was delivered via C-section.

It is normal to go through a range of emotions after birth such as happiness and excitement. It is also normal to experience mood swings, difficulty sleeping, anxiety, depression, lack of appetite, and sadness. However, if these emotions are persistent and/or intense, it is important to speak with someone immediately as these are signs of postpartum depression (PPD). PPD is not a sign of weakness, and it does not make you a bad parent, and by seeking treatment you will be better able to manage your symptoms and bond with your child.

 POINT OF INTEREST

Vaginal intercourse is not advised for 6-weeks post-delivery. The 6 weeks rule is not one-size-fits-all when it comes to sex after pregnancy, and some people may need longer than that, either because the provider has recommended it because your body needs longer to heal, or because you are not feeling up to resuming sexual activity. Have open discussions with you partner, and do not rush into having sex until you feel like you have recovered enough to be intimate.

Pregnancy Loss

There are times a pregnancy may not make it to term, a reality that is known as a miscarriage. A miscarriage refers to the loss of a pregnancy during the first 20 weeks. It is estimated that 1 in 4 pregnancies end in miscarriage, with most of them occuring during the first trimester.[151] Other occurrences in pregnancy include stillbirths, which is a miscarriage after 20 weeks. Losing a pregnancy in any way can be a difficult experience, and might cause feelings of blame and guilt, but it is not your fault.

 POINT OF INTEREST

Sometimes doctors use the same procedure (known as a D&C) preformed during an abortion when a person experiences a miscarriage or ectopic pregnancy. Medically, the procedures can be identical and are reported as such on medical records. This can be a source of discomfort and trauma for those who do not consider their experience to be the same as an elective abortion. Moreover, given the politicization around abortion, the legal definition of abortion in some states can result in unfairly criminalizing women who have experienced pregnancy loss due to a miscarriage.[152]

ECTOPIC PREGNANCY

An ectopic pregnancy is when a fertilized egg attaches outside of the uterus, usually attaching to the fallopian tube or cervix. When this happens, the egg is unable to develop further and poses health risks to the pregnant person. Ectopic pregnancies tend to develop during the first trimester, and there is no way to predict them. It is important to see a healthcare provider if you have any symptoms of an ectopic pregnancy such as:

- Severe abdominal and/or pelvic pain and bleeding
- Dizziness or fainting
- Shoulder or neck pain

Ectopic pregnancies are not viable, and your healthcare provider may either give you medication to induce abortion or surgically remove the embryo.

ABORTION AND PREGNANCY TERMINATION

Abortion, also known as, pregnancy termination, is a lived experience that is much more common than is spoken about in Muslim communities. Abortion is not only a decision that can be elective, but there are many circumstances in which abortions may be deemed medically necessary. The decision to terminate may not be an easy one. In fact, this is often a decision that can cause great distress to many people. There are counseling services to help think through this option. Moreover, the sociopolitical context of where you live and access to financial resources can play a large role in whether or not this is an option that is available and accessible to you.[153]

[151] Tommy's Pregnancy Hub. (2022). *How Common is Miscarriage?* Retrieved from: https://www.tommys.org/ pregnancy-information/im-pregnant/early-pregnancy/how-common-miscarriage.

[152] Weigel, G., Sobel, L., & Salganicoff, A. (2019). *Understanding Pregnancy Loss in the Context of Abortion Restrictions and Fetal Harm Laws* - Glossary. KFF. Available at: https://www.kff.org/womens-health-policy/issue-brief/understanding-pregnancy-loss-in-the-context-of-abortion-restrictions-and-fetal-harm-laws/.

[153] To check state restrictions based on where you live, visit https://www.guttmacher.org/state-policy/explore/overview-abortion-laws.

DID YOU KNOW?

While the rate of abortion has continued to decline in the past decade, the need to make abortion widely accessible for all is still critical. Contrary to popular belief, **the majority of abortions (88%—93%) occur before 12 weeks gestation.**[154] The politicization and stigmatization of abortion in this country has attached a pejorative narrative to abortion—that only a certain "type" of person would want to get an abortion, or that they are using abortion as a method of birth control—i.e. having an abortion simply because having a child is inconvenient for them. These are all unfair and dangerous stereotypes. **In reality, abortion is a lived reality of 1 in 4 people ages 15-45 of all backgrounds and identities.**[155] In fact, a third of women (33.1%) who get abortions already have two or more children and almost a quarter had a college degree or higher. Fourteen percent of those who obtained abortions in 2014 were married.[156] The rate of abortion has declined among teenagers due lower teen pregnancy rates, and currently the largest percentage of abortion patients are in their 20s.[157] Moreover, 58% of abortion patients have not had a previous abortion, and less than a fifth have had two or more, as reported by the *New York Times*, so the claim that abortion is being widely used as a method of birth control is inaccurate.[158] People consider abortion for many reasons including unplanned pregnancy, fetal anomalies, risk to mother's life, etc. **In fact, abortion can often be a life-saving medically necessary procedure.** Banning abortion or restricting access to abortion impacts anyone who has the ability to get pregnant and does not result in a decrease in abortions. Rather, the rate of unsafe abortions actually increases.[159]

[154] Guttmacher Institute. (N.d.). *Induced Abortion in the United States.* Retrieved from: https://www.guttmacher.org/fact-sheet/induced-abortion-united-states?gclid=Cj0KCQiA_JWOBhDRARIsANymNOYnCM5TFEaufUwhlvjK9rITNM3g4CqXojHr9UfSgGvOKKMCPMUKT6EaAvZFEALw_wcB; Sangor-Katz, M, Miller C C, and Bui Q. (2021). Who gets Abortions in America? *The New York Times.* Retrieved fromt: https://www.nytimes.com/interactive/2021/12/14/upshot/who-gets-abortions-in-america.html.

[155] Guttmacher Institute. (2017). *Abortion is Increasingly Concentrated among Poor Women.* Retrieved from: https://www.guttmacher.org/news-release/2017/abortion-common-experience-us-women-despite-dramatic-declines-rates; Korstmit K, Jatlaoui TC, Mandel MG, et. al(2020). *Abortion Surveillance—United States—2018. Surveillance Summaries.* 69(7);1–29 retrieved from: https://www.cdc.gov/mmwr/volumes/69/ss/ss6907a1.htm; Ireland, L. (2019.) Who are the 1 in 4 American women who choose abortion? *For the Conversation.* Retrieved from: https://www.umassmed.edu/news/news-archives/2019/05/who-are-the-1-in-4-american-women-who-choose-abortion/.

[156] Guttmacher Institute. (N.d.). *Table 1: Percentage distribution of U.S. Women Obtaining Bbortions in Nonhospital Settings and of all U.S. Women aged 15-44, and Abortion Index, by Selected Characteristics, 2014 and 2008.* Retrieved from: https://www.guttmacher.org/sites/default/files/report_downloads/us-abortion-patients-table1.pdf.

[157] Sangor-Katz, M, Miller C C, and Bui Q. (2021). *Who gets Abortions in America?* The New York Times. Retrieved fromt: https://www.nytimes.com/interactive/2021/12/14/upshot/who-gets-abortions-in-america.html.

[158] Ibid.

[159] Amnesty International. (N.d.). *Key Facts on Abortion.* Retrieved from: https://www.amnesty.org/en/what-we-do/sexual-and-reproductive-rights/abortion-facts/.

For those from faith communities, abortion—whether elective and/or medically necessary—is an option that is often considered taboo and controversial, and many might try to pressure you to continue the pregnancy to term, regardless of the circumstance. You are your best advocate, and you know what is best for you and your future. The Islamic opinion on the permissibility of abortion varies. The majority of scholars will agree that abortion is permissible if it is before a certain time period, although there is a difference of opinion regarding the gestational age of the pregnancy. Some say it is only permissible until 40 days into the pregnancy while others say it is as long as 120 days. Moreover, there are a number of other considerations, such as the life of the mother or severe fetal abnormalities are regarded on a case by case basis.[160] Zahra Ayubi, Ph.D. provides detailed context on abortion and the diverse range of opinions in her paper "Muslim Biomedical Ethics of Neonatal care: Theory, Praxis, and Authority:"

> Most religious scholars across various sects are unanimous about the permissibility of abortion in cases of danger to the mother's life. Many, based on Quranic verses and hadith, say that a breastfeeding woman may terminate a subsequent pregnancy because it is believed that the 'living child has priority [of receiving nutrition] over the fetus,' though this permission is not universal and again, must take place before 120 days—reiterating that a fetus is considered a living child only after the 120-mark. More relevant: since the 1980s, muftis from several countries including Kuwait, Saudi Arabica, Iran, and Pakistan have ruled that abortion is permissible if fatal abnormalities, genetic disorders leading to a severely compromised life, or severe physical or mental defects are detected—some argue before three months, some maintain the 120-day mark, and some have even ruled permissibility after 120 days.[161]

---

[160] There are not that many resources on abortion in Islam in English as we'd like. Also see Yaqeen Institute's article available at: https://yaqeeninstitute.org/omar-suleiman/islam-and-the-abortion-debate/.

[161] Ayubi, Z (2019). Muslim Biomedical Ethics of neonatal care: Theory, Praxis, and Authority. *Religion and Ethics in the Neonatal Intensive Care Unit.* Oxford University Press. See also Muslim Women's League "When the mother's life was in danger from the pregnancy, when continuation of the pregnancy would compromise the life of a child already living (e.g., by depleting the supply of breast milk on which the child depended), or when the fetus suffered from a lethal anomaly (which means death was certain at the time of birth.)" Muslim Women's League. (2001). *Birth Control and Islam.* Available at: https://www.mwlusa.org/topics/health/contraception.pdf.

ISLAMIC RULINGS: SOME CONSIDERATIONS

The rulings regarding the permissibility of abortion across the various *madhabs* (schools of thought) draw from Quranic verses and various *hadith* about the stages of creation for a fetus and the sanctity of life. The ethical considerations that contribute to the rulings around abortion deal with:[162]

The point that the soul enters the fetus
Each *madhab* determines this differently, but generally it is as follows:

The threat of harm/endangerment to the mother
This can include physical, emotional, and mental health.

The presence of fetal anomalies
This can include chromosomal abnormalities such as Trisomy 13 and Trisomy 18.

The motivation or reasoning to terminate, which also differs by school of thought

INDUCED ABORTION BREAKDOWN[163]

FIRST TRIMESTER
- **Timeframe:** can be performed up to 13 weeks.
- **Medical abortion:** drugs taken orally or inserted vaginally through suppositories to induce an abortion. Can be taken at home with visits to a provider afterwards. Average Cost: $551
- **Surgical abortion—suction curettage:** cervix is dilated prior to or at the time of the procedure using medication or dilators. Once dilated, a thin plastic tube with a suction/vacuum is inserted into the uterus to remove the pregnancy. Average cost at 10 weeks: $495

SECOND TRIMESTER
- **Timeframe:** performed after 13 weeks of pregnancy.
- **Medical abortion:** drugs taken orally, vaginally, injected into the uterus or through IV to induce an abortion—administered in a hospital or clinic setting.
- **Surgical abortion—dilation and evacuation (D&E):** outpatient surgery where cervix is dilated, general or regional anesthesia administered for pain relief, and fetus is removed through vagina with a suction used for any remaining tissue. Average cost at 20 weeks: $1,670

LATER ABORTIONS
- **Timeframe:** performed at or after 21 weeks.
- **Surgical abortion—dilation and extraction (D&E):** cervix is dilated and labor is induced. The fetus is removed. Average cost: $1,350

[162] Bowen, D.L. (2006). Reproduction: Abortion and Islam: Overview. Encyclopedia of Women & Islamic Cultures, In: *Joseph, S (ed.) Encyclopedia of Women and Islamic Cultures Volume IIIL Family, Body, Sexuality, and Health.* Leiden and Boston: Brill.; Al-Matary and Ali, J (2014). Controversies and Considerations Regarding the Termination of Pregnancy for Foetal Anomalies in Islam. *BMC Medical Ethics.*15:10.
[163] American College of Obstetricians and Gynecologists, 2021; Kaiser Family Foundation, 2021; Witwer, E., Jones, R. K., Fuentes, L., & Castle, S. K. (2020). Abortion Service Delivery in Clinics by State Policy Climate in 2017. *Contraception:* X, 2, 100043.

 **TRY IT OUT**

If you are faced with having to make a decision around pregnancy termination, here are some questions to reflect on:

1. If you have received a concerning diagnosis, and the doctor is recommending termination, **what medical information do you need** to understand the full scope of the diagnosis?

   - For example, **consider getting a variety of perspectives:** from obstetricians to pediatricians, genetic counselors, and other specialists who can provide you with the necessary context of what to expect if you choose to take the pregnancy to term.

2. If you want to gain a deeper understanding of whether your decision is aligned with your religious and spiritual values, **consider seeking an opinion from a trusted spiritual guide or resource (or several).**

3. Does the geography of where you live and the sociopolitical context factor into your decision?

   - Some states have stricter laws around abortion, and at some point into the pregnancy, it may no longer be legal to get an abortion.

   - Do you live in a rural area where safe and affordable access to abortions is limited?

4. Do you have access to the **necessary insurance or funds** you need to seek an abortion?

5. **Who are your people?** Who are your trusted family and friends who can hold space with you as you make a decision around terminating a pregnancy, without judgment, and with full trust in you that you know best?

6. **How will the decision impact your personal mental, spiritual, and physical health?** Would it help to discuss what anxieties you are holding around the decision and discuss potential scenarios with a trained mental health professional?

7. **What support systems do you need moving forward**, whether postpartum after a full term pregnancy, or postpartum after termination?

8. Navigating a pregnancy after loss can also bring its own challenges and anxieties: it is important to remember that **every pregnancy is different and your decision-making process may be very different in subsequent pregnancies.** Consider talking to a trained mental health professional who can help you navigate the simultaneous emotions of grief and joy that you may feel in subsequent pregnancies.

POINT OF INTEREST

Abortion in the pre-modern period (before Western imperialism) was a decision that often did not include religious scholars, men, or the state. The decisions were generally between pregnant people and their providers.[164] Scholars have documented that there were numerous classic Islamic texts in the 9th-11th centuries that explained in detail ways to prevent pregnancy and induce abortion.[165] Most abortions occurred at home with women being the ones to implement the procedures, and the "knowledge of these medicines and procedures gave women the power to determine their fertility to some extent."[166] Despite this, there were male scholars in the past that did attempt to "use religious discourses to reassert male authority over reproduction in rejection of the previously held exclusivity of women caring for women in childbirth."[167] Yet this exclusive female control over maternity no longer exists in contemporary Muslim societies, due to the introduction of colonialism and medicalization of reproduction, and now instead "the Islamic decision-making process which discusses permissibility of abortion is carried out by male jurists and scholars."[168]

Infertility

While the most common way people plan pregnancies through vagina sex, there are a few other options couples may consider to get pregnant, either by choice or circumstance. Sometimes, a couple needs to consider other options because they are having trouble getting pregnant and may be experiencing infertility. Other times, a pregnancy may not be biologically possible, but the couple still desires a child.

It's important to ask what your medical history and other tests may indicate about your fertility. With your physician, explore how your age and lifestyle may impact your fertility and ask for a general timeline on diagnosis and treatment. If you are infertile, thoroughly explore possible treatment plans and the potential side effects associated with each plan. Make sure to find additional resources for support, as infertility can be emotionally and physically challenging.

[164] Ayubi, Z. (2019). Muslim Biomedical Ethics of neonatal care: Theory, Praxis, and Authority. *Religion and Ethics in the Neonatal Intensive Care Unit.* Oxford University Press.

[165] Bowen, D L. (2006). Reproduction: Abortion and Islam—Overview, In: Joseph, S (ed.) *Encyclopedia of Women and Islamic Cultures Volume IIIL Family, Body, Sexuality, and Health.* Leiden and Boston: Brill.

[166] Ibid.

[167] Ayubi, Z. (2019). Muslim Biomedical Ethics of neonatal care: Theory, Praxis, and Authority. *Religion and Ethics in the Neonatal Intensive Care Unit.* Oxford University Press.

[168] Mattson, I. (2018). Gender and Sexuality in Islamic Bioethics. *Islamic Bioethics: Current Issues and Challenges.* (2): 57 - 83; Ayubi, Zahra (2019). *Muslim Biomedical Ethics of neonatal care: Theory, Praxis, and Authority.* Religion and Ethics in the Neonatal Intensive Care Unit. Oxford University Press.

? DID YOU KNOW?

Both men and women can experience infertility. While often the burden of infertility may land on cisgender women and people with uteruses, this is not always the case. Cisgender men and people with penises can also struggle with infertility.

Medically, infertility is a result of many factors—20–35% being female infertility, 20–30% male infertility, 25-40% are due to combined causes in both individuals, and no cause is found in 10–20% of cases.[169] Those who identify as or are perceived as women are often blamed for the lack of fertility, which can lead to conflict with a spouse and other family members. In Muslim communities, those with fertility issues may be stigmatized and ostracized by members of their family and community. Muslims who are shamed for their infertility can likely experience psychological distress.

A lack of information and misconceptions can lead to insensitive and sometimes hurtful comments, and it can be difficult to speak to family and friends about fertility issues. Two conditions which are major causes of infertility, PCOS and endometriosis, disproportionately affect Black, Asian, and racially marginalized people with uteruses. There is little to no representation of infertility among BIPOC Muslims, which can leave these women feeling isolated and afraid.

If you and your partner are having difficulty conceiving, fertility treatments may help increase your chances of having a baby. Fertility treatment refers to medications or procedures that stimulate egg or sperm production. Once again, the Islamic opinions on the permissibility of infertility options varies with each school of thought. Many opinions allow for infertility treatment, especially if the sperm and the egg belong to the biological parents.[170]

Treatment can also include surgical interventions, lifestyle changes, weight loss, or treatment of an underlying medical condition. A treatment plan will depend on the causes behind the infertility and personal circumstances. It is important to note that not all infertility is treatable, and in many cases couples may have to consider other ways to become parents. On the next page is a chart of the available fertility treatments and other options for having a baby. Note that fertility treatment options and their costs will vary not only from state to state, but also from what health insurance a person has. Many health insurance plans may not cover certain types of fertility treatments, and dependign on how many cycles or stages of a particular treatment plan a person chooses, the price may vary. For example, for some treatments such as egg freezing, a person will be looking at separate costs for retrieval, medications, and storage.

[169] Mayo Clinic. *Female Infertility*. Available at: https://www.mayoclinic.org/diseases-conditions/female-infertility/symptoms-causes/syc-20354308.
[170] Al-Bar MA, Chamsi-Pasha H. (2015). Assisted Reproductive Technology: Islamic Perspective. *Contemporary Bioethics: Islamic Perspectives*. Available at: https://www.ncbi.nlm.nih.gov/books/NBK500175/.

Female Fertility Treatment Options

HORMONE MEDICATION

Purpose:
Regulate or stimulate ovulation, often used when ovulation disorders lead to infertility; can also be used for women who ovulate regularly, but cannot conceive by stimulating extra/better eggs.

Cost
Relatively inexpensive compared with other treatments; oral medications are often paired with IUI and regular ultrasounds to range in total from $500 and $1000 a month for a single cycle (on its own, meds cost about $10–$100 month). If injecting hormones through shots (paired with IUI and ultrasounds), it can cost about $3,000-$5,000 per month.

Considerations
Can increase risk of twin pregnancies and higher-order multiple pregnancies; certain drugs can cause swollen and painful ovaries and, if taken for a long time with no pregnancy, may increase your risk for ovarian tumors.

SURGERY

Purpose:
For structural problems that can be treated surgically to increase the chances of conception, surgery might be the best option. Surgery can be used for the removal of uterine fibroids, polyps, pelvic adhesions, and endometriosis tissue.

Cost
The cost of surgery for fertility can range from $2,000 to $10,000, depending on the specific surgery and insurance coverage.

Considerations
Patients must consider whether the surgery will be minimally invasive or "open." With minimally invasive fertility surgery, you can expect less pain and recovery time than traditional 'open' surgery.

ASSISTED REPRODUCTIVE TECHNOLOGY—IVF

Purpose:
In Vitro Fertilization: To combine the egg and sperm outside of the body (in vitro) and then implant that embryo in the uterine lining; medications are needed to control hormones and ovulation, and minor surgical procedures are used to retrieve and implant the egg.

Cost
Health insurance only covers some of the costs of IVF if patients meet certain requirements, and IVF can be very costly. One cycle can cost up to $15,000-$20,000 when one includes the cost of treatment and medication, and the national average is $11,500.

Considerations
IVF can be time-consuming, expensive, and invasive. Both partners as well as the person who is performing the procedure may suffer from depression or anxiety during the process. IVF may take several months to complete, and oftentimes more than one round may be necessary for pregnancy. However, everybody is different, and it might not work/work differently for everyone, depending on age and the cause of infertility.

ASSISTED REPRODUCTIVE TECHNOLOGY—IUI

Purpose:

IUI, also known as intrauterine insemination or artificial insemination, can be used to increase the number of sperm that reach the fallopian tubes and subsequently increase the chance of fertilization. A physician uses a soft catheter that is moved into a woman's uterus to deposit the semen at the time of ovulation.

Cost

Depending on insurance coverage and specific fees, IUI usually costs about $300–$4,000 (less expensive than IVF) without insurance. The type of medication, pricing for monitoring and bloodwork, and cost of insemination (injecting sperm into the uterus) are all factors that may change the cost of IUI.

Considerations

IUI is not recommended for women who have severe disease of the fallopian tubes, have a history of pelvic infections, or anyone who has moderate to severe endometriosis. The procedure may result in infection, spotting (small amounts of vaginal bleeding), and an increased risk of a multiple pregnancy (twins, or more which may result in early labor and low birth weight).

EGG FREEZING

Purpose:

In the situation that an individual with ovaries gets a serious disease, such as cancer, or plans to have children at a later stage in life, they can harvest and freeze their eggs to use later when they are ready to have children.

The main purpose of egg freezing is to ensure there are lower chances of serious complications if they choose to have a child in the future.

Cost

The average national cost of egg freezing is $7,500, but can also range even higher, closer to $30,000-$40,000 if you include the combination of treatment and storage.

Considerations

Consider what you expect your life timeline might be, such as an ideal age you plan to have children or making a financial plan to secure the future of your family.

The cost of egg freezing is definitely out of range for many individuals, couples, and families, so consider income, family planning, savings, and the reality of the situation.

People under 38–40 are usually given the option to freeze their eggs, since it is typically harder to have children past the age of 40.

SURROGACY

Purpose:

For couples who cannot carry a pregnancy safely to term, finding another person to carry your embryo can be an option.

Cost

The cost can vary from state to state, depending on their requirements, however, average surrogacies can be between $100,000–$200,000; this can include agency fees if there is an agency involved, psychological evaluations, legal fees, healthcare costs, and compensation for the surrogate.

Considerations

Among the criteria often considered for choosing surrogate mothers is medical history, past pregnancy and delivery history, lifestyle, specific needs—financial and otherwise—of the surrogate. It is important to note that it is difficult to find an Islamic opinion that approves the permissibility of surrogates.

Male Fertility Treatment Options

HORMONE MEDICATION TREATMENT

Purpose:
Hormone therapy can be used to increase the number of sperm.

Cost
The cost of hormone therapy can range from $10–$300 monthly depending on the type of treatment and the number of medications a person is taking.

Considerations
With all medication, there can be side effects from hormone treatments. Side effects can include, but are not limited to: changes in libido (sex drive), mood, aggression, and energy levels, as well as headaches, blurred vision, and acne. Speak with your care provider to help manage these side effects.

SURGERY

Purpose:
For structural problems that can be treated surgically to increase the chances of conception, surgery might be the best option. Surgery can be used for treatments for varicocele (swollen veins), azoospermia (semen lacking sperm), vasectomy reversals and ejaculatory duct blockages.

Cost
The cost of surgery for fertility can range from $7,000-$10,000, depending on the specific surgery and insurance coverage.

Considerations
Depending on the type of infertility, patients must consider which surgery may be the best option for them through discussions with their care providers.

SPERM FREEZING

Purpose:
In the situation that an individual with testicles gets a serious disease, such as cancer, or plans to have children at an older age, they can freeze their sperm to use later when they are ready to have children.

Cost
It costs about $100–$500 yearly to store frozen sperm.

Considerations
Although sperm freezing is safe, sperm may undergo damage during the thawing process, though over 50% of sperm will usually survive this.

 **TRY IT OUT**
Get to Know Your Fertility

Too often, the conversation around fertility doesn't happen until later, right when a person or couple is ready to have a child. While much of fertility is not in anyone's hands, there are still measures you can take to better understand your body, your fertility, and your options. This can help lessen the anxiety in the future if you do encounter trouble. Here are some suggestions on how to get started.

- **Get to know your cycle.** Do you have regular periods (approximately 28 day cycles), or are they more or less frequent?

- **Understand your medical history.** There are some conditions that may have implications on your fertility, such as polycystic ovary syndrome, endometriosis, or chronic illness like cancer. Talk with your doctor about how this may impact your fertility and if there are any protective measures you can take.

- **Consider planning ahead.** Egg freezing for those who are undergoing chemotherapy or those in a certain age bracket is an option for those who want to have children in the future, but are not ready to have children in that moment.

Chapter 4 Key Resources

This list is not comprehensive, and for full citations please see the works-cited at the end of the book.

For Low-Cost Care in Your Community

- Department of health and human services website at **www.hhs.gov**. More information on where you can find low-cost care is available under the "FAQ" and "insurance reform" sections.
- healthcare.gov website for more information on where you can find low-cost care near you. More information can be found by searching "How to find low-cost health care in your community" in the search bar.
- Free clinics website at **www.freeclinics.com** for more information on where you can find low-cost care near you.

How to Prepare for a Gynecological Visit

- Scarleteen (website) at **www.scarleteen.com**. Recommended articles include "Your First Gynecologist Visit" by Heather Corinna.

Reproductive Health for Trans Men

- Please take a look at this article on the "check it out guys" website about reproductive health for trans men. Available on the way back machine website at **https://web.archive.org/web/20170424225956/ http://checkitoutguys.ca/**.

Pap Smears

- HEART pap smear video on YouTube for more information on pap smears. The video can be found on the HEART Women and Girls channel or by searching "HEART pap smear" into the search bar.

Human Papilloma Virus (HPV)

- World Health Organization (website) at **www.who.int** for more information on HPV and cervical cancer. Information can be found under the "newsroom" and "factsheets" tabs.
- CDC (website) **www.cdc.gov** for more information about the HPV and men. Please search the "HPV and Men factsheet".
- "I Have HPV, and I Got The Vaccine" (article) by Evette Dion published on the 9th July 2014 in Bustle Magazine. **www.bustle.com**.

Self-Breast Exams

- HEART video on performing self-breast exams and mammograms on YouTube. The video can be found on the HEART Women and Girls channel or by searching "HEART to HEART: Breast Self-Exams and Mammograms" into the search bar.

Health Disparities in Black Communities

- HEART video on Health disparities in Black communities on YouTube. The video can be found on the HEART Women and Girls channel or by searching "HEARTfelt Conversations with Kamilah Pickett, Part 1 of 3: Foundations of Public Health" into the search bar.

Ghusl

- @VillageAuntie's video "A Quick & Dirty Guide to Ghusl! Part 2" posted on the 19th of February 2020. Available on Instagram.

Emergency Contraception

- Guttmacher Institute website at **www.guttmacher.org**.
- Planned Parenthood website at **www.plannedparenthood.com**. More information can be found under the "learn" and "birth control" tabs.

Pregnancy

- CDC (website) **www.cdc.gov/pregnancy/during.html** Additional topics can be found under the
  - "before pregnancy" tab
  - "planning for pregnancy" tab
  - "During Pregnancy" tab.
  - "reproductive health" and "contraception" tabs.
  - "pregnancy and whooping cough" tab.
- Parenthood (website) **www.plannedparenthood.com**. More information is located under the "learn" and "pregnancy options" tabs.

Pregnancy and Abortion Support Hotlines

- Exhale – call or text 617-749-2948. The exhale website URL is **www.exhaleprovoice.org**.
- All-Options @ 1-888-493-0092.
- All-Options website at **www.all-options.org**. The All-Options website contains a wealth of pregnancy resources.

Abortion in Islam:

- Dr. Omar Suleiman's article titled "Islam and the Abortion Debate" (article) by Dr. Omar Suleiman. The article can be found online at the Yaqeen Institute website, the URL to the article is **https://yaqeeninstitute.org/omar-suleiman/islam-and-the-abortion-debate/**.
- "Muslim Biomedical Ethics of neonatal care: Theory, Praxis, and Authority" (article) by Zahra Ayubi in *Religion and Ethics in the Neonatal Intensive Care Unit*. Available online on the Oxford Medicine website.
- "Reproduction: Abortion and Islam – Overview." By Donna Lee Bowen In the *Encyclopedia of Women and Islamic Cultures, Volume III: Family, Body, Sexuality and Health*. Available online at **www.brillonline.com**.

- "Abortion Bans Trample on the Religious Freedom of Muslims, Too" (article) by Asifa Quraishi-Landes–San Francisco Chronicle.
- "How Islam Settled Roe v Wade Centuries Ago," (article) by Rashad Ali and Anna Lekes Miller, Newsline Mag.
- "Family Planning, Contraception, and Abortion in Islam: Understanding Khilafah." (article) by Sa'diyya Shaikh in Maguire, D.C. (ed.). *Sacred Rights: The Case for Contraception and Abortion in World Religions.* Oxford University Press, Inc.
- *New Handbook for a Post Roe America: The Complete Guide to Abortion Legality, Access, and Practical Support.* (book) by Robin Marty. Available on Amazon.
- *Reproductive Justice: An Introduction.* (2017). (book) By Loretta Ross and Rickie Solinger. Available on Amazon.
- "Authority and Epistemology in Islamic Medical Ethics of Women's Reproductive Health." (article) by Zahra Ayubi. *Journal of Religious Ethics.*

Abortion, Adoption, and More:

- Planned Parenthood (website) **www.plannedparenthood.org/learn/abortion** for more information on pregnancy termination.
- National Network of Abortion Funds (website) **www.abortionfunds.org**. Includes e resources and information on organizations in every state that with individuals seeking abortion care and funding.
- To see adoption laws by state, please visit the Adoptive Families website at **www.adoptivefamilies.com/adoption-laws-by-state/.**
- Parent center hub (website) at **www.parentcenter.org** for more information on foster and adoptive parenting. More information can be found by searching "foster parenting" in the search tab.
- "Why So Many Women are Forced to Lie about Terminating Wanted Pregnancies" (article) by Jessica Zucker Published on 13th Oct 2020. Available at: **www.instyle.com**.

Miscarriages:

- Please check out the work of Dr. Jessica Zucker, a psychologist specializing in reproductive health. Dr Zucker runs the "I had a miscarriage" account on Instagram and has published a book titled "I had a miscarriage", which is available online.
- Miscarriage Matters Inc. (website) **www.mymiscarriagematters.org** for more information on miscarriage.
- Share: Pregnancy and Infant Loss Support (website) **www.nationalshare.org** for more information on miscarriages.

Infertility:

- Very Well Family website at **www.verywellfamily.com**. Recommended readings includes the article "How to Track Ovulation When Trying to Conceive" by Krissi Danielsson. Article can be found under the "trying to conceive" section.
- "Detection of ovulation, a review of currently available methods" (articlie) by Su Hsiu-Wei et al. Available online at **wiley.com DOI:10.1002/btm2.10058**

- "What's That Stuff Coming Out of My Vagina?: Vaginal and Cervical Secretions 101" (2020) video post (HEART instagram post).
- Taking charge of your fertility **website at www.tcoyf.com** for more information on fertility.
- Planned parenthood website at www.plannedparenthood.org for more information on fertility treatments. More information can be found by visiting the fertility treatment section.
- "Costs of infertility treatment: Results from an 18-month prospective cohort study" (article) by Patricia Katz, Jonathan Showstack et al. The article is available online at the US national library of medicine. Search PMID 21130988.
- "Supporting Muslim Women Dealing with Infertility: The Amal Support Group" (article) by Chelby Daigle for more information on fertility treatments on www.muslimlink.ca.
- Mayo Clinic website at **www.mayoclinic.org**. More information on infertility can be found by searching "infertility" in the search bar.

Chapter 5: Relationships: The Good, The Bad, and the In-Between

In This Chapter	Quick Snapshot
Taking a deeper dive into the RIDHA framework from Chapter 1, this chapter will provide you with the foundational knowledge on healthy, unhealthy, and abusive relationships. It will also offer additional resources for how to identify abuse and seek help for it.	

Relationships: Not One-Size-Fits-All

Relationships aren't just about sex; most of the time, sex is just one aspect of a healthy, thriving relationship. While human relationships are one of the most fundamental aspects of our lives, many people do not have the language or skills to distinguish a healthy relationship from an unhealthy or abusive one. This section will take a deep dive into relationships: the good ones and the not-so-good ones. Using the RIDHA framework we introduced in Chapter 1 to define healthy relationships, we will explore each component in the framework and give examples of what it looks like when it is put into practice, what it can look like when it is not, and how that could have implications on the health of your relationship.

The information on healthy sexual relationships in this chapter can apply to both marital and non-marital relationships, as relationships come in many forms. These include courtship, dating, engagement, and marriage. Sexual intimacy can be present (or absent) in any of these relationships, depending on the individuals' culture, comfort levels, religious practices, personal boundaries, family traditions and expectations, and more. Because unhealthy intimacy, violence, and abuse can occur outside of a marital relationship as well as within one, having comprehensive, accurate information about how to identify, address, and seek help for violence and abuse—irrespective of marital status—can be life saving for many. Everyone should have safe and easy access to this information, so that they have resources to seek help when they need it, especially those with additional marginalized identities.

Additionally, some of the topics covered in this section, particularly around marriage and divorce, may feel focused or limited to straight couples, especially a husband and wife in a marriage. This is because most of the classical Islamic texts have approached marriage as being between a man and a woman. While we recognize this may feel like the information excludes other lived experiences such as queer or nonmarital relationships, we invite you to consider the ways in which you can still apply these lessons in your life context. The elements of the RIDHA framework can be relevant to all forms of relationships, and thus the practical tools offered in this chapter (such as the utility of the marriage contract) can still be helpful for all people navigating their relationships.

Applying the RIDHA Framework to Build and Maintain Healthy Intimate Relationships

Remember the RIDHA framework we introduced in Chapter 1? HEART created this as a way to connect its research on healthy relationships and intimacy to the guidelines that Islam provides Muslims on living spiritually-fulfilling lives.

Here's a short but detailed summary of the RIDHA Framework to refresh your memory:

R **Rahma**

Rooted in compassion (*rahma*) and mutual pleasure
The Quran speaks of how God has created us in pairs, putting love and compassion between them, so that we may find tranquility.[171] This means that our intimate relationships and the physical, spiritual, and emotional intimacy and gratification we find in them are a divine gift—a mercy (*rahma*)—to be cherished and nourished.

I **'Ilm**

Informed by communication and knowledge (*'ilm*)
Open, honest dialogue and seeking knowledge (*'ilm*) is key between partners to uphold informed consent, build trust, facilitate an ongoing connection and communicate boundaries, needs and desires.

D **aDalah**

Driven by equity and fairness (*'adalah*)
All people are created equal and have integrity before God. A relationship which reflects this equality in shared power and privilege by both partners will help create a healthy partnership rooted in fairness (*'adalah*).

H **Hurma**

Housed in safety and security (*hurma*)
A relationship should provide each partner with a sense of safety and security (*hurma*). Any threat, or actual acts, of any kind of violence, abuse, or coercion is in conflict with the Islamic ideal of love and mercy between partners.

A **'Aqd**

Affirmed in commitment (*'aqd*) and fidelity.
Sexual intimacy in Islam is preceded by a clear agreement (*'aqd*) between the partners, thus affirming their commitment to each other and honoring the reality of sex as a sacred, spiritual, and mutually beneficial experience.

[171] Quran 30:21.

In this chapter, we will elaborate on each of these components in more detail. Here we will lay out what we think the RIDHA framework looks like in real life, with specific attention to the essential ingredients of healthy sexual intimacy, and then we will explain what it looks like when it is not in practice. While each component of the framework has its own unique focus, it is also important to note that they all intersect with each other, and you may notice that they each seem to presume the other components are there. This is because this framework is meant to be applied in its entirety; holistically. If one component is missing, or weak, then it is likely the relationship's health is in jeopardy. As such, it is important to think about each component as a necessary pillar of a 5-pillared building: each one works with all the others to contribute to the overall health of the relationship.

The RIDHA framework is our best effort to create a user-friendly roadmap to building and sustaining a healthy, intimate relationship. Cultivating such a relationship is no easy task. First, no one is a mindreader, so there have to be clear and direct conversations not only around each other's expectations, but also interests and experiences. Further, a healthy relationship requires both individuals to become comfortable with vulnerability and sharing any parts of themselves that might be wounded. How well we get to know our partner depends on how much we are willing to invest in knowing all the parts of them as well as sharing all the parts of ourselves.

Keeping all this in mind, we have prioritized the following important components of a healthy relationship:

- Compassion and pleasure
- Non-judgmental and direct communication
- Individual awareness and a commitment to sharing power
- Consent, boundaries, and safety
- Trust and commitment

Each of these components are found and elaborated in the RIDHA framework, explained in more detail on the next page.

R (RAHMA) ROOTED IN COMPASSION AND MUTUAL PLEASURE

The first component of our framework is that healthy sexual relationships are rooted in compassion (*rahma*) and mutual pleasure. *Rahma* is the Arabic word for compassion and known as one of Islam's core values. God is *ar-Rahman*, the Most Compassionate, and Muslims are called to take inspiration from God's compassion and be compassionate with all living beings.

Compassionate relationships are spaces where intimacy, trust, empathy, and mutual respect thrive, as partners are committed to the well-being and pleasure of each other. Having compassion with each other can look like identifying stressors outside of the bedroom such as work, health, and taking care of the family that may contribute to a lack of sexual satisfaction. Moreover, a commitment to mutual pleasure involves both partners being equally supportive of each other experiencing sexual pleasure—including achieving orgasm. Because achieving orgasm is complex and nuanced for women, it is especially important that their partners be supportive, flexible, and creative in sexually intimate settings. This includes not insisting on [vaginal] intercourse as the only means of sexual intimacy and having a great deal of understanding if a woman is unable to orgasm.

There are many *hadiths* and religious texts that reflect the importance that Islam puts on mutual pleasure in sex. The significance of foreplay before intercourse, for example, has especially been affirmed by Muslim jurists. For example, fourteenth-century Hanbali Scholar Ibn Qayyim al Jawziyya in his book Tibb-an-Nabawi (*Healing with the Medicine of the Prophet*)[172] states that the Prophet forbade spouses from engaging in sexual intercourse before foreplay. It is important to note that this foreplay was not just for the husband's pleasure. As Ibn Qudama, another classical Hanbali scholar noted, the Prophet (peace be upon him) is reported to have said, "Do not begin intercourse until she has experienced desire like the desire you experience, lest you fulfill your desires before she does."[173]

 Green Flags:

- Being treated with kindness and respect
- Being touched with gentleness and with prior permission
- Finding pleasure in physical intimacy
- Your partner/spouse takes interest in what pleases you and what does not and actively seeks out ways for you to feel sexual pleasure
- Your partner/spouse is committed to helping you orgasm and reach sexual climax
- Your partner/spouse is understanding and kind when you don't feel like having sex

---

[172] Al-Jauziayah, Ibn Qayyim. (1999). *Healing with the Medicine of the Prophet*. Dar-us-Salam Publications; First Edition. Available at: https://www.kalamullah.com/Books/Medicine.pdf.

[173] Ibn Qudamah "Al Mughni" 8:36, cited in Zuberi, Hena. (2016). Intimacy for Muslim Couples: the Anti-Climax. *Muslim Matters*. Available at: https://muslimmatters.org/2016/01/05/intimacy-for-muslim-couples-the-anti-climax/.

DID YOU KNOW?

There are multiple types of orgasms for women. Orgasms from penetration (vaginal or g-spot orgasms) may be most commonly known, but women can experience orgasm through other forms of sexual stimulation as well. In fact, these other forms of orgasm are more common, as research shows that only about 25% of women are able to orgasm from intercourse alone.[174] Clitoral stimulation is usually the easiest way for women to achieve an orgasm. Stimulation of the breasts, nipples, anus, and mouth can also lead to orgasms without directly touching the genitals.[175] Outside of sexual touching, orgasms can be achieved through exercise and sleep as well.[176]

 **TRY IT OUT**
Get to Know Sexual Pleasure

Sexual pleasure is both a science and an art. There are ways to increase sexual pleasure that have been documented for centuries, and dedicating time to learning what works for you and your partner is an excellent way to foster deeper intimacy with your partner and be more intentional with each other's pleasure.

Here are some tips to get you started.

1. **Learn about your erogenous zones.** These are areas of the body that have heightened sensitivity located throughout the body to experience pleasure.[177]

2. **Learn about sexual pleasure techniques.** Ancient practices such as *kunyaza* from East Africa[178] and books such as the *Kama Sutra* or *The Perfumed Garden* offer explicit descriptions for various sex positions and techniques to enhance pleasure.

3. **Get playful.** Sex toys, lingerie, lube, and other products can set the tone, add playfulness, and introduce new things to your sex life.

4. **Explore different types of touch.** Sensual massage techniques can activate senses and pleasure for both the partner receiving the massage as well as the partner giving the massage.[179]

5. **Explore pleasure through foreplay and non-penetrative sex.** Foreplay and oral stimulation such as cunnilingus, fellatio, and partner masturbation can offer ways to experience sexual pleasure and orgasm without penetration.

6. **Maintain a healthy lifestyle.** Exercising, eating healthy, and reducing stress can go a long way to increase libido and sexual pleasure.

7. **Get armed with knowledge.** Education about women's pleasure is a rather new concept, despite the reality that the topic has been written about for centuries. Grab some books, explore online, take workshops— decide what mechanism of learning is comfortable for you, and dive in with an open mind!

[174] Castleman, M. (2009). *The Most Important Sexual Statistic There is Today.* Psychology Today. Available at https://www.psychologytoday.com/gb/blog/all-about-sex/200903/the-most-important-sexual-statistic.

[175] Akande, H. (2018). "14 Types of Orgasms" Kunyaza: *The Secret to Female Pleasure.* Rabaah Publishers.

[176] Boutot, M. (2019). How Many Types of Female Orgasms are There Really? *Hello Clue.* Available at https:// helloclue.com/articles/sex/researching-orgasm-how-many-types-of-female-orgasms-are-there-really.

[177] Younis, I., Fattah, M., Maamoun, M. (2016). Female Hot Spots: Extragenital erogenous zones. *Human Andrology* (6)1: 20-26; Akande, H. (2018). "14 Types of Orgasms" *Kunyaza: The Secret to Female Pleasure.* Rabaah Publishers.

[178] Akande, H. (2018). Kunyaza: *The Secret to Female Pleasure.* Rabaah Publishers. Pg 258.

[179] Akande, H. (2015). *A Taste of Honey: Sexuality and Erotology in Islam.* Rabaah Publishers.

Masturbation and Self-Pleasure

Depending on your personal comfort and religious beliefs about self-pleasure, or masturbation, you may be able to explore your body on your own before trying it out with your partner. Like most *fiqh* rules, the Islamic legal rules pertaining to the permissibility of masturbation vary greatly, but there is a general understanding that if nothing else, masturbation is an option to avoid premarital sex, and some scholars even deemed it as a type of medicine.[180] One such 12th-century scholar Ibn Aqeel said:

> If a woman is without a husband, and her craving becomes intense, some of our companions have said it is permissible for her to take hold of the *akranbij*, which is an object made from the shape of a penis that a woman can insert, or something similar to it made from a cucumber or squash.[181]

Additionally, masturbation can be used in partnered sexual activity as well as a technique to stimulate one's partner and achieve sexual pleasure.

 TRY IT OUT

Questions to Ask Yourself as You Implement the RIDHA Framework

Rooted in compassion and pleasure

- Does my partner show me compassion and empathy?
- Is this relationship mutually pleasurable?
- Is my partner taking interest in what pleasures me (and what doesn't)?

Use this space to jot down a few thoughts on what a relationship rooted in compassion and pleasure means to you.

_____

_____

_____

_____

_____

_____

_____

_____

_____

_____

---

[180] Adam, M. I. (n.d.). "Female masturbation and Islam." Retrieved from https://rabaah.com/female-masturbation-and-islam.html; Muslim Women's League. (1995). Sex and Sexuality in Islam. Available at: https://www.mwlusa.org/topics/sexuality/sexuality.html; Akande, Habeeb. (2021). *Women of Desire: A Guide to Passionate Love and Sexual Compatibility.* Rabaah Publications.

[181] Akande, H. 2022. https://www.instagram.com/p/CbScAL-ong4/?igshid=YmMyMTA2M2Y=.

Far too often, relationships are lacking in compassion and attention to mutual pleasure. There are many reasons for this, including the hesitance to talk about intimacy in Muslim communities. This hesitance can cause Muslims to lack the necessary skills for healthy sexual relationships. Stereotypical gender roles for relationships and cultural expectations can also contribute to these relationships not being grounded in compassion or mutual pleasure. Moreover, both secular communities and Muslim communities tend to include hypersexual messaging that emphasize male pleasure and deprioritize women's pleasure. This messaging can lead to a misalignment of values between partners and can also cause individuals to have unrealistic ideas about sexual pleasure. This can result in them seeking outlets outside of the relationship, such as pornography, to fulfill these mistaken expectations. This behavior can lead to sex addiction and strained sexual relations that leaves one or both partners' needs unmet.

 Red Flags:

- Your partner/spouse demands sex when they feel like it, irrespective of your needs/desires.
- Your partner/spouse insists that you participate in sexual activity that makes you feel uncomfortable or safe.
- Your partner/spouse gets angry and makes you feel guilty if you decline sex.
- Your partner/spouse doesn't want to have sex with you often and blames you when you try to talk about it.
- Your partner/spouse no longer desires intimacy with you.
- Your partner/spouse is having sex outisde your relationship without your knowledge and/or agreement.
- Sex is a painful experience physically, emotionally, or spiritually. (Please note that here we do not mean physical pain due to medical reasons after sex (as opposed to pain due to forced sex). Normally, physical pain during sex is not a red flag. If you want to have sex, and you are experiencing physical pain, please see a medical professional to provide you the appropriate tools.

Pornography

Contrary to the general assumption, not only men watch porn. People are attracted to porn for universal reasons: curiosity, easy access, and as a way to explore desire. Because pornography is increasingly readily available and provides a way to explore sexual acts without actually having sex, some may turn to it as a way to avoid premarital or extramarital sex, especially in places where sexual relationships are highly regulated. According to Google statistics from 2015 searches, Muslim nations were six out of eight of the top porn-consuming countries in the world.[182] A recent study surveying 350 Muslim youth by the Family and Youth Institute indicates that 59% of Muslim youth report having viewed pornography, and 40.7% view it weekly.[183] More interestingly, this study found that religiosity was not part of the equation. In other words, a respondent's religious practice or beliefs did not impact whether or not they watched porn: specifically, "of those who reported viewing pornography (N=199), 70% describe themselves as regularly or very practicing and believe that viewing pornography is immoral."[184]

---

[182] Wessiman, C. (2015). Why Porn is Exploding in the Middle East. *Salon*. Available at: https://www.salon.com/2015/01/15/why_porn_is_exploding_in_the_middle_east_partner/

[183] Tahseen, M. (2022). Muslim Youth & Pornography. The Family and Youth Institute. Retrieved from: https://www.thefyi.org/porn-findings/

[184] Ibid.

There are certainly numerous ethical and moral issues with pornography, as numerous research studies and anti-violence experts have pointed out. Some of these are:

- The exploitation and objectification of women (especially women of color) and the message that women are objects, not human beings to be in relationship with[185]
- Unrealistic attitudes about sexual dynamics in a relationship (seen in most heterosexual and non-heterosexual porn)
- Unrealistic body standards showcased in professional porn (where men have super-sized penises and women exhibit fake breasts and bleached anuses)
- A negative impact on human sexual relationships, including dissatisfaction, sexual dysfunction, or delayed ejaculation[186]

Moreover, watching porn also can create spiritual concerns for Muslims, as watching two (or more) people have sex may feel inappropriate or compromising of one's *haya* (modesty) and certain elements of *adab* (Islamic manners). These spiritual concerns are supported by research, which also shows that extended viewing of porn and other sexually-explicit media can rewire the brain and leave one dissatisfied with real-life sex.[187] It can make it harder for men to ejaculate in a reasonable amount of time, and it can also change their attitudes toward sexual experimentation.[188] Perhaps the biggest issue with pornography, though, is that it isn't real. In many cases, female actresses aren't experiencing pleasure. The depiction of female desire, bodies, and sexuality in male-produced and male audience-targeted porn is often misleading and inaccurate.

In Your Own Words   **#THEFIRSTTIME SURVEY RESPONDENT**

"Sadly as a male my only exposure to the female body, beyond sex ed in school, was through pornography which objectifies women. So my first time involved a lot of curiosity about what was real and what was not about a woman's body based on that. I found that the reality and beauty of physical intimacy made porn completely irrelevant and thus I never went back to it."

Despite these risks, some couples choose to view pornography together as a way to become stimulated to enhance their sexual activity with each other. These couples often have an agreed-upon understanding of when and how often pornography will be consumed and to what end. Given the dangers involved in pornography: it is important to remember that, if it is brought into one's life or relationship, there must be a clear understanding of its purpose and a clear line of communication (with oneself and one's partner) to make sure it is managed in a productive and not destructive way. If you notice your partner hinting that you need to be more like pornographic images that they have encountered, it is important to have a conversation with them to get to a place of mutual understanding and intimacy. Sometimes an inundation

[185] Paul, P. (2006). *Pornified. How Pornography is Damaging Our Lives, Our Partnerships, and our Families.* St. Martin's Griffin; First edition.

[186] Akande, H. (2015). *A Taste of Honey: Sexuality and Erotology in Islam.* Rabaah Publishers. Pg 154.

[187] The Conversation. (2019). Watching Pornography Rewires the Brain to a More Juvenile State. *Neuroscience News.* Available at: https://neurosciencenews.com/neuroscience-pornography-brain-15354/.

[188] Paul, P. (2006). *Pornified. How Pornography is Damaging Our Lives, Our Partnerships, and our Families.* St. Martin's Griffin; First edition.

of pornographic imagery can numb one's sense of excitement towards their partner, and new, non-pornographic tools might be needed to reverse this trend. This includes having a conversation with the partner, setting goals and creating an environment that can help avoid and/or trigger one to view, pornography. In the end, each couple needs to decide how to handle this issue based on their own mutual comfort, values, and interpretation of Islamic beliefs around the matter.

Sex Addiction / Porn Addiction

Excessive watching or obsessing over porn (i.e. needing to watch porn several times each day) can lead to addiction. Porn addiction is defined as a preoccupation with and psychological dependency on sexual imagery over an extended period of time (some say six months or more) that results in obsessive behavior to the point of disrupting of normal daily activities. It is a compulsion, done in secret, and at the expense of intimacy with one's partner and failing in other relationship responsibilities. Research has shown that porn can have a negative impact on relationships and families, including less time spent with each other or children due to watching porn, and changing attitudes such as not wanting a family.[189]

Porn addiction is one type of sex addiction. Sex addiction more generally, is a "progressive intimacy disorder characterized by compulsive sexual thoughts and acts."[190] This often includes porn consumption and may extend to obsessive masturbation and infidelity and sexual activity outside of one's primary intimate relationship.

Sex addictions are not about high sex drives. In fact, sex addiction is rarely about sex.[191] Rather, it is often about the failure to develop emotional intimacy and filling that void with sexual behavior. Many addicts are challenged with additional feelings of guilt and shame around their behavior. Muslims struggling with sex addiction experience enhanced complications because Muslim conversations around sex are already often shame-based. Many Muslims are unaware that sex addiction is a diagnosable psychological state and that help is available.

Addictions are strong forces, and can be extremely painful for both partners to navigate when one partner is an addict. If you are in such a relationship, you should not feel like you have to fix you or your partner's problem on your own. If you are able to, and want to try to work through the relationship, seek help from a marriage counselor or professional therapist. Sex addiction, like other addictions, is tied to emotional, clinical, and possibly mental health issues that the other partner cannot address simply by offering more sex, adjusting one's physical appearance, or displaying more affection. Seeking help for sex or porn addiction is often challenging, especially in Muslim communities, due to stigma, shame, and misconceptions. A common misconception, as noted above, is that religious people don't watch porn or struggle with porn addiction and therefore hesitate to seek help.[192]

Similar to an alcoholic or drug addict, a sex addict may not recognize that they have a problem. Interventions normally occur only after a sex addict is caught and has little choice but to admit to something, although it may take a long time to admit to everything. It is unusual for an addict to initially own the destructive nature of their behavior. They may even lie or attempt to minimize the situation. In fact, some may turn the tables to make their partner feel at fault, such as suggesting that they are imagining things (gaslighting) or blame the lack of sexual activity in the relationship as justification for

189 Paul, P. (2006). *Pornified. How Pornography is Damaging Our Lives, Our Partnerships, and our Families.* St. Martin's Griffin; First edition.

190 Gillette, H. (2021). What Is Sex Addiction? *Psych Central.* Retrieved from https://psychcentral.com/lib/what-is-sexual-addiction.

191 Murphy, S. (2011). It's Not About the Sex. *Counseling Today.* Available at: https://ct.counseling.org/2011/12/its-not-about-sex/.

192 Mirza, S and Issra K. (2022). *3 Things You Should Know About Porn Addiction.* Retrieved from: https://www.thefyi.org/3-things-about-porn-addiction/.

seeking it out with others.

Recovery from addiction is a long process, and the discovery of sex addiction in a partner could result in the relationship ending. If you are in a relationship where sex addiction has been discovered, therapy is a necessary part of treatment for both of you, whether you decide to continue your partnership or not. If you feel that you might be struggling with infidelity or sex addiction yourself, do not use the fear of being rejected or losing the relationship as an excuse to avoid seeking help. The most important thing you can do is move beyond that place of powerlessness. Open the door to honest communication as your way out. Fear, guilt, and shame create a cycle of behavior that traps you in addiction.

TRY IT OUT
Seeking Help for Sex Addiction

If you think you or your partner is struggling with sex addiction, there are resources to help. The diagnosis of sex addiction will normally occur in therapy or by a mental health professional. Consider the following tips to get help: Does my partner show me compassion and empathy?

- **Get professional help.** Find a licensed therapist (preferably one specializing in sex addiction) and build a community of support.

- **Consider group therapy.** Most areas around the United States have Sex Addicts Anonymous (SAA) meetings. These are modeled on the 12-Step Program and provide perspectives from others in recovery. The hotline is 800-477-8191. You may also try Pornography Addicts Anonymous (PAA).

- **Explore online resources.** PurifyYourGaze.com is a Muslim site dedicated to compassionately supporting those struggling with porn and sex addiction. There is an online questionnaire to assess if your attitudes and behaviors around sex might indicate an addiction. The site also provides religiously appropriate resources and an online support community. Sexualrecovery.org is another group that can help.

- **Get help for the non-addict, too.** Codependents of Sex Addicts (COSA) (https://cosa-recovery.org/) is an organization with chapters around the country and offers a 12-step recovery program for those that are impacted by their partner's compulsive sexual behavior.

('ILM) INFORMED BY COMMUNICATION AND KNOWLEDGE

The next component of the RIDHA framework is to be informed through communication and knowledge. The pursuit of knowledge ('ilm in Arabic) is a central Islamic value. Not only did the Prophet (peace be upon him) tell us that the pursuit of knowledge is an obligation on every Muslim,[193] but he also reminded us to be wise in how we use that knowledge:

> A servant of God will remain standing on the Day of Judgment until he is questioned about his (time on earth) and how he used it; about his knowledge and how he utilized it; about his wealth and from where he acquired it and in what (activities) he spent it; and about his body and how he used it.[194]

Another hadith compares seeking knowledge to the journey of a martyr: The ink of a scholar is equal to the blood of a martyr.[195] Moreover, the Islamic idea of 'ilm is more expansive than the English word "knowledge" in that it includes not just theoretical knowledge, but also "theory, action, and education.[196]"

As such, a critical component to healthy sexual relationships is to be informed through knowledge and then put that knowledge into action. That is, we must equip ourselves with the necessary information about our bodies, about sex, and have the right kinds of conversations with our partners so that we are informed about each other and can act productively with this knowledge.

The starting point of all this is communication—an essential skill for any relationship, but even more crucial for sexually intimate ones. In a relationship, effective communication allows all parties to express their expectations, feelings, and needs. It is necessary for building trust, decision-making, establishing goals, and resolving conflicts. Successful relationships involve hard work in communicating and active listening.

In addition to verbal communication, nonverbal behavior can also be a significant way to express yourself and understand your partner. In Chapter 3, we discussed in detail some of the conversations that an individual can have with their current or future partner/spouses specifically about their needs and preferences around sex. Talking about boundaries, consent, past sexual history, future plans, and commitment are all important topics to discuss before moving forward with a sexual relationship. Consider the prompts and reflection activities offered in Chapter 3 as a way to build strong communication with your partner.

Additionally, clear communication can go a long way in maintaining a healthy relationship outside of sex. Having the ability to communicate and resolve conflicts effectively is empowering because it allows people to convey what matters to them in a relationship. Little or poor communication between partners can lead to misunderstandings, conflict, and secrecy, and can contribute to degrading the trust between them and maybe even the breakdown of a healthy relationship. (There are also communication methods that may also be abusive, which we will explore later in this section.)

[193] "Seeking knowledge is an obligation upon every Muslim man and woman." Source: Sunan Ibn Mājah 224, Grade: Sahih.
[194] Al-Tirmidhi.
[195] Zahid, A. W., & Tabasum, M. (2012). The Islamic Era and its Importance to Knowledge and the Development of Libraries. *Library Philosophy and Practice.* Retrieved from: https://digitalcommons.unl.edu/libphilprac/718/.
[196] Asra. (2011). *'Ilm: Knowledge.* Available at: https://islamic-dictionary.tumblr.com/post/5470765752/ilm-arabic-%D8%B9%D9%84%D9%85-translates-into-knowledge.

Green Flags:

- You and your partner are open to hearing a different perspective, rather than insisting you/they are always right.
- You and your partner have the ability to process issues together, as they come up.
- You feel comfortable sharing your opinions with each other.
- You have clear expectations of each other that do not result in harmful consequences when those expectations are not met.
- You are able to share/discuss your feelings without fear of being judged or facing a consequence.
- You are able to communicate a boundary around sex to your partner without feeling ashamed or fear of being judged.
- You are able to have a healthy disagreement and work through conflict.
- You and your partner have worked to build open and transparent communication with each other.
- You and your partner are each able to express when you/they need space or time to reflect.
- You and your partner are mindful of body language and nonverbal communication.

 # TRY IT OUT
Healthy Communication Tactics

Open and honest communication between partners is crucial, but often, many things are left unsaid. Most of the time, this happens because of a fear of hurting the other person's feelings, or from minimizing one's own feelings. Here are some tips to help you communicate well with your partner:

1. **Reflect.** Before you bring a concern to your partner, analyze what is agitating you. Are there certain experiences in your past that impact your triggers today? Is this a one-time situation or are there patterns in your partner's communication skills that are repeatedly showing up?

2. **Consider timing and delivery.** When is the best time that your partner is open to feedback, or having uncomfortable conversations? Are they more open to a face-to-face conversation, or would writing them a letter give them time to process before they talk with you? What do you need to feel safe and comfortable having this conversation?

3. **Develop shared agreements for dialogue.** Sometimes, hard conversations become even harder when there aren't tools or shared agreements in place to guide the conversation. This can include not talking over each other, listening to each other with respect and no name-calling, and focusing on "I" statements, so your partner doesn't feel attacked.

4. **Learn each other's love language.**[197] Does your partner perceive love through physical touch, acts of service, words of affirmation, gifts, or quality time? And how do they show love? What about your love language? Learning more about what makes each of you feel loved can help you effectively communicate your love and affection for each other.

5. **Practice active listening.** This is a skill both partners can work to build. Active listening requires reflecting back to your partner what you heard, and not necessarily jumping to problem-solving mode. It also means not interrupting each other and validating each other's feelings.

---

[197] Chapman, G. (2015). Discover Your Love Language - The 5 Love Languages®. Retrieved February 2, 2022, from https://www.5lovelanguages.com/.

6. **Name what is happening.** If you feel disrespected or hurt, be clear about what happened that made you feel that way, and how your partner can show up differently next time.

7. **Close with a clear understanding of what's next.** Part of active listening is also being supportive and asking your partner what they need from you and what you need from them to move forward in a way that makes your relationship stronger.

IMPORTANT NOTE: Sometimes, one partner does not communicate with the other because there is a legitimate fear of safety (i.e. one partner feels that the other will retaliate or harm them if they say what's on their mind). If this is happening to you, these tips will not work. Instead, please read later sections where we discuss how to identify these situations and where to get help.

Understanding Consent

Another important component of being informed is understanding the nature of consent. As discussed in Chapter 1, we developed our healthy relationships framework around the concept of *ridha*, the Arabic word that depicts the fullness of choice, and honoring a Muslim's right to full consent and be in control of their life's decisions, including those about sexual health.

No matter the situation, for healthy sexual intimacy, consent is always specific to each moment in time, and is something that can always be revoked. Thus, **consenting to one behavior does not obligate you to consent to other sexual behaviors, nor does it obligate you to consent to the same sexual activity on another occasion with the same person.** Again, consent is specific to each present moment. In other words, respecting someone's agency around sexuality and sex means respecting consent as a process— one that involves constant awareness and communication.

Moreover, there may be times where consent isn't actually possible, even though it might seem that both parties are agreeing. According to the law in many states, consent is definitely not present in certain situations, such as when:

- consent is not given in person, but through email, text, or social media.
- one of the individuals is incapacitated under the influence of drugs or alcohol.
- one of the individuals is asleep, unconscious, or going in and out of consciousness.
- one of the individuals is a minor (under 17 in most states) and the other is an adult.
- one of the individuals is in a position of authority (i.e. doctors, clergy members, teachers) over the other.
- one of the individuals has a severe physical, developmental, or mental disability that inhibits their ability to understand, and thereby give, consent.

If a sexual encounter occurs under the above-mentioned circumstances and where consent is compromised or void, it is no longer simply "sex," but instead becomes an act of sexual violence, which can be prosecuted as a crime. More detail about these situations will be discussed later in this chapter.

REFLECTION

What are some ways message about consent can be conflicting? What messages do you get from the media about consent? Your peers? Your faith?

The Question of Marital Rape

It is worth repeating that consent can be given and taken away, even during the course of a date or a sexual encounter. It is crucial to recognize this because it disrupts the idea that someone can presume consent—such as within a marriage/legal partnership, or even a dating relationship. This may be a new way of thinking about consent for many Muslims, because some classical *fiqh* rules presume that a wife's consent to sex exists automatically simply as an attribute of marriage. Specifically, classical Muslim jurists have argued that once a husband has paid the *mahr* (bridal gift) and provides basic marital support such as food, shelter and clothing, he has a right to have sexual relations with his wife, and she has no right to deny her husband sexual access.[198] On the other hand, Islam advocates that people—including spouses—should treat each other with care and compassion and without causing harm. In this context, it is important to recognize that a husband's insisting on a right to have sex with his wife whenever he wants to—regardless of her feelings— not only creates an unhealthy power dynamic, but it also can cause resentment or feelings of dread around sex. These feelings can in turn lead to a strained, dysfunctional, and unhappy sexual relationship for both parties. The five categories of behavior defined by the *fiqh* in Chapter 1 remind us that just because you can, doesn't mean you should. Thus, from the perspective of the RIDHA framework, we conclude that marital rape unequivocally goes against Islamic ethical behavior.

---

[198] Quraishi-Landes, A. (2013). A Meditation on Mahr, Modernity, and Muslim Marriage Contract Law. *Feminism, Law, and Religion* (1st ed.) p. 179-181. essay, Routledge. Retrieved from https://www.routledge.com/Feminism- Law-and-Religion/Failinger-Schiltz-Stabile/p/book/9781409444213.

Moreover, sex without consent is a form of sexual and/or intimate partner violence, and causes harm to the nonconsenting partner. Research has shown that women who are victims/survivors of marital rape have high rates of post traumatic stress disorder, depression, sexual dysfunction, and other psychiatric disorders as people who are victims/survivors of other forms of rape.[199] When victims of marital rape choose to stay with their partners, this increases the severity of the stress and trauma for the individual and leaves little room for healing and care.[200] Other complications from marital rape can also include STIs, sexual dysfunction, miscarriage, and chronic genital pain.

In summary, physical intimacy is a place of refuge and trust between two people who have consented to the experience. In marriage, this is also a way to praise God, not bring harm to His creation. Islam highly values the institution of marriage, encouraging both spouses to act with kindness, love, and mercy with each other, and consent to sexual activity is very much a part of that equation.

TRY IT OUT
Questions to Ask Yourself as You Implement the RIDHA Framework

Informed by communication and knowledge

- Do I know my partner/spouse's (and my own) needs? Boundaries? Likes? Dislikes? Past sexual history?
- Have we discussed our beliefs around abstinence and contraception?
- Do I have enough information about my body and reproductive processes?
- Do I understand how to prevent pregnancy and sexually transmitted infections, if I need to do so?
- Do I have full and complete information about any other sexual partners who may be involved with my partner/spouse currently?
- Do I have enough information about the commitment we are making to each other and the terms of our relationship moving forward?

Use this space to jot down a few thoughts on what being informed means to you.

---

[199] Bennice, J A., Resick, P A., Astin M. (2003). The Relative Effects of Intimate Partner Physical and Sexual Violence on Post-Traumatic Stress Disorder Symptomatology. *Violence and Victims* 8,(1) 87-94. doi:10.1891/vivi.2003.18.1.87.

[200] Boucher, S. et al (2009). Marital Rape and Relational Trauma. *Sexologies*. 18 (2): 95-97. https://doi.org/10.1016/j.sexol.2009.01.006.

Poor Communication

While it's normal for couples to disagree, occasional disagreements and tension should be differentiated from ongoing toxicity, abuse, and violence. Conflict is a natural part of every relationship because each person has their own perspective, opinions, thoughts, feelings, and preferences. But conflict should not be ugly or violent. It can be resolved peacefully when people communicate effectively and are interested in finding a solution that works for both parties. Ultimately, your partner/spouse should not cause you harm through their words or nonverbal body language. Repeated patterns of this kind of behavior may constitute emotional abuse and can damage your sense of self—eroding the bond and trust between you and your partner.

 Red Flags:

Every unhealthy or abusive relationship is unique to the individuals involved and red flags can vary from relationship to relationship, but here are some common ones that might help you figure out if you are in a potentially unhealthy or abusive relationship:

- **Irrational irritability leading to physical or emotional threats:** threatening you because you didn't do what they asked you to, or responding with threats when you raised a concern or gave them feedback.

- **Temperamental communication:** communicating to you in a way that is inconsistent and unpredictable, and connected more to their moods than to responding in a timely way to a need or a concern.

- **Emotional blackmailing:** making you feel guilty to manipulate you to do something they want you to do.

- **Physical confrontations of any sort:** using physical force or intimidation to silence you (for example if your partner is taller and larger than you, towering over you to make you feel small).

- **Silent treatment:** not speaking to you as a way to make you feel like you did something bad.

In some situations, red flags signal extremely unsafe conditions that threaten physical and emotional health—and sometimes life itself. For this reason, it is important to recognize certain relationship red flags and address them if possible. In later sections in this chapter, we will be discussing resources for how to address situations when they are unsafe.

 # TRY IT OUT
Questions to Ask Yourself When Checking for Red Flags

1. Is this not an isolated incident, but rather part of a pattern of repeat behavior?
2. Has a third-party individual (like a friend or family member) ever commented/alerted you to their concerns about how you or your partner/spouse communicate?
3. Have you felt unsafe multiple times because of the ways your partner/spouse talks to you?

If you have answered "yes" to any of these questions, it may be helpful to consider speaking to a therapist or an advocate at your local domestic violence organization to consider whether you need to take certain precautionary measures.

D (ADALAH) DRIVEN BY EQUITY AND JUSTICE

The third principle of our framework—equity and fairness (*adalah*)—is a central component of a healthy relationship. *Adalah* is another core value in Islam. God is known as *Al-'Adl* (the Most Just), one of the 99 Names. There are several translations of '*adalah*: justice; fairness, impartiality; probity, integrity, honesty, equitableness; decency, proper conduct; honorable record. The depth of this word reflects the richness and the spirit that we hope this component of the RIDHA framework communicates. When a relationship is driven by '*adalah*, both partners share power and have their needs met equitably, treating each other with justice and fairness. Relationships void of equity and fairness run the risk of being unsafe and insecure, and can ultimately result in violence and abuse. For this reason, the D ("driven by equity and fairness") and H ("housed in safety and security") in the RIDHA framework are very closely interconnected.

Equitable power between partners means that both people in the relationship make decisions together, or have a mutual understanding and agreement about how decisions will be made and by whom. Equity does not mean that both partners have to be equally involved at all times or that each partner will make the same number of decisions. It simply means that the partners have discussed and mutually agreed upon a process for how their decisionmaking will happen, and considers both partners' needs fairly.

As noted in Chapter 1, all human beings are created spiritually equal before God. In fact, some Muslim scholars have asserted that not believing in this equality and instead creating a hierarchy between people is at the root of violence and oppression. Specifically, violence against another, such as domestic violence, is akin to satanic logic or *shirk* (associating another being with God—the gravest sin in Islam): because it stems from arrogance and the notion of being better than another. This is exemplified by the story of Iblis's refusal to bow to Adam upon God's command, claiming that he (made of fire) was superior to Adam (made of clay).[201] As Azizah al-Hibri describes this story:

> Iblis adopted a value system based on an arbitrary hierarchical principle (i.e. fire is better than clay), which served his own arrogant and selfish purposes. Iblis was so committed to this hierarchical principle that he was willing to incur God's eternal wrath rather than violate it. In effect, Iblis deified his principle, for he permitted it to supersede Divine Will. Consequently, he violated the fundamental principle of tawhid and fell into shirk (the opposite of monotheism, that is a belief in mdore than one Supreme Being or will).[202]

In her analysis, al-Hibri asserts that any posture of hierarchy between humans is an un-Islamic Iblis-like behavior. This includes domestic violence because it demonstrates an attitude of hierarchy and superiority on the part of the abuser, or in other words, exerting power and control over another person, which is at the root of domestic violence.[203] She further points out that some classical *fiqh* scholars embraced this idea by prohibiting men from getting married if they were likely to harm or oppress their prospective wives.[204]

[201] al-Hibri, A. (2003). An Islamic Perspective on Domestic Violence. *Fordham International Law Journal*, 27(1), 195. https://doi.org/http://ir.lawnet.fordham.edu/ilj.
[202] Ibid.
[203] Abugideiri, S. E. (2010). *A Perspective on Domestic Violence in the Muslim Community*. Retrieved from https://www.faithtrustinstitute.org/resources/articles/DV-in-Muslim-Community.pdf.
[204] al-Hibri, A. (2003). An Islamic Perspective on Domestic Violence. *Fordham International Law Journal*, 27(1), 195. https://doi.org/http://ir.lawnet.fordham.edu/ilj.

Keeping all of this in mind, HEART identified these "green flags" for what an equitable relationship can look like:

 Green Flags:

- Your partner interacts with you with respect and not a condescending attitude.
- Both partners are equally accountable to each other.
- Both partners take responsibility for when they are wrong and apologize.
- Your partner treats you as an equal partner, and not as someone over whom they have power or authority.
- Both partners have freedom to make decisions about what they wear, who they see, who their friends are.
- When there is disagreement, you can talk through that conflict without either party using force.
- You and your spouse/partner discuss big decisions that may involve finances, children/family, housing, education, etc. and come to mutual agreement before proceeding.
- Both partners are transparent about individual and shared finances, especially about how they're spent.
- Both partners are open to compromise if the other partner does not feel like they have equitable say and/or decisionmaking power.
- Both partners feel like their needs are being considered, heard, and addressed.
- Both partners share power, especially during conflict, and work together to find solutions.
- Both partners use clear and direct communication regarding desires and needs without fear of disagreement and rejection.

 TRY IT OUT
Questions to Ask Yourself as You Implement the RIDHA Framework

- Does my partner treat me with dignity and integrity?
- Does my partner respect my values, beliefs, and personhood?
- Do I feel like I am an equal partner in this relationship?
- Are my needs considered fairly and equitably alongside my partner's needs?
- Is my partner fair to me during disagreements?
- Is my partner accountable when they harm or hurt me?

Reflect on what being driven by equity and justice means to you. If you have answered "no" to any of the questions above, consider finding a time when your partner is open to receiving feedback and try to discuss your feelings about the issue. Keep mutuality and equality in mind as you approach the subject, and practice the communication techniques listed above under I ("Informed by Communication and Knowledge") in the RIDHA framework.

If you have answered "no" to more than 3 of these questions above, and conversation and communication has not improved things, consider a couples' counselor/therapist who can help with guiding questions and help you and your partner/spouse get a deeper look into what is going on in the relationship.

Contentious and Abusive Relationships

Now that we have explored what equitable power can look like, we will now consider what starts to happen when that power dynamic shifts. A consistent, unequal power dynamic can result in the health of that relationship deteriorating, and ultimately can lead to abuse and violence. In an unhealthy relationship, there is an imbalanced distribution of power, resulting in an inequitable dynamic between partners. In such a relationship, power ultimately becomes contentious, with one person often attempting to assert their dominance and control over the relationship by making unilateral decisions without the other person's knowledge or consent. Transforming a relationship of imbalanced power into a balanced one can be difficult, and counseling may be helpful to address concerns and unhealthy tendencies in the relationship. For example, a couples or sex therapist can help a couple explore questions about their relationship—and work through some of the tense power dynamics.

In an abusive relationship, there is a complete imbalance of power. The exercise of power in these relationships involves inflicting harm and creating an unsafe or oppressive environment where one partner is disempowered. Couples counseling is **not** usually recommended for abusive relationships because of safety concerns: the dominant partner will often make it dangerous to address the problematic issues in the relationship. In such cases, we recommend seeking out an advocate from a gender-based-violence direct service organization. They can support the vulnerable partner with safety planning. A safety plan considers options that work best for each situation—taking individualized safety and security into account. More details about abusive and violent relationships will be explored in the fourth component of the RIDHA framework ("Housed in safety and security"), below.

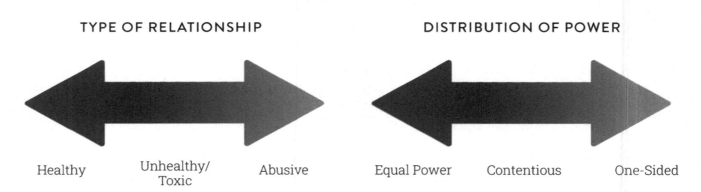

Figure 1. Power Distribution in different types of relationships. (HEART, 2022)

It's not always easy to tell if a relationship is violent and abusive or merely contentious. As shown in the graphic above, an abusive relationship might start off as contentious and then move into abuse, but not always. Contentious relationships are subtle in the ways an individual may experience harm and can involve a power struggle between partners.

What is important to recognize is that if you find yourself in a contentious relationship, it has more of a potential to slide down the slippery slope into an abusive one than one that is not contentious. There are some "red flags" that you can keep an eye on and monitor closely, so you can stay alert to possible sliding and address it early.

Red Flags of an Inequitable Relationship:

- **Your partner isolates you away from your friends and family.** They can do this, for example, by wanting to occupy all your time and getting upset when you try to make plans with someone else.
- **Your partner controls all aspects of your finances.** This could mean keeping your money in a bank account that only they can access, or making financial decisions for you and controlling how you spend your money, or constantly monitoring how much and where you spend.
- **Your partner makes your medical decisions for you.** This may include but is not limited to: forcing you go on or off birth control, or to get or/not get an abortion, or to go on or off medication to treat mental health or other medical issues.
- **Your partner makes all or most life decisions** for you and your family without your input or consideration.

 # TRY IT OUT
Is Your Relationship Contentious?

Here are some questions designed to see if your relationship is contentious—these are "red flags" to see if you should watch for a possible abusive relationship in the future. You may experience all, a combination of a few, or even none.

Even if you experience one of the following, it may be best to consider speaking with a mental health professional and/or an advocate that may help you process whether there are potential next steps.

When you are with your partner:

- Do you feel safe when you have an argument with each other?
- During an argument, do you feel like you aren't able to express how you feel because you are afraid they will either judge you, or not receive your perspective calmly?
- Do you avoid an argument because you anticipate being emotionally hurt?
- Have you ever ended an argument for fear that things may lead to something physical (even if things have not yet escalated to any physical harm)?
- Do feelings of distrust arise during a confrontation?
- Do you feel as though your partner is always defensive and is not open to feedback?
- Does this leave you feeling like you can never express yourself? Do you find that sometimes, you don't trust yourself when trying to speak up?
- Do you frequently decide not to speak up because it's not worth it—due to your partner's reactions to past discussions?
- Do you consider how things could have been done differently regarding a situation after it has happened?

We recognize that not many couples or individuals can access therapy, or want to access therapy. If you feel like you are sitting in the gray zone of what we are naming as a contentious relationship, then consider the following:

- Ask yourself: do you want to end the relationship?
  - If you do, is it safe for you to do so? Will you face retaliation from your partner or others?
  - If you don't, find ways to directly communicate to your partner that you don't feel heard. Share what you would like to see done differently.

Power and Control in a Relationship

Another way to look at the power distribution in relationships is through the lens of power and control. Below is a power and control chart developed by HEART and Justice for Muslims Collective, which is modeled after the Power and Control wheel developed in the 1980s by Domestic Abuse Intervention Programs in Duluth, MN.[205] This wheel describes how an abuser may secure control over their partner. While this wheel is specific to situations of sexual violence, many of the techniques referred to in the wheel can exist through other forms of violence as well, such as spiritual abuse and domestic violence.[206]

[205] HEART. (2020, May 29). Power and Control: Sexual Violence in Muslim Communities. HEART. Retrieved from https://hearttogrow.org/resources/power-and-control-wheel/.

[206] Please also refer to the power and control wheel specific to domestic violence developed by Peaceful Families Project available at: Peaceful Families Project. (n.d.). Power and Control in Muslim Families. Peaceful Families. Retrieved from https://www.peacefulfamilies.org/uploads/1/1/0/5/110506531/providers%E2%80%99_fact_sheet_.pdf.

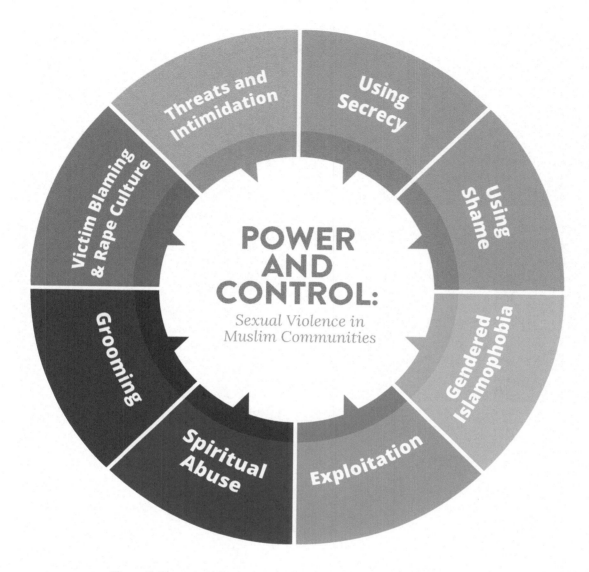

Figure 2. Power and Control: Sexual Violence in Muslim Communities[207]

Power and Control Wheel

In this diagram, we've broken down eight specific ways an abuser can gain power and control. Each "slice" shares in depth how that particular technique can be used to exert power over another and perpetuate sexual violence. For example, a person may threaten to take away financial support or may intimidate another person into having sex with them. Or, a person may misuse religious tradition to coerce someone to have sex, a tactic known as spiritual abuse.

[207] This diagram is created for a project that is supported by Grant No. 2017-UD-AX-0006, awarded by the Office on Violence Against Women, "Grants for Outreach and Services to Underserved Populations Program," US Department of Justice. The opinions, findings, conclusions, and recommendations expressed in this graphic are those of the authors and do not necessarily reflect the views of the Department of Justice, Office on Violence Against Women.

Victim Blaming & Rape Culture

Relying on societal attitudes and gender stereotypes to justify abuse. Examples: saying victim tempted the abuser; wouldn't have been assaulted if they just followed Islam; gaslighting the victim to question their reality by insisting it didn't happen the way the victim describes it, or that they are angry and seeking revenge; in instance of male rape, using homophobia to question the masculinity or sexuality of the person because "men don't get raped."

Threats and Intimidation

Using threats or intimidation to blackmail, coerce, shame, or disclose personal details about the victim publicly. Examples: will expose the relationship to others to shame the victim (in premarital, extramarital, or same sex situations); will call Child and Family Services to take the kids away or get custody; intimidating the victim to not call police or receive counseling in order to protect "family honor."

Using Secrecy

Insisting that the relationship needs to remain private for the time being and making false promises. Examples: telling the victim that the relationship has to be secret because no one will understand; that they will get married soon; that their marriage will only have to remain a secret for a short while.

Using Shame

Shaming the victim into silence by using emotional manipulation, which could result in excommunication from a community or family. Examples: using arguments like "no one will believe you," "what will people say," or "no one will want to marry you if you leave me" to coerce victims to stay; threatening to publicly ruin their or their family's reputation, or generally destroying their reputation (e.g. slut shaming, isn't a virgin, mentally unstable, bad character.)

Gendered Islamophobia

Using current fearmongering techniques to coerce victim to not report. Examples: threatening to call immigration enforcement, FBI, or threatening to report the victim as a potential terrorist; silencing the victim to not report abuser because they are bringing shame upon the community and responsible for, or contributing to, Islamophobia; coercing victim to not report because abuser will be tried as a terrorist.

Exploitation

Using immigration, financial dependence, housing, mental health or health status to silence a victim. Examples: threatening financial instability or deportation if abuse is reported; makes victim dependent on them; demands sex in exchange for housing, food, employment, medications and other life needs, controlling access to key documents, the victim's physical living, work, school, and other spaces; threatening to or transmitting STDs/STIs and then threatening to disclose that information.

Spiritual Abuse

Using religious doctrine, religious authority and male privilege to justify behavior. Examples: abuser may try to escape accountability by saying "I know more than you," "Secret marriage is lawful," "Men have a degree over women;" abuser may demand that they have sexual rights, or use the threat of polygamy to coerce their spouse to have sex; abuser may control what the victim wears under the guise of "modesty" or dictate what "appropriate" gender interactions are and aren't.

Grooming

The majority of victims—child and adult—know their abusers, who use emotional tactics to gain the victim's trust. Examples: buying lavish gifts or grand, romantic gestures; showering extra attention on a victim or giving them special treatment, crossing boundaries and demanding sexual acts in order to keep the gifts and attention; using religious authority or otherwise to make the victim believe their relationship is normal and lawful.

TRY IT OUT
How Does Power and Control Show Up?

Here are three case studies designed to help identify the various ways in which power and control can show up—in the form of spiritual abuse, exploitation, gendered islamophobia, secrecy, shame, threats and intimidation, victim blaming and rape culture, and grooming. Please note that you may see more than one form of power and control show up in each case study. To see the answers, please refer below.

Case Study 1

A couple has a six-month old baby. The husband works from home in the basement from 9am to 6pm, while his wife juggles caring for their baby and a part-time consulting job. The husband suggests to his wife that they should have sex once the baby is asleep. The wife tells the husband that she is exhausted and hasn't even had time to eat or shower, let alone feel emotionally ready to have sex with him. The husband reminds her about a wife's Islamic obligations and threatens her with *hadiths* regarding the sin of denying one's husband his sexual rights. Further, he mentions that if she does not oblige, he will report her to the authorities and get her deported. He raises his voice, which concerns the wife about waking up their baby. She agrees to his request. What type of power and control is showing up from the wheel?

Case Study 2

A victim of a prominent sexual assault case drops charges after meeting with the defense attorneys who told her that there is not enough evidence to take the case forward. When speaking to a friend, the victim shares that the religious leader had told her to keep their interactions a secret for a long time and that she had already felt guilty about doing that, until he sexually violated her. If she drops the charges, she is now afraid her community could outcast her as a liar and accuse her of spreading gossip and slander about a respected religious leader. What type of power and control is showing up from the wheel?

Case Study 3

A male scholar-in-residence at an Islamic school is supervising the female lead teacher at the Sunday school. He asks the teacher to stop wearing skinny jeans and expresses disappointment when he notices her speaking with a male colleague, admonishing her that "you wouldn't want men here to get distracted, would you?" Further, he schedules a series of face-to-face, one-on-one meetings with this teacher in his office. During those meetings, he not only supervises her work, but also finds ways to give her gifts and compliments in private. What type of power and control is showing up from the wheel?

Answers:

Case Study 1: Spiritual abuse, threats, and intimidation
Case Study 2: Spiritual abuse, victim blaming, shame, threats and intimidation, secrecy
Case Study 3: Grooming, rape culture, spiritual abuse

Referring back to figure 1 on page 160, abusive relationships fall on the end of the relationship spectrum because elements of power and control are showing up. Abusive relationships, because there is a threat of power and control, fall on one end of the relationship spectrum. An abusive relationship differs from an unhealthy relationship in that one partner may be afraid for their safety and the partner with control has shown a pattern of coercive/threatening behavior. Later in this chapter, we will address violence and how it can appear in relationships in more detail.[208] For now, here is a chart that shows elements of healthy, unhealthy, and abusive relationships and how they might manifest.[209]

	Healthy	**Unhealthy**	**Abusive**
Communication	Partners can talk about their feelings and show empathy toward each other.	One or both partners feeling uncomfortable about expressing feelings or emotions	One partner controls another partner's thoughts, feelings, technological/electronic devices, who they see, who they don't see.
Disagreements	There are disagreements in the relationship and there is still respect for one another.	Disagreements turn into fights more often than not.	Someone is afraid to disagree because they fear their partner's anger, abuse, belittling, or violence.
Intimacy and Affection	Partners have open, honest communication about intimacy, physical affection, and sex.	Someone feels ignored or disrespected by their partner.	One partners' needs and wants are ignored and/or are coerced into intimacy, physical affection (abuse), and/or sex (rape).

⚙ TRY IT OUT

Using the box above, can you name examples of healthy, unhealthy, and abusive relationship signs?

_____

_____

_____

_____

_____

_____

_____

[208] See "H" Housed in security and safety.

[209] This list is adapted from Office of Victim Assistance. (n.d.). *The Difference Between Healthy, Unhealthy and Abusive Relationships*. Office of Victim Assistance. Retrieved from https://www.colorado.edu/ova/sites/default/files/attached-files/ova_knowthedifference_flyer.pdf.

Weaponizing Sex

Weaponizing sex happens when sex is used as a means to an end. There are a number of ways this can happen. First, someone may weaponize their partner's sexual history by threatening to expose it as a means to coerce them into obedience or to get something from them. Another way is to force sex as a means of control and domination, withhold sex as a condition for some behavior, or to convey anger for some past behavior. Both are very harmful to developing healthy sexual intimacy. Withholding sex is akin to silent treatment in that it lacks compassion and can result in the other partner's humiliation and degradation of their self worth. Forcing sex disregards the dignity and agency of the partner being forced, which creates obstacles to healthy sexual intimacy. It might even be said that using sex as a weapon violates the general Quranic recommendation that we should treat all humanity with dignity (*karamah*).[210]

While both partners can participate in withholding sex from each other, we have also seen how wives in particular can be guilted into having sex, and husbands can weaponize sex as an act of obedience to them: potentially citing a *hadith* to insist that if she is not obedient, then she will be cursed by the angels.[211] As we described earlier, HEART believes that this understanding of sexual obligation between spouses is not an appropriate *fiqh* interpretation because it interferes with healthy relationship intimacy. Moreover, that particular *hadith* is said to have a weak narrative chain (*isnad*), thus giving us another reason to not feel obligated to treat it with unquestionable authority.[212] Finally, it is inconsistent with the Prophet's own example of expressing love and mercy toward his wives—including honoring their agency to decline sex. As such, it is better to interpret all these verses and *hadiths* with a focus on the Islamic centering of "affection, mercy and tranquility in family relations."[213]

---

[210] "We have given dignity (karamah) to the Children of Adam." (Quran 17:70).

[211] "If the husband calls his wife to bed and she refuses, the Angels will curse her until she gets up in the morning" Sahih Bukhari, as cited in al Hibri, Azizah and Ghazal, Ghada. (2018). "Debunking the Myth: Angels Cursing Hadith." Available at: https://karamah.org/debunking-the-myth-angels-cursing-hadith/.

[212] al Hibri, Azizah and Ghazal, Ghada. (2018). Debunking the Myth: Angels Cursing Hadith. Available at: https://karamah.org/debunking-the-myth-angels-cursing-hadith/.

[213] Ibid.

H (HURMA) HOUSED IN SAFETY AND SECURITY

Relationships that are not grounded in equity can challenge the health of a relationship, and ultimately compromise a partner's safety. In our RIDHA framework, the "H" is critical: it is essential in a healthy relationship for both parties to feel a sense of security (*hurma*) and safety with each other. This means being safe from various forms of violence, oppression, or deception, with each individual upholding and protecting the general well-being of the other. As the Quran says, we are garments for each other.[214] Garments can keep us safe and warm, protected from cold and irritants, as well as beautifully adorned. They should never be the cause of harm or fear.

REFLECTION

What do you need to feel safe in a relationship? Physically? Emotionally? Spiritually?

In Chapter 1, we introduced the concept of *hurma*, or the sacred inviolability of the human body. We take the concept of *hurma* to mean that boundaries should be respected within intimate relationships too. While many people tend to focus on safety from physical violence, this section will take an expansive view of *hurma*, and address all forms of violence that can compromise one's physical, emotional, and spiritual safety, all of which are crucial to one feeling secure in a relationship. That is, if there is any kind of violence, abuse, coercion, or deception in a relationship, it interferes with *hurma*, and with a partner's/spouse's ability to feel safe and secure. Many classical and contemporary Muslim scholars have argued that violence and abuse contradicts both the Quran and Prophetic example. The Prophet never hit his wives or harmed them in any way; his behavior is an example of kind treatment of women.[215] In fact, he is reported to have said "the best of you will not strike."[216]

---

214 Quran 2:187.

215 Ibrahim, N., & Abdalla, M. (2010). A Critical Examination of Quran 4: 34 and its Relevance to Intimate Partner Violence in Muslim Families. *Journal of Muslim Mental Health*, 5(3), 327-349.

216 Ali, K. (2006). "The Best of you will not Strike": Al-Shafi on Quran, Sunnah, and Wife-Beating. *Comparative Islamic Studies*. 2(2): 143-155.

A Deeper Dive into 4:34

Despite this Prophetic example, we know that violence and abuse continue to exist. Although all people are created spiritually equal before God, some Muslims believe that this equality does not extend to the relationship between spouses in a marriage, citing *fiqh* opinions that wives should be obedient to their husbands, and moreover that husbands can physically enforce this obedience. This idea of obedience comes from a particular interpretation of Quranic verse 4:34 which provides guidance on conflict resolution if a wife is "disobedient." Specifically, verse 4:34 states:

> Men are in charge of women by [right of] what Allah has given one over the other and what they spend [for maintenance] from their wealth. So righteous women are devoutly obedient, guarding in [the husband's] absence what Allah would have them guard. But those [wives] from whom you fear arrogance—[first] advise them; [then if they persist], forsake them in bed; and [finally], strike them. But if they obey you [once more], seek no means against them. Indeed, Allah is ever Exalted and Grand.[217]

The majority of classical and contemporary scholars argue that this verse does not encourage physical violence or harm toward one's wife, but do differ in their interpretations. Some argue this verse grants permission to strike lightly while others contend it means a nonviolent physical separation.[218] Specifically, some *fiqh* scholars conclude from this that a husband has the right to physically discipline a wife whom he deems to be "disobedient."[219] But these same *fiqh* scholars also insist that husbands should never physically injure their wives, rather only use a symbolic gesture. They insist that use of disciplinary action must "have the potential to help the marriage...and restore the relationship."[220]

Unfortunately, we at HEART have seen a great deal of harm resulting from Muslims taking advantage of this interpretation of this verse and—ignoring the *fiqh* scholars' admonitions against harm, using it to justify committing domestic and intimate partner violence, ranging from emotional abuse to actual physical injury and even death. Such harm is in direct violation of the Quran, which emphasizes the principle of "do no harm," as reflected in the verse "Say: My Lord has forbidden all atrocities, whether overt or disguised, and harm (*ithm*)."[221] In addition, it is also notable to consider the Prophet's response to this verse's revelation, as Dr. Laury Silvers explains:

> It is widely reported that Muhammad was disturbed by the commandment/permission when the verse was revealed to him, limited it to non-violent tapping, and did not act on it himself. *Because the Prophet rejected violence against women, we would be justified in accepting the reading of non-violent separation as that which was intended by God and be done with it.*[222]

Considering all of this, we continue to explore below some alternative interpretations of this verse, especially those offered by contemporary Muslim women scholars. First, they reject the notion that wives

[217] Quran 4:34.
[218] Ibrahim, N., & Abdalla, M. (2010). A Critical Examination of Qur'an 4: 34 and its Relevance to Intimate Partner Violence in Muslim Families. *Journal of Muslim Mental Health*, 5(3), 327-349.; Silvers, L. (2008). 'In the Book we have left out nothing': The Ethical Problem of the Existence of Verse 4:34 in the Quran. *Comparative Islamic Studies* (2)2: 171-180.
[219] The Muslim Vibe. (2019). *Analyzing the so-called Wife-Beating Verse: 4:34 of the Holy Quran*. Retrieved from: https://themuslimvibe.com/faith- islam/in-practice/434-of-the-holy-quran-analysing-the-so-called-wife-beating-verse.
[220] Your Vibe. Analyzing the so-called Wife-Beating Verse: 4:34 of the Holy Quran. *The Muslim Vibe*. Available at: https://themuslimvibe.com/faith-islam/in-practice/434-of-the-holy-quran-analysing-the-so-called-wife-beating-verse.
[221] Quran 7:33.
[222] Silvers, L. (2008). 'In the Book we have left out nothing': The Ethical Problem of the Existence of Verse 4:34 in the Quran. *Comparative Islamic Studies* (2)2: 171-180.

are to owe their husbands' obedience, and second, reject that they may use any from of control of physical discipline to assert this obedience. For example, amina wadud explains:

> The Quran never orders a woman to obey her husband. It never states that obedience to their husbands is characteristic of the 'better women' (66:5), nor is it a prerequisite for women to enter the community of Islam... However, in marriages of subjugation, wives did obey their husbands, usually because they believed that a husband who materially maintains his family, including his wife, deserves to be obeyed. Even in such cases, the norm at the time of the revelation, no correlation is made that the husband should beat his wife into obedience. Such an interpretation has no universal potential, and contradicts the essence of the Quran and the established practices of the Prophet. It involves a severe misreading of the Quran to support the lack of constraint in some men.[223]

Additionally, it is critical to consider verse 4:34 in context with the verse following it: 4:35, which states "if you [believers] fear that a couple may break up, appoint one arbiter from his family and one from hers. Then if the couple want to put things right, God will bring about a reconciliation between them: He is all knowing, all aware."[224] Given that the Quran offers reconciliation as an immediate next step, it is clear that the process outlined in 4:34 does not in any way encourage an environment where domestic violence or intimate partner violence (IPV) can be present. As explained further by Ibrahim and Abdallah:

> In situations where a wife's safety may be at risk as a result of intimate partner violence (IPV), this process of arbitration may place the wife at further risk, which is why a desire for reconciliation is stressed in verse 4:35, implying a process that has overcome any danger that may exist. It seems that the method the Quran uses is more results-oriented than dogmatic, where both parties are dealt with equitably and with justice. If reconciliation with the help of arbitrators from each side fails, and marital harmony does not seem to be restorable, then the couple may seek divorce.[225]

Every *fiqh* opinion is fallible, so every Muslim has to determine for themselves if what they believe is aligned with their core values. As Ayesha Chaudhry explains, this verse can be read both in violent and nonviolent ways, and the responsibility lies with the reader to determine how they want to approach it:

> The fact is that 4:34 can legitimately be read both ways—violently and non-violently, either as sanctioning violence against wives or as offering a non-violent, non-hierarchical means for resolving marital conflict. Muslims may follow whichever interpretation they choose, and the inescapable truth is that the interpretation chosen says more about the Muslim in question than it does about the verse. This marvelous agency comes with a heavy responsibility: Rather than holding 4:34 responsible for what it means, Muslims can and must hold themselves responsible for their interpretations.[226]

Dr. Laury Silvers makes a similar argument, as she writes of classical scholar Ibn 'Arabi's take on it, arguing that "God may intend all meanings, but it does not follow that He *approves* all meanings...the

223 wadud, amina. (1999). *Quran and Woman: Rereading the Sacred Text from a Woman's Perspective.* Oxford University Press. Pg 77.

224 Quran 4:35.

225 Ibrahim, N., & Abdalla, M. (2010). A Critical Examination of Quran 4: 34 and its Relevance to Intimate Partner Violence in Muslim Families. *Journal of Muslim Mental Health,* 5(3), 327-349.

226 Chaudhry, A. (2014). Does the Koran Allow Wife-Beating? Not If Muslims Don't Want It To. *The Globe and Mail.* Retrieved from https://www.theglobeandmail.com/opinion/its-muslims-who-give-voice-to-verse/article17684163/.

227 Silvers, L. (2008). 'In the Book we have left out nothing': The Ethical Problem of the Existence of Verse 4:34 in the Quran. *Comparative Islamic Studies* (2)2: 171-180.

purpose of the existence of this verse would be to remind human beings of the extraordinary burden of freedom."[227] Put differently, it is possible to read this verse not as God's command, but rather as an invitation to exercise free will and not harm their partner.

All this considered, even those who choose to follow an interpretation of Quran 4:34 that justifies wifely obedience and a husband's power to discipline a disobedient wife must also consider the very important principles of Islamic ethics, and that "not all possible interpretations of the divine will are considered ethically equal."[228] The *fiqh's* five categories of behavior from Chapter 1 remind us that just because you can, doesn't mean you should. Simply put, it just makes for deeper and more fulfilling emotional connection—and a better sex life—when obedience is not wielded as a tool in a relationship.

 Green Flags For Relationships That Are Grounded In Safety And Security:

- You feel heard and your boundaries are respected and honored.
- If there is conflict or harm, there is an apology and intentional change in behavior instead of a repeat pattern of harmful, aggressive, or violent behavior.
- You feel like you are in control when it comes to making decisions about your body.
- Sex is not used as a weapon to force you to have sex or as a punishment when you do not want to have sex or withheld from you as a mechanism to force other behavior.
- Religious scripture or tradition is not used to denigrate or shame you or coerce you into any particular behavior.
- If you approach your partner/spouse with a concern, they consider your concern rather than shame you or punish you for it.

 # TRY IT OUT
Questions to Ask Yourself as You Implement the RIDHA Framework

Housed in Security and Safety:
- Do I feel emotionally, spiritually, and physically safe with my partner?
- Does my partner know that they are not entitled to my body without considering whether I want to be intimate?
- Do I have what I need to be safe if I want to prevent pregnancy and/or sexually transmitted infections?
- Is my relationship being kept a secret from my partner's family and friends (or my own)? If yes, for what reasons is it being kept secret?
- Does my partner isolate me from my family and friends or control who I can see or talk to?

Use this space to jot down a few thoughts on what being in a safe and secure relationship means to you.

_____

_____

_____

_____

_____

_____

[228] Silvers, L. (2008). 'In the Book we have left out nothing': The Ethical Problem of the Existence of Verse 4:34 in the Quran. *Comparative Islamic Studies* (2)2: 171-180.

Relationships and Violence

As mentioned earlier, there is a difference between normal conflict and an unhealthy relationship that is violent or abusive. The transition from one to the other can be subtle and sometimes hard to recognize, let alone disrupt. Being emotionally invested in your partner can result in blind spots or denial that your partner is mistreating you. Nevertheless, the more you understand what makes a relationship abusive, the various forms of violence that can occur between people, and your rights (both under U.S. law and Islamic law), the more you will be equipped to identify and address when your relationship is no longer safe, or support a friend when they are experiencing an unsafe relationship.

 Red Flags of an Abusive or Violent Relationship

- Your partner constantly puts you down, shames, or blames you for things that are not your fault.
- Your partner emotionally, mentally, spiritually, or even physically harms you but denies it—causing you to believe that either nothing happened or that it was all your fault (also known as gaslighting).
- You are afraid of ending your relationship with your partner because you fear them hurting you, them hurting themselves, or how they might react/respond.

As mentioned earlier, violence and abuse is not limited to marriage, but can happen in many types of relationships, including courtship and dating, and can also continue after a relationship is over. At the root of these forms of violence is power and control, discussed in the previous section ("D"—Driven by Equity and Fairness). It is easy to see how a relationship rife with inequities can lead to abuse and violence.

There are various forms of violence that may occur in a relationship, and some that can also occur outside of one. You may remember some of these from the power and control wheel in the previous section. These include the following:[229]

Physical Abuse: The intentional use of force or threats of force on another person in an attempt to control behavior and/or intimidate. Examples include: hitting, slapping, punching, strangulation, shoving, throwing, pulling hair.

Verbal Abuse: The use of words to manipulate, intimidate, and maintain power and control over someone. This can include insults, humiliation and ridicule, silent treatment, attempts to scare, isolate, and control.

Emotional Abuse: Often falls into one or more of these categories:

- **Degrading:** A person receives messages about not being good enough
- **Ignoring:** A person is given mixed messages—welcomed in some situations and ignored in others.
- **Isolating:** Individuals are cut off from normal social interactions and/or family and friends. They become emotionally dependent on their abusers.
- **Terrorizing:** Fear is created using insults and by verbal and nonverbal threats. This intimidates a person and destroys his/her independence and self-esteem.
- **Corrupting:** An individual is encouraged to participate in illegal, destructive behavior.

[229] Creative Interventions. (2012). *Creative Interventions Toolkit A Practical Guide to Stop Interpersonal Violence.* Retrieved from https://www.creative-interventions.org/wp-content/uploads/2020/10/CI-Toolkit-Final-ENTIRE-Aug-2020-new-cover.pdf.

- **Exploiting:** A person is making use of a partner to meet inappropriate needs, or for economic or social gain.
- **Controlling:** One partner expects, compels, or requires the other partner to cater to their needs and desires at the other's expense.
- **Gaslighting:** a type of psychological abuse in which the abuser denies the victim's reality, causing them to question themselves, their memories, or their perceptions.

Sexual Violence: All unwanted sexual acts—whether harassment, abuse, or assault—committed against another person, without that person's freely given consent, is sexual violence and could be prosecuted as a crime.

Spiritual Abuse: Using religion to manipulate, control, and bully or shaming to manipulate, control, bully, and harm for their own personal gain, such as sexual or financial.

Economic Abuse: The use of financial assets to control the victim. Examples include: denying access to money, preventing the victim from viewing or having access to bank accounts, stealing money from the victim or their family and friends.

Digital Abuse: The use of technology and/or social media to control the victim. Examples include: telling the victim who they can or can't be friends with on Facebook, using email, social media, and tweets to harass, threaten, or insult them, and looking through their phone frequently.

Violence that occurs between intimate partners is commonly known as domestic violence, or intimate partner violence, but it is important to note that domestic violence can also include violence inflicted in the home by other family members. In an intimate relationship, domestic violence is a pattern of behaviors used by one partner to maintain power and control over another partner.

 DID YOU KNOW?

Domestic violence is more common than people like to admit. The National Domestic Violence Hotline (the Hotline) reports that 1 in 4 women (24.3%) and 1 in 7 men (13.8%) aged 18 and older in the United States have been the victim of severe physical violence by an intimate partner in their lifetime.[230] The Hotline also reports that almost 1 in 4 children report having witnessed some form of intimate partner violence in their home.

Sexual violence is also jarringly frequent. According to the Rape, Abuse, Incest National Network (RAINN), 1 in 6 women and 1 in 33 men have experienced an attempted or completed rape in their lifetime.[231] According to the Centers for Disease & Control (CDC), 1 in 4 girls and 1 in 6 boys have experienced some form of sexual violence before the age of 18. Unfortunately, the actual numbers are probably much worse, because nearly 68% of sexual violence goes unreported, and in communities of color, we have reason to believe this percentage is even higher.

[230] The National Domestic Violence Hotline (2021). *Domestic Violence Statistics.* Retrieved from https://www.thehotline.org/stakeholders/domestic-violence-statistics/.
[231] Rape Abuse Incest National Network (2021). *Victims of Sexual Violence: Statistics.* Retrieved from https://rainn.org/statistics/victims-sexual-violence.

A recent study by HEART surveying 792 Muslims ages 18-45 in the United States and Canada revealed alarming rates of sexual violence. Specifically, 1 in 5 (22.9%) Muslims have experienced forced penetration (23.5% of women, 11.4% of men, 33.3% of Transgender noncomforming (TGNC) people) and 18.8% of Muslims have experienced unsuccessful rape (19.1% of women, 7% of men, 34.8% of TGNC people). Finally, 46.5% of Muslims (47.9% of women, 20.9% of men, and 70% of TGNC people) experienced unwanted kissing, touching and/or groping.[232]

These statistics are disturbing and can cause fear and anxiety. As we review these numbers with an eye to how to respond to this injustice, we can find direction in the statistics themselves, by looking at them from a different angle. Dr. Juliane Hammer explains that, for example, "the statistical approach focuses on the victims rather than on the perpetrators: if one in three women experience domestic violence, then how many men in our society are current or former perpetrators? How do statistics define and limit people to their status of victims of domestic violence?"[233] In sum, domestic and sexual violence is sadly a lived reality of many in our communities and families. If we do not respond to both victim needs as well as addressing those who harm, we will not be able to eradicate it.

Sexual Violence

All nonconsensual sexual acts committed against another person—whether harassment, abuse, or assault—is sexual violence and could be prosecuted as a crime in the United States. As noted above, sexual violence is less about sex, and more about the power and control one person has over the other. It not only violates a person's body, but also their sense of safety and autonomy over their life.

While it is common to think about sexual violence as being limited to rape or attempted rape, sexual violence includes a number of offenses that have specific legal definitions and can be considered criminal in a court of law. These can range from verbal to physical, and can be either of the following:

- **Sexual harassment is unwanted sexual attention.** It can be visual, physical, or verbal. Examples include sending explicit photos or making sexual jokes.

- **Sexual assault is nonconsensual sexual penetration or contact.** Examples include rape, attempted rape, molestation, or penetration with an item or body part.

- **Sexual abuse is nonconsensual sexual contact where someone in a position of power or authority takes advantage of a person's trust.** Examples include rape, attempted rape, molestation, touching, or exposure to sexually explicit photos.

- **Child sexual abuse is any sexual activity between a minor (under 17)* and an adult.** Examples include rape, attempted rape, touching, exposure to explicit photos or body parts.[234]

[232] Ceesay, H., Tricic, M., Khayr, Y. W., Bdaiwi, M., Spitz, G., Akhtar-Khaleel, W. Z., Rahman, S., & Mohajir, N. (2022). *Perceptions and prevalence of sexual violence in North American Muslim communities*. Manuscript submitted for publication.

[233] Hammer, J. (2019). *Peaceful Families: American Muslim Efforts Against Domestic Violence*. Princeton: Princeton University Press.

[234] See rainn.org for state-specific definitions of minor.

Other important definitions pertaining to sexual violence:[235]

Victim blaming is when the victim of a crime or any wrongful act is held entirely or partially responsible for the harm that occurred.

"Stealthing"[236] is the pop culture name to describe a new sex trend reported to be on the rise. It refers to the act of deliberately removing a condom during sex without your partner's knowledge or consent. This new term doesn't actually mean it's a new trend, but it coins a new term for this kind of sexual assault.

Rape culture refers to the ways in which society blames victims of sexual assault and normalizes male aggression and sexual violence. It is a complex set of beliefs that portrays violence as sexy and sexuality as violent.

Coercion is a tactic used to intimidate, trick or force someone to have sex without resorting to physical force. Examples include constantly putting pressure on someone and refusing to take "No" for an answer, implying sex is owed in return for financial favors, making someone feel guilty for not engaging in sex, and so on.

Revenge porn is the distribution of nude and/or sexually explicit photos and/or videos of an individual without their consent. In many cases, the pictures or footage are obtained by a partner during a relationship and posted after a break-up. Posts can also be made by acquaintances, former partners, or hackers hacking into someone's personal electronic device(s).

"Rape by Drugs" is when a substance is used to incapacitate a person in order to sexually assault them. Rape by drugs is a crime regardless of the relationship between the victim and their aggressor. (Although this practice is often associated with dating, it is best practice to not use the term date rape because it doesn't only happen on dates or between romantic partners.)

Common drugs used to incapacitate an individual:

- Alcohol
- Marijuana
- Cocaine
- Over the counter drugs: antidepressants, tranquilizers, or sleeping aids
- Known as club drugs (but can be used outside of this context): flunitrazepam (Rohypnol), gamma-hydroxybutyric acid (GHB), gamma-butyrolactone (GBL), and ketamine[237]
- These drugs can be used in combination with the aforementioned drugs, and oftentimes do not have any smell, taste, or color. They may be hard to decipher when added to a drink or food.
- These drugs may also be used in non-alcoholic drinks or outside a party environment.

Unfortunately, many downplay the seriousness of a rape that happens on a date, with a romantic partner, or with drug-induced incapacitation. This dismissive attitude perpetuates rape culture and victim blaming, adding another layer of harm to those who experience this sort of assault.

[235] More definitions from this sheet here: https://heartwomenandgirls.org/wp-content/uploads/2014/01/Important-Definitions_final.pdf.
[236] Pemberton, B. (2021). What is Stealthing and is Removing the Condom During Sex Assault? *The Sun*. Retrieved from https://www.thesun.co.uk/living/3488839/what-is-stealthing-sexual-trend-assault-risks/.
[237] Victim Witness Assistance Program. (2017). *Drug-facilitated Sexual Assault*. U.S. Department of Justice, Drug Enforcement Administration. Available at: https://www.dea.gov/sites/default/files/2018-07/DFSA_0.PDF.gov/sites/default/files/2018-07/DFSA_0.PDF.

According to the CDC, about 11.0% of women experienced completed alcohol/drug-facilitated penetration at some point in their lifetime. Preliminary data analysis of a national study exploring the prevalence rates of sexual assault for Muslims ages 18-45 shows that Muslims experience drug-alcohol related sexual assault at a similar rate, with 10.3% of women reporting being assaulted while incapacitated.[238] While the rates of alcohol/drug facilitated assault tends to be higher on college campuses where party and dating culture are prevalent, this type of assault can happen to anyone in any context. Even if you are not going to a party, an unattended beverage still has a chance of being laced with a drug. This can occur in places as discreet as a library, coffee shop, or a friend's home.

Here are some precautions to take and consider:

- Make sure to keep your beverage with you at all times. Don't lose sight of your beverage and/or food.
- Do not accept any drink or beverage that you have not seen poured in front of you, from a sealed bottle/can. Especially if it's from someone you just met, just started dating, don't know as well, etc.
- When in public places, make sure to keep your beverage sealed/covered and always in close proximity to you.
- If there are large containers of liquid, make sure you are cautious of taking a drink and are informed of what is in the container.
- If you feel strange after drinking your beverage, make sure to stop drinking and ask for assistance from a trusted friend and/or go to the doctor or emergency clinic.

Being informed about red flags can help protect you, but remember, if you do experience sexual assault due to being drugged, it is never your fault and there are people who can help you.

REFLECTION

What are some of the ways you've seen victims of sexual violence blamed in your community? What are some of the ways you've seen them supported?

[238] Ceesay, H., Tricic, M., Khayr, Y. W., Bdaiwi, M., Spitz, G., Akhtar-Khaleel, W. Z., Rahman, S., & Mohajir, N. (2022). *Perceptions and prevalence of sexual violence in North American Muslim communities*. Manuscript submitted for publication.

Figure 3. Spectrum of Sexual Violence (HEART 2022)[239]

Another way to understand sexual violence is to see it as a continuum. In other words, the various forms of sexual violence are not on a hierarchy but rather a spectrum. Viewing sexual violence as a continuum dismantles the idea that someone who experienced a more "extreme" form of violence deserves more attention or should be taken more seriously than someone who is a victim of a "less extreme" form of violence. Thus, an individual who experiences sexual harassment may experience similar trauma or trauma responses as an individual who was raped. All forms of sexual violence have the potential to violate another person's physical, emotional, and spiritual safety and well being. This is especially important to keep in mind because survivors and victims often struggle to be believed. When a community places types of violence on a spectrum/ hierarchy, it tends to minimize, silence, or even erase forms of violence that may be viewed as less extreme.

 POINT OF INTEREST

Arousal is not the same as desire.

It is possible for your body to respond physically to a non-consensual sexual act by becoming aroused, even though you don't want it or feel desire for it. This is a concept called "arousal non concordance," which is where a person's body can respond involuntarily to physical touch, such as by getting an erection, having vaginal wetness, or even an orgasm, but does not mean that they desired, wanted, or consented to the interaction.[240] As such, in reflecting about your experiences, it is important to remember that even if your body responded to physical touch in a certain way, it does not mean you wanted it or consented to it happening.

---

[239] This project is supported by Grant No. 2017-UD-AX-0006, awarded by the Office on Violence Against Women, "Grants for Outreach and Services to Underserved Populations Program," US Department of Justice. The opinions, findings, conclusions, and recommendations expressed in this publication are those of the authors and do not necessarily reflect the views of the Department of Justice, Office on Violence Against Women.

[240] Nagoski, E. (2014). *Unwanted Arousal: it Happens. What Science Says About those Times your Genitals Respond to Sexual Violence.* Available at: https://enagoski. medium.com/unwanted-arousal-it-happens-29679a156b92.

Due to pervasive victim blaming in certain Muslim communities, sometimes sexual assault, such as rape, is talked about in the same context as *zina* or pre-marital or extramarital sex. However, this is a false comparison.[241] *Zina* is an act of sex between two consenting adults, while sexual assault is an act that is forced upon one of the parties involved. This is especially poignant when we realize that the Quran strongly condemns those who accuse a woman of *zina* without bringing actual eyewitnesses, but at the same time, the Prophet did not hesitate to severely punish a man who raped a woman. Clearly, rape is a serious crime involving tangible harm, whereas *zina* is a sin that has so many obstacles to proving that it occured, that it is unlikely anyone would ever be convicted of it, if we followed the Quranic rules of evidence.[242] To conflate rape and *zina* in our conversations is to turn the Quranic verses upside down: it replicates the very accusations of *zina* against women that the Quran specifically warns us not to do. In fact, the Quran says anyone who does this should be punished for slander.[243]

POINT OF INTEREST

You need four witnesses that witnessed for themselves the act of penetration to prove someone has committed *zina*, or sex outside of marriage. But you do not need four witnesses to prove rape.

This high evidentiary standard is set by Islamic law is a reminder to society to not violate each others' privacy regarding sexual intimacy, until it becomes a public matter, as it would if it happened in front of four people.[244] In fact, Muslim scholars have argued that the high evidentiary support is to "prevent carrying out punishment for this offense... [the Quran] authorizes the Muslim legal system to prosecute someone for committing [*zina*] only when the act is performed so openly that four people see them without invading their privacy."[245] In fact, in most schools of *fiqh*, even a pregnancy in an unwed mother is not—on its own—enough evidence to prosecute *zina*.[246]

Moreover, in the past, a person who spread news about another committing *zina* without this high evidentiary standard would have been charged with slander in a classical *qadi* (Islamic judge) court. Thus, the communities we live in today that are quick to spread gossip and rumors about others' sexual behavior are not upholding the spirit of *sharia*—which takes protecting privacy very seriously. As Dr. Asifa Quraishi-Landes explains:

> Quranic principles honor privacy and dignity over the violation of the law, except when the violation becomes a matter of public indecency... In the face of any hint of a woman's sexual impropreity, the Quranic response is: walk away. Leave her alone. Leave her dignity intact. The honor of a woman is not a tool, it is her fundamental right."[247]

---

[241] Here is a resource in which you can learn more about other ways religious and cultural tradition has been misused to blame survivors and protect those who do harm: https://hearttogrow.org/resources/facts-about-sv/.

[242] Quraishi, A. (1997). Her Honor: An Islamic Critique of the Rape Laws of Pakistan from a Woman-Sensitive Perspective. *Michigan Journal of International Law*, (18)287.

[243] Kongden, O. (2018). Unfounded Accusation of Unlawful Sexual Intercourse (qadfh). *The Codification of Islamic Criminal Law in the Sudan.* Brill.

[244] Mattson, I. (2018). Gender and Sexuality in Islamic Bioethics. *Islamic Bioethics: Current Issues and Challenges.* (2):57–83; Quraishi, A. (1997). Her Honor: An Islamic Critique of the Rape Laws of Pakistan from a Woman-Sensitive Perspective. *Michigan Journal of International Law*, (18)287.

[245] Quraishi, Asifa. (1997). "Her Honor: An Islamic Critique of the Rape Laws of Pakistan from a Woman-Sensitive Perspective." *Michigan Journal of International Law*, (18)287.

[246] The Maliki school of fiqh is the exception, allowing prosecution to begin on the basis of an unwed pregnancy, shifting the burden to the accused to prove that it was not consensual. But even the Maliki school goes to great lengths to avoid actual punishment. See Quraishi, Asifa, Islamic Legal Analysis of Zina Punishment of Bariya Ibrahim Magazu, Zamfara, Nigeria, 2001, available at http://www.mwlusa.org/topics/marriage&divorce/islamic_legal_analysis_of_zina.htm. Quraishi, Asifa. (1997). "Her Honor: An Islamic Critique of the Rape Laws of Pakistan from a Woman-Sensitive Perspective." *Michigan Journal of International Law*, (18)287.

[247] Quraishi, A. (1997). Her Honor: An Islamic Critique of the Rape Laws of Pakistan from a Woman-Sensitive Perspective. *Michigan Journal of International Law*, (18)287.

Getting Help for Violence and Abuse

If you think you have experienced sexual violence or any form of gender-based violence, consider seeking help from a medical professional, mental health professional, crisis center, spiritual leader, community member, friend, relative, or someone you trust. All your feelings and emotions after a sexual assault are valid and real. You deserve proper support as you work through them.

Some people may be ready to discuss their experience in a hospital setting or with a friend. For others, it can take years, sometimes decades, to process what happened. There are many barriers to disclosing experiences of the various forms of gender-based violence. Often, people may fear not being believed or being judged harshly by others in their family or community—even being blamed for the violence they experienced. Still others may fear other consequences—such as not being able to get married or compromising their immigration or financial status. These are real concerns and the experience of far too many survivors in Muslim communities. Coming forward and seeking help for the sexual, domestic, and intimate partner violence one has experienced is an act of courage and bravery, and our communities must work toward building spaces that are safe for those who disclose and seek help.

 POINT OF INTEREST

In Muslim communities, it is common for people who experience sexual, domestic, or intimate partner violence to experience spiritual abuse as well.

Spiritual abuse is when a person uses religious tradition, scripture, or shaming to manipulate, control, bully, and harm for their own personal gain, such as sexual or financial. There are two types of spiritual abuse. The first is the type perpetuated by a religious leader like an imam or a chaplain. They are using their positional power and religious authority to gain control or obedience over someone. The second is when a person uses religious tradition or scripture to shame or control behavior.

The impact of spiritual abuse is similar to the impact of other forms of violence and abuse, and can also result in the survivor struggling with their faith identity, leaving certain religious practices, or leaving the faith entirely. Examples of spiritual abuse include:

- Forcing religious practice using physical force or emotional manipulation such as dressing a certain way, prayer, or other forms of worship;
- Misusing religous scripture to enforce obedience;
- Misusing relgious scripture or tradition to force sex or other intimate acts;
- Asserting that one has religious authority over another to isolate someone or justify where they go and who they see.

It can be scary and overwhelming for someone to realize that they've experienced a form of violence or abuse. However long it takes, your experience is a part of your life, and you can choose how you want to respond. Your decisions about your body and your life can be as public or private as you want. Know that you are not alone, and that you have many options as you think about how you want to move forward.[248] Everyone deals with trauma in their own way, whether it is talking to a medical professional, distracting oneself with an activity, or acting like it didn't happen at all. Some options include:[249]

- **Getting a medical exam and rape kit:** If you or a friend has experienced sexual assault or rape within the past 72 hours, consider contacting a rape crisis center or going to the nearest emergency room. Most hospital emergency rooms have medical professionals who are trained to deal with cases of sexual assault and rape.[250]
- **Seeking counseling:** If you think you have been the victim of sexual violence in the past, know that there are many options for you, such as seeking counseling from a licensed therapist, social worker, or psychiatrist.
- **Calling a hotline:** In addition to rape crisis centers, counselors, and healthcare facilities, there are also hotlines you can call. The National Sexual Assault Hotline is available 24 hours every day at 1-800-656-4673.
- **Filing a restraining order:** This is usually filed with law enforcement to keep someone from harming you. This is commonly filed during divorce or civil cases, but if the danger is established, it can be available in other situations too.
- **Filing a protective order:** This is used in cases of domestic violence when there is a likelihood of violence reoccurring. It can include many provisions like: no contact, a physical distancing from the abusive partner, a firearms provision, etc. If violated, the abuser/person who harms may be charged with a criminal offense.
- **Ending the relationship:** If you are married, this can involve filing for divorce. If you have children, additional considerations about custody may be relevant.
- **Safety planning:** You may decide that it is not the right time to leave the relationship. Most advocates recommend that if you choose to stay with your partner, it is still helpful to engage in a safety planning process. A safety plan is a personalized, practical plan that you can develop by yourself, with a friend, or with an advocate to help you avoid dangerous situations and offer a framework for what to do when you are in danger.[251]

If you are not the person who experienced violence, but rather a friend or a loved one has disclosed this to you, check out our avenues of support flow chart on the next page, to see how to help them navigate their options.[252]

---

[248] A fuller list of resources is available at the end of this chapter.

[249] Please note these options are specific to the United States.

[250] If you are not sure if you live in an area with an emergency room with this option or a local rape crisis center, see: https://www.nsvrc.org/find-help.

[251] To learn more about safety planning, please see here. https://www.thehotline.org/2013/04/10/what-is-safety-planning/.

[252] If a friend or a loved one has disclosed to you that they experienced sexual violence, refer to our Responding with RAHMA framework to help you respond to their disclosure. Specifically, Respond by listening, Affirm and believe, Honor cultural and religious context, Maintain privacy, and Assist with providing resources. Full framework available here: https://hearttogrow.org/resources/responding-with-rahma/.

Avenues of Support

An individual just disclosed to you that they were sexually assaulted. How you respond in that moment of disclosure is crucial, and can have a profound impact on the survivor's healing journey. The RAHMA Principles offer an easy framework to help you respond with compassion. Specifically, the five step framework is: Respond by listening, Affirming and believe, Honor cultural and religious values, Maintain privacy, and Assist with providing resources. This guide will help you support the individual by offering them resources for additional support. Many survivors feel like they have lost control, so it's important to meet them where they are at rather than telling them what they should do or what they need. It may take time to seek help or decide what to do, but giving them control is crucial for their healing.

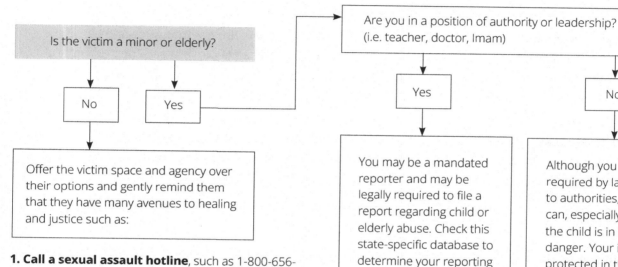

Is the victim a minor or elderly? → No / Yes

Are you in a position of authority or leadership? (i.e. teacher, doctor, Imam) → Yes / No

No/Yes (victim minor or elderly): Offer the victim space and agency over their options and gently remind them that they have many avenues to healing and justice such as:

Yes (authority): You may be a mandated reporter and may be legally required to file a report regarding child or elderly abuse. Check this state-specific database to determine your reporting requirements.

No (authority): Although you are not required by law to report to authorities, you still can, especially if you think the child is in immediate danger. Your identity is protected in this process.

1. Call a sexual assault hotline, such as 1-800-656-HOPE (4673). This hotline is for both victim and their support systems, is free, confidential, and open 24 hours a day.

2. Engage in restorative justice mediation process. This emerging field works to repair harm caused by crime by bringing victims, offenders, and community members together.

3. File a police report. If there is reasonable evidence for a case to be made, the city attorney or district attorney will then pick the case up.

4. Get a rape kit. If it has been 72-120 hours since the assault, the victim has the option to visit a healthcare facility to get a rape kit. The victim can test it either now or later.

5. File a Title IX Report. If the abuse occured by someone on campus, a victim can file a Title IX complaint through their campus.

6. Engage in self-care. Sometimes even a scent or simple sentence can trigger feelings of anguish.

Identifying these triggers and taking good care of the mind and body can be helpful.

7. Seek trauma-informed counseling. Mental health professionals are trained in helping victims process their trauma. Psychology Today is a great resource to find local therapists.

8. File a civil lawsuit against the perpetrator or institution. The victim may sue the perpetrator or institution for financial damages.

9. Talk with a trusted friend, relative, community, or faith leader about additional sources of social support.

10. If the victim decides not to leave their abusive situation or relationship, they can **create a safety plan**—a practical plan preparing them to seek refuge if it happens again

11. File a report with human resources if it is a case of workplace sexual assault.

12. Take no immediate action. Victims always have the option of not doing anything about their assault.

Being supportive of sexual assault survivors can be emotionally intensive. Remember that it is equally important to take care of your needs to prevent burnout. Consider taking time to yourself to relax, to journal, talk to a counselor, or call a hotline.

DID YOU KNOW?

Communities of color are less likely to call law enforcement.

In the United States, the system to get help for a situation of sexual or domestic violence is closely connected to calling the police, and yet many victims and/or survivors in communities of color are less likely to call the police.[253] Here are some reasons documented by research that people may not want to rely on law enforcement:

- **Fear of being harmed.**[254] People are afraid law enforcement may harm them. For example, for members of Black communities that frequently experience police brutality, this legitimate fear may keep members in those communities from turning to law enforcement as a reliable source of help.

- **Islamophobia and anti-blackness.** Due to rising surveillance of Muslim communities and being labeled as terrorists, many Muslims choose not to report crime as a way to "protect" their communities from additional negative scrutiny. The racialization of Muslims, particularly Black Muslims, adds an additional layer of a sense of obligation to maintain a positive image of their faith, community, and men.[255]

- **Fear of state consequences.**[256] If the survivor/victim is undocumented, they may fear this may result in the police finding out they are undocumented and deporting them. If they have children, they may fear that the investigation may result in their children being taken away from them.

If reporting to law enforcement is not an option, there are still other ways to address safety concerns. These can include:

- **Community Support.** If you trust and feel safe with folks from your community, reach out to them and create a safety plan that involves them. Consider pod mapping to identify who is in your safety network and what their roles can be.[257] For example, if your partner/spouse is less likely to harm you in front of other community members, can you arrange shifts with neighbors and other community members to spend more time in your home, so your partner doesn't harm you?

- **Advocate Support.** Sometimes you don't need to report, but still need support. Getting connected to an advocate at a direct service organization can be helpful in getting linked to resources and information.

- **Restorative / Transformative Justice.**[258] Using both your community and an advocate as well as a transformative justice practitioner, you can seek out an accountability process with the person who has harmed you. If you do not wish to directly be involved, a community accountability process can still happen with the person who has caused harm.[259]

[253] Petrosky, E., Blair, J. M., Betz, C. J., Fowler, K. A., Jack, S. P., & Lyons, B. H. (2017). Racial and Ethnic Differences in Homicides of Adult Women and the Role of Intimate Partner Violence — United States, 2003–2014. *MMWR. Morbidity and Mortality Weekly Report,* 66(28), 741-746. doi:10.15585/mmwr.mm6628a1.

[254] Oyewuwo-Gassikia, O. B. (2020). Black Muslim Women's Domestic Violence Help-Seeking Strategies: Types, Motivations, and Outcomes. *Journal of Aggression, Maltreatment & Trauma,* 29:7, 856-875, DOI: 10.1080/10926771.2019.1653411.

[255] Kiely-Froude, C and Abdul-Karim, S. (2009). Providing Culturally Conscious Mental Health Treatment for African American Muslim Women Living with Spousal Abuse. *Journal of Muslim Mental Health,* 4:175– 186.; Oyewuwo-Gassikia, O. B. (2020). Black Muslim Women's Domestic Violence Help-Seeking Strategies: Types, Motivations, and Outcomes. *Journal of Aggression, Maltreatment & Trauma,* 29:7, 856-875, DOI: 10.1080/10926771.2019.1653411.

[256] Cho, H., Shamrova, D., Han, J., & Levchenko, P. (2017). Patterns of Intimate Partner Violence Victimization and Survivors' Help-Seeking. *Journal of Interpersonal Violence,* 1–25.

[257] Podmapping is a concept developed by activist Mia Mingus for those who want to create a community-centered approach to violence prevention and community care. For more information on pod mapping, see https://www.yesmeansyes.com/2021/02/what-is-pod-mapping/.

[258] To learn more about transformative justice processes, visit https://transformharm.org/.

[259] Mohajir, N and Qureshi, S. (2020). *Responding with RAHMA: Removing Roadblocks for Muslim Survivors.* Hurma Project Conference. Retrieved from: https://hurmaproject.com/wp-content/ uploads/2021/03/Responding-with-RAHMA-Removing-Roadblocks.pdf.

Safety Planning Guide

As explained by the National Domestic Violence Hotline, "a safety plan is a personalized, practical plan that includes ways to remain safe while in a relationship, planning to leave, or after you leave. Safety planning involves how to cope with emotions, tell friends and family about the abuse, take legal action, and more."[260]

With this safety planning guide, you can be equipped with a strategy either for yourself or for someone else to feel safe from their abuser/the person who harms them. This guide is not exhaustive, and you can find out more at the National Domestic Violence Hotline.[261]

Emotional safety planning:

- **Find and/or connect with people you trust** who can help you process and support you when needed. This can be a friend or family member or a trained professional like a therapist.
- **This will be a difficult an unnerving time.** Remind yourself of your resilience, strength, and value.
- **Create realistic, actionable goals.** Work on your own timeline and remember that you are not obligated to do anything uncomfortable. A realistic, actionable goal can look like calling a local resource center.

Safety planning while staying with the person who harms:

- **Create a safety bag** to be kept with a trusted person, which has either originals or copies of the following documents: birth certificate, driver's license/state ID/passport, children's birth certificates and passports (if applicable), immigration documents, medical records and health insurance cards, legal documents/order of protection/restraining order, cash, a few items of clothing, keepsakes, a new phone or prepaid phone with important contacts saved, and a spare set of keys.

- **Inform trusted friends, family, and/or colleagues** of what is going on and develop coded language to signal for help.
- **Identify safe areas** in the home that are possible to retreat to when your partner is getting violent.

Preparing to leave the person who harms:

Note that leaving an abusive partner may result in escalated harm.

- **Inform someone you trust** about what is happening and that you are leaving, so that they can support and provide protection as deemed necessary.
- **Reach out to a local domestic violence (DV) shelter** or agency to continue safety planning and to consider safe options of relocation.
- **Keep records of the violence and abuse** such as photos of injuries, screenshots of messages, recordings of calls, etc.

---

[260] The National Domestic Violence Hotline. (2021). Create a safety plan. The Hotline. Retrieved from https://www.thehotline.org/plan-for-safety/create-a-safety-plan/.
[261] Ibid.

When leaving the person who harms:
- **Reach out to the people you trust** and who are aware of your situation to create a plan of escape.
- **Request a trusted friend and/or community member to escort you out.**
- **Remember to grab your safety bag** (whether it is in your home or with a trusted person).

After leaving the person who harms:
- **Change your phone number.**
- **Change your locks** if you are residing somewhere else, or are still residing in your own home separate from your partner.
- **Reschedule any appointments** that the person who harms may be aware of. This may also mean disconnecting from any shared online calendars.
- **Inform your job** about what is happening and request changing work hours. Change your route to work and any other familiar places the person who harms may be aware of.

 POINT OF INTEREST

It's hard to leave an abusive or violent relationship.

If you are supporting a survivor or victim, you may be wondering: "Well why don't you just leave this person? Why are you still staying with them?" Be aware that this question comes from not fully appreciating the psychological impact of trauma. There are several reasons a survivor or victim cannot or does not want to leave.[262] Studies show that it may take up to seven tries to successfully leave an abusive/harmful partner. Moreover, research suggests the barriers to leaving an abusive partner are even greater for communities of color and faith as "social identity constructs—such as race, culture, and religion – shape women's domestic violence help-seeking experiences."[263]

Please note that asking or telling a survivor or victim to leave an abusive partner can put them at a safety risk, depending on the tenuousness of their situation. A survivor or victim knows their situation better than anyone else. This also means that they know what safety looks like, and leaving may not be the answer.

Here are some reasons why a survivor or victim may stay in an abusive relationship:

They love their partner. This particular reason may be hard to believe or empathize with, but it's true. The person causing harm is not always a stranger and is often someone that the survivor or victim has built a relationship with. They may have a family together. The survivor and victim may share memories, many that are actually very loving and ones that bring joy.

They feel shame and stigma.[264] Many faith communities and communities of color stigmatize and shame people who divorce, or worse, blame them for the divorce. This makes it harder for those experiencing abuse to leave, especially if they do not think they have enough community or family support.

[262] See our Barriers to Disclosure video at https://www.youtube.com/watch?v=a0apc3FMRHA&t=114s and accompanying handout at https://hearttogrow.org/resources/barriers-to-disclosure/.

[263] Oyewuwo-Gassikia, O. B. (2016). American Muslim Women and Domestic Violence Service Seeking: A Literature Review. *Affilia*, 31(4), 450–462. doi:10.1177/0886109916654731.

[264] Hassouneh-Phillips, D. (2001). American Muslim Women's Experiences of Leaving Abusive Relationships. *Health Care for Women International*, 22, 415–432.

It is not financially feasible to leave.[265] Sometimes a survivor or victim may rely or are dependent on their partner who is causing them harm. Leaving them could mean a threat to their own safety in terms of losing access to housing, transportation, food, childcare, funds or access to healthcare, etc.

They may be facing pressure or expectations from their families or religious community.[266] Messaging from family or faith that encourages trusting God, being patient, and relying on prayer through hardship can influence a person's decision to seek help. They may also think getting a divorce is a sin or rooted in disobeying their husband.[267]

They may be worried about their immigration status.[268] If the survivor or victim is not a citizen, the abusive partner can threaten them with reporting survivors or victims to authorities to remove their status and potentially get them deported.

They may have children together. If the survivor or victim has children with their abusive partner, they often stay to protect the children or family unit or there is a reliance on the partner to provide for both children and the survivor or victim.

They may have a trauma bond. This is when a survivor or victim is loyal to the person who is causing them harm. This often occurs due to cycles of abuse followed by intermittent love or reward, resulting in a powerful psychological bond that is extremely hard to break and leave.[269]

It might be safer to stay.[270] If we want to take a survivor-centric approach, then we must believe that survivors and victims are able to assess their own safety. Oftentimes, survivors and victims don't leave because it is just not an option: they know the person who is harming them will escalate if they try to escape, and they have adapted their own safety measures to keep themselves as safe as possible.

[265] Freefrom. (2021). Prioritizing Financial Security in the Movement to End IPV: A Roadmap. Retrieved from: https://www.freefrom.org/wp-content/uploads/2021/07/Prioritizing_Financial_Security_Report.pdf.

[266] Kiely-Froude, C and Abdul-Karim, S. (2009). Providing Culturally Conscious Mental Health Treatment for African American Muslim Women Living with Spousal Abuse. *Journal of Muslim Mental Health*, 4:175–186; Hassouneh-Phillips, D. (2003). Strength and Vulnerability: Spirituality in Abused American Muslim Women's Lives. *Issues in Mental Health Nursing*, 24(6–7), 681–694; Oyewuwo-Gassikia, O B (2020). Black Muslim Women's Domestic Violence Help-Seeking Strategies: Types, Motivations, and Outcomes. *Journal of Aggression, Maltreatment & Trauma*, 29:7, 856-875.

[267] Hassouneh-Phillips, D. (2001). American Muslim Women's Experiences of Leaving Abusive Relationships. *Health Care for Women International*, 22, 415–432.

[268] Cho, H., Shamrova, D., Han, J., & Levchenko, P. (2017). Patterns of Intimate Partner Violence Victimization and Survivors' Help-Seeking. *Journal of Interpersonal Violence*, 1–25.

[269] Reid, J., Haskell, R., Dillahunt-Aspillaga, C., & Thor, J. (2013). Trauma Bonding and Interpersonal Violence. *Psychology of trauma*. Nova Science Publisher; T. Van Leeuwen & M. Brouwer (ed.), Reid, J. A., Haskell, R. A., Dillahunt-Aspillaga, C., & Thor, J. A. (2013). Contemporary Review of Empirical and Clinical Studies of Trauma Bonding in Violent or Exploitative Relationships. *International Journal of Psychology Research*, 8(1), 37.

[270] Kiely-Froude, C and Abdul-Karim, S. (2009). Providing Culturally Conscious Mental Health Treatment for African American Muslim Women Living with Spousal Abuse. *Journal of Muslim Mental Health*. 4:175–186.

A ('AQD) AFFIRMED IN COMMITMENT AND FIDELITY

The final component of our framework is a relationship affirmed in commitment. Whether this looks like a commitment to God, your marriage, yourself, your partner, or some combination thereof, it is important to have a strong sense of awareness of what commitment means to you before engaging in sexual activity. In Islam, commitment is most commonly thought of in terms of two parties freely agreeing to the terms of their relationship with a contract ('aqd)—usually a marriage contract. There are other ways people can commit to each other outside of a formal contract, but it is the idea of a conscious commitment that is important in any healthy sexual union.[271] Understanding what kind of commitment you want for yourself before saying yes to a sexual relationship is key to feeling informed and empowered.[272]

As such, intention-setting becomes important when thinking about a healthy relationship. What are the intentions of both partners in this relationship? It is crucial for both partners to agree upon an understanding of what commitment and fidelity looks like to them. This will involve really understanding each other's values and beliefs about what commitment entails. Breaches of commitment can mean a variety of things, but more serious breaches of commitment are when a partner/spouse is having an affair, or if they choose to engage in polygyny without notice or consent to the first wife.

 Green Flags:

- Both partners respect the other's religious and spiritual boundaries and commitments.
- Both partners share their vision for the relationship and periodically engage in reviewing it to see if it's working in order to keep the relationship healthy.
- When one partner wants to re-evaluate the relationship structure, there is direct and clear communication instead of secrecy and silence.
- If there is a disagreement, instead of neglecting one partner's concerns and going forth with a decision, there is a pause and acknowledgement to work on a solution together (if there is one).
- Both partners have a clear understanding of the purpose of their relationship and are aligned on the commitments they are making to each other
- Both partners honor their relationship agreements, marital vows, or contractual commitments.
- One or both partners consider a couples therapist or individual therapist to address needs with professional support.

---

271 These include: courtships, casual and exclusive dating, engagement, marriage (including monogamy, polygamy, temporary marriage (mut'a), and secret marriage).
272 Arriaga, X. B., & Agnew, C. R. (2001). Being Committed: Affective, Cognitive, and Conative Components of Relationship Commitment. *Personality and Social Psychology Bulletin*, 27(9), 1190-1203.

 **TRY IT OUT**
Questions to Ask Yourself as You Implement the RIDHA Framework

Affirmed in commitment and fidelity:

- Is entering into this relationship aligned with my commitment to God? To myself? To my values and religious beliefs? To my partner?

- If applicable, is entering into this relationship honoring the commitment I have made to my current partner/spouse?

Use this space to jot down a few thoughts on what being affirmed in commitment and fidelity means to you.

The Islamic Marriage Contract ('aqd al-zawaj/nikah)

If you choose to enter a marital partnership, we have included below some key points to keep in mind about marriage, the marital contract, and divorce. For most Muslims, marriage to their life partner is a significant part of faith and an indisputable milestone. It can also be a powerful tool to help build a healthy long-lasting partnership affirmed in commitment. Because Islamic law designates marriage as the primary means by which Muslims engage in legitimate sexual activity, marriage gets a lot of attention in the *fiqh* literature. Although the ways of performing marriage ceremonies differ from culture to culture, the *fiqh* requirements for a permanent Islamic marriage to be valid are quite simple:[273]

- both partners must consent to the marriage;[274]
- (for *Sunnis*[275]) witnesses must observe the taking of the vows
- a *mahr* must be agreed upon by both partners

The marriage agreement is usually solemnized in a written contract.[276] The process of drafting this contract is a powerful opportunity for future spouses and/or their families to openly discuss and decide how they will merge their lives, careers, finances, and lifestyles together, and what their compromises and deal breakers will be. In fact, many of the features of the RIDHA framework above can be addressed in a Muslim marriage

---

[273] Hammer, Juliane. (2021). Weddings: Love and Mercy in Marriage Ceremonies in Kecia Ali, ed. *Half of if Faith: American Muslim Marriage and Divorce in the Twenty-first Century*. Boston: Open BU, 4-16. https:// hdl.handle.net/2144/42505.

[274] The schools of *fiqh* disagree over whether a guardian of the bride (*wali*) is required as part of the bride's consent. For the *Hanafi* and *Ja'fari madhhabs*, if the bride is mature a *wali* (legal guardian) is not required; for the *Shafi'i, Maliki* and *Hanbali* schools, it is. All the *fiqh* schools (*Sunni* and *Shia*) allow a father to arrange the marriage of his minor child (boy or girl) without their consent. See: Ali, K. (2008). Marriage in Classical Islamic Jurisprudence: A Survey of Doctrines 11-42, in *The Islamic Marriage Contract: Case Studies in Islamic Family Law*. Vogel & Quraishi, ed.s, Harvard University Press; Farooq, M. (2019). Walayah (Guardianship) and Kafa'a (Equality) in Muslim Marriage verses the Woman's Consent. Available at SSRN: https://ssrn.com/abstract=3497607; Khan, A A. (2017). Marrying Without the Consent of the Wali (a Case Study of Pakistan) Compatibility of Pakistani Family Laws with UDHR Available at SSRN: https://ssrn.com/abstract=3067457; Fadel, M. (1998). Reinterpreting the Guardian's Role in the Islamic Contract of Marriage: The Case of the Maliki School. *Journal of Islamic Literature*, 3, 1.

[275] The Ja'fari school does not require witnesses in order for a marriage contract to be valid. See Iqbal, R. (2015). *A Thousand and One Wives: Investigating the Intellectual History of the Exegesis of Verse Q4:24*. Dissertation. Georgetown University.

[276] Hammer, J. (2021). Weddings: Love and Mercy in Marriage Ceremonies in Kecia Ali, ed., *Half of Faith: American Muslim Marriage and Divorce in the Twenty-First Century Boston: OpenBU* pp. 4-16. https://hdl.handle.net/2144/42505; Jaafar-M I and Lehmann, C. (2011). Women's Rights in Islam Regarding Marriage and Divorce. *Journal of Law and Practice*: Vol. 4, Article 3.

contract, such as equity, communication, the consequences of violence, stipulations about monogamy, equal access to divorce, division of household labor, timing and care of children, daily decisionmaking, and much more.[277] Throughout history, many Muslim women have used the contract drafting process as an important tool to protect their rights and plan the contours of their married life.

Because there is no ordination or formal clergy in Islam, there are no particular religious qualifications required of the person officiating a Muslim wedding: anyone whom both parties respect can conduct such a ceremony.[278] (In order to be recognized by the secular law of the land, it is important to also register one's marriage according to local state law—such as getting a civil marriage license registered in your local city hall.)

 POINT OF INTEREST

Officiating a wedding

A person does not have to be a religious authority or even a man to officiate a wedding. Islamic law does not specify the gender of the officiant, and the role of an imam is mainly ceremonial. What makes a marriage a marriage is the agreement of partnership by the two parties. Any person with an understanding of Islamic tradition is able to oversee the vows and deliver the wedding sermon. The decision on who you may want to officiate your wedding is fully up to you.[279]

Mahr

The *mahr*, or marital gift, deserves special attention as it is an essential component of any Islamic marriage contract. The *mahr* is any item of value (money, or property, or even intangible) given to the bride from the groom at the time of the marriage.[280] The *mahr* is solely the bride's property, not to be owned or controlled by anyone else. Among other things, a *mahr* can serve as a means by which a wife can achieve and maintain financial independence—she could save or invest it, and thus not be completely financially dependent on her husband, or she could spend it. A significant *mahr* can be especially useful to maintaining financial independence for a wife who is planning stay-at-home time, such as caretaking a family instead of earning an external income.[281]

The *mahr* can be paid up-front or delayed. Deferred *mahr* is often set to the event of divorce or widowhood. This means that a large *mahr* can operate as an effective deterrent against unexpected and unilateral divorce by a husband—a form of divorce called *talaq*, which we will discuss shortly.[282]

[277] Quraishi-Landes, A. (2013). A Meditation on Mahr, Modernity, and Muslim Marriage Contract Law. in Kecia Ali, ed., *Half of Faith: American Muslim Marriage and Divorce in the Twenty-First Century Boston: OpenBU*, 2021. https:// hdl.handle.net/2144/42505; Ayubi, Z. (2022). Premarital Counseling and Nikkah Contract Writing Guide. in Ali, Kecia, ed. *Tying the Knot: A Feminist/Womanist Guide to Marriage in America*. Boston: OpenBU. https://hdl.handle.net/2144/44079; Quraishi-Landes, A. (2022). Drafting a Muslim Marriage Contract: A Summary of Mandatory and Optional Clauses. in Ali, Kecia, ed. *Tying the Knot: A Feminist/Womanist Guide to Marriage in America*. Boston: OpenBU. https://hdl.handle.net/2144/44079.

[278] Ali, K. (2022). Making it Official: A Guide to Officiating at Muslim American Weddings. in Ali, Kecia, ed. *Tying the Knot: A Feminist/Womanist Guide to Marriage in America*. Boston: OpenBU. https://hdl.handle.net/2144/44079.

[279] Kecia Ali, (2013). Acting on a Frontier of Religious Ceremony," in Kecia Ali, ed., *Half of Faith: American Muslim Marriage and Divorce in the Twenty-First Century* (Boston: OpenBU, 2021), pp. 17-21. https:// hdl.handle.net/2144/42505.

[280] Currently, the literature available on marriage contracts and mahr are in the context of heterosexual partnerships. Further research needs to be done on how or if these traditions can be applied to non-normative relationships. That being said, a similar framework can still be used for pre-nuptial agreements.

[281] Quraishi-Landes, A. (2013). A Meditation on Mahr, Modernity, and Muslim Marriage Contract Law. in Kecia Ali, ed., *Half of Faith: American Muslim Marriage and Divorce in the Twenty-First Century* (Boston: OpenBU, 2021). https:// hdl.handle.net/2144/42505.

[282] Ibid.

POINT OF INTEREST

The classical Islamic marriage contract is based on the model of a contract of sale (where the groom "purchases" access to the bride for sexual intercourse).[283] Importantly—this "sale contract" model is not dictated by the Quran, but is rather a creation of human scholars, which means that other contract models are possible and could create a very different collection of doctrinal rules for Muslim marriage law. Scholar Asifa Quraishi-Landes, for example, suggests a "partnership contract" model for the Islamic marriage contract which could result in different rules on everything from spousal obedience to marital rape to divorce.[284]

 TRY IT OUT
What to Include in Your Marriage Contract

As you discuss your future marriage with your partner, consider the conditions you may want to include in your marriage contract. Here are a few reflection exercises for you to get this process going.[285]

Mahr

1. What would you like as your *mahr*? Would you like it to be monetary or another type of asset, such as jewelry or property?
2. If you decide on a monetary gift, do you want it as a lump sum, or deferred to a specified time or event in your marriage (e.g. death or divorce, completion of a degree, retirement)? Another idea is that it could be paid as installments during certain marital milestones.

Assets and Finances

3. If you have any assets such as property or significant finances, consider if you want to share or separate those assets. (Note, according to classical Islamic law, women have no obligation to spend their income or assets on family expenses, whereas a husband does.)[286]
4. If there are any family heirlooms, consider what should happen to them in the event of a divorce.

Raising a Family

5. Do you want to have children? If so, what is important to you as you raise a family?
6. If having children is important to you or your fiancé, consider discussing conditions around openness to adoption and fertility treatments.
7. If the financial situation allows, do you want paid help for the home/children?
8. If either of you have children from a previous marriage, what do you expect from each other in terms of caregiving? Sharing finances? Dealing with each other's exes?
9. How will you handle caregiving for family members who are ill? Parents?

---

[283] Ali, K. (2003). Progressive Muslims and Islamic Jurisprudence: the Necessity for Critical Engagement with Marriage and Divorce Law. *Progressive Muslims on Justice, Gender, and Pluralism*, edited by O. Safi. Oxford: Oneworld Publications 163-89; Quraishi-Landes, A. (2013). A Meditation on Mahr, Modernity, and Muslim Marriage Contract Law. in Kecia Ali, ed., *Half of Faith: American Muslim Marriage and Divorce in the Twenty-First Century* (Boston: OpenBU, 2021). https:// hdl.handle. net/2144/42505.

[284] Quraishi-Landes, A. (2013). A Meditation on Mahr, Modernity, and Muslim Marriage Contract Law. in Kecia Ali, ed., *Half of Faith: American Muslim Marriage and Divorce in the Twenty-First Century* (Boston: OpenBU, 2021). https:// hdl.handle.net/2144/42505.

[285] We also love the guide of questions offered in the following article: Ayubi, Z. (2022). Premarital Counseling and Nikkah Contract Writing Guide. in Ali, Kecia, ed. *Tying the Knot: A Feminist/Womanist Guide to Marriage in America*. Boston: OpenBU. https://hdl.handle.net/2144/44079.

[286] Ali, Kecia. (2003). Marriage Contracts in Islamic Jurisprudence. *The Feminist Sexual Ethics Project*. Brandeis University. Retrieved from https://www.brandeis.edu/projects/fse/muslim/marriage.html.

10. Do you care where you live? Do you want to be sure you are not too far from your family/support system? If you are far from family, do you want to protect time to travel for visits? To ensure children get contact with extended family?

Polygyny

11. What are your ideas about polygyny? Is this something you are open to?
12. If not, what kinds of stipulations do you want to put in your contract regarding polygyny?[287]

Education and Career Goals

13. Do you have any particular education or career goals that you want your partner (and in-laws if applicable) to honor and uphold? For example, if you are pursuing a graduate degree, do you want to delay starting a family until after you graduate?
14. Do you want to work outside the home? Do you want to be able to travel for work? Do you want your spouse gone from the home for extended periods of time? How much/how far?

In the Event of a Divorce

15. What will happen to your assets?
16. If you gave up an income to care for the children, what expectations do you want to set with your partner about ongoing maintenance?
17. Do you want to follow the state's rules about community property, or do you want the state to recognize income earned by each spouse during the marriage as their own separate property (and not to be divided equally upon divorce)?

Other Types of Marriage

A permanent marriage between one man and one woman, although more common and recognized by all schools of thought, is not the only form of valid marriage recognized in the *fiqh*. Classical Islamic law recognizes several other types of marriage—temporary marriage (*mut'a*), marriage of "ease" (*misyar*), and polygynous marriage (and sometimes combinations of all of the above). It is not within the mission of this book to recommend whether a Muslim should or should not enter any of these types of marriages. But, because we aim to be inclusive of different intimate relationships that our readers might be exposed to, we will address these alternative forms of marriage below. We urge our readers to focus not so much on the Islamic permissibility of these types of marriages, but rather on whether and how such marriages can follow the RIDHA Framework for healthy intimacy.

It is also important to provide a trigger warning for this section, as we know that too many have been harmed by these alternative forms of marriage, and we will talk about the ways they have been misused—by men in particular—to harm and exploit women. On a global scale, where matchmakers are frequently utilized, vulnerable women and families have been exploited to agree to such arrangements.[288] Just like other topics in this book, having more information about the purpose of these types of marriages can help individuals feel equipped with the right information to have honest conversations with their (potential) partners, ask the right questions, and ensure that consent is at the forefront of any arrangement they enter. If you or someone you know are considering entering into any of these alternative forms of marriage, think

287 Ahmad, N., Ghazali, N. M., Othman, R., & Ismail, N. S. (2019). Women's Rights in Marriage: Between Quranic Provision and Malpractice. *Pertanika Journal Of Social Science And Humanities.* 27 (4): 2721 - 2730.

288 Badran, S. and Turnbull, B. (2019). Contemporary Temporary Marriage: A Blog analysis of First-Hand Experiences. *Journal of International Women's Studies.* (20)2: 241-256.

carefully about whether it is the right choice. This includes being clear about both partners' intentions and the ultimate purpose for the arrangement. It is important to be fully informed of your rights in these types of marriages, and to ensure that consent and communication are at the forefront.

It is also worth remembering that not all Muslims recognize these alternative forms of marriage as valid, so anyone choosing to enter one of these marriages should be prepared for the negative judgment and stigma that might come with it.[289] This stigma, combined with the fact that some of these marriages can exist without any public announcement or witnesses, means that a spouse may find it very hard to reach out for help if there are challenges or abuse in the relationship. Always remember: just because you can, doesn't mean you should.[290]

All this considered, the RIDHA Framework can be especially helpful for anyone considering one of these forms of marriages, to prevent harm and abuse from occurring to either partner.

Temporary Marriage (*Mut'a*)

The Twelver Shi'is[291] recognize the validity of a marriage that is set to end at a specified time. This is called a *mut'a* marriage (commonly referred to as "temporary marriage"). In order for a *mut'a* marriage to be valid according to this school, two of the above requirements of a typical Muslim marriage contract must be fulfilled: consent from both parties, and a *mahr* agreement betwen the bride and groom. (In some cases, the *fiqh* also requires a guardian for the bride.) In addition, a *mut'a* marriage contract includes a clause clearly setting forth the end date of the marriage (this could be a calendar date, or the occurrence of an event, such as a graduation or relocation to another city). There is no requirement for witnesses, consistent with the *Ja'fari Shi'a* rule that witnesses are not required for a marriage contract. For the duration of a *mut'a* marriage, the couple operate as any ordinary (permanently) married couple - such as living together, the husband providing for the wife and any children born to the marriage and so on. Children born from a *mu'ta* marriage have the same rights as children born in permanent marriages, but there are no inheritance rights between *mut'a* spouses. Unless the contract is renewed, a *mut'a* marriage ends automatically on the date specified in the contract, with an *'iddah* period of two menstrual cycles or 40 days.[292]

Mut'a relationships, like all intimate relationships, hold great potential for harm as well as can serve a specific utility.[293] On the one hand, because they facilitate sexual intimacy without any long-term commitment, *mut'a* marriages have the potential to be exploitive and harmful.[294] Without careful attention to communication and shared vulnerability that is usually built over time, these relationships risk being unhealthy hookups and one-night stands. On the other hand, if two parties are sexually attracted to each other, but are not ready (emotionally or financially) to make a lifetime commitment, *mut'a* offers a way for them to take their relationship to a physical level within Islamic parameters.[295] If used honorably, a

---

[289] Specifically, there is agreement among both *Sunni* and *Shia* Muslims that temporary marriage was a practice the Prophet Muhammad allowed, but there is disagreement about whether this practice was later denounced by the Prophet or his companions such as Omar (may God be pleased with him). See Badran, Sammy and Turnbull, Brian. (2019). Contemporary Temporary Marriage: A Blog analysis of First-Hand Experiences. *Journal of International Women's Studies.* (20)2: 241-256.

[290] See Chapter 1, where we discuss how this is a core principle of the five categories of action laid out in the *fiqh*.

[291] The majority Ismaili and *Zaydi fiqh* (like *Sunni fiqh*) does not recognize the validity of *Mut'a* marriages. See Iqbal, Roshan. (2015). *A Thousand and One Wives: Investigating the Intellectual History of the Exegesis of Verse Q4:24.* Dissertation. Georgetown University.

[292] Rabbani-Lubis, A. A. A. M., Muzakki, M. H., Rizal, F., & Makmun, A. R. (2021). Mut'ah Marriage: Between Human Rights and Maqashid Shari'ah. *Proceedings of the 2nd International Conference on Islamic Studies, ICIS 2020*, 27-28.

[293] Badran, S and Turnbull, B. (2019). Contemporary Temporary Marriage: A Blog analysis of First-Hand Experiences. *Journal of International Women's Studies.* (20)2: 241-256; Yusouf, S., and Yusouf-Sadiq N. (2022). Temporary Pleasure, Permanent Effects: Practical Advice on Mut'a Marriage. in Ali, Kecia, ed. *Tying the Knot: A Feminist/Womanist Guide to Marriage in America.* Boston: OpenBU. https://hdl.handle.net/2144/44079.

[294] Ibid.

[295] Ibid.

mut'a marriage contract could be an important tool to assure consent before sexual intercourse, as well as ensuring parental responsibility in the case of pregnancy. Moreover, these types of marriages can also be a particularly useful option for divorced or widowed Muslims—especially those who had previously abusive marriages—to help protect themselves from getting entangled in another permanent marriage before having certainty that this is the right partner for them.[296]

In short, although the *fiqh* on *mut'a* allows such a marriage to be kept secret, it does not presume these temporary marriages to be merely casual sexual encounters. Rather, they are another way to Islamically make the serious commitment of becoming sexually intimate with another person. Nevertheless, in current day practice, many of these marriages do not uphold that spirit: some people use it to give superficial Islamic legitimacy to what is really casual sex and possible exploitation. Because *mut'a* can be done without witnesses, and because the *fiqh* rules allow men (but not women) to have multiple marriage partners, there is also a high risk that men will manipulate the system to have multiple sexual encounters, while married permanently to a wife who might not know about these affairs. In these situations, claiming such behavior is allowed by *sharia* is a thin technicality that ignores the spirit of relationship intimacy described in the Quran and modeled by our Prophet.

Marriage of "Ease" (*Misyar*)

Misyar is a rather recent term[297] used to describe a permanent marriage in which the wife waives obligations that ordinarily attach to the husband with a Muslim marriage contract, such as financial support and the provision of food and housing. This means that it is possible (and quite often likely) that a *misyar* couple will not cohabitate. Instead, a *misyar* husband and wife could have an ongoing sexual relationship, but live quite separate lives.[298] A *misyar* marriage is contracted just like a permanent marriage according to the rules of *Sunni fiqh* (e.g., consent of the parties, witnesses, an agreed *mahr*, and a guardian for the bride in some circumstances), but the contract includes a clause specifying the rights waived by the wife.[299] A *misyar* marriage does not have a specified length of time, as according to *Sunni fiqh* this is contrary to the purpose of marriage. It can be ended in the same way as a permanent marriage: through divorce. As with all marriages in Islam, children born of a *misyar* marriage are legitimate and the responsibility of both parents.

Like any relationship, a misyar marriage can be healthy or unhealthy. On the one hand, when a woman is financially secure on her own, a waiver of a husband's financial obligations could be a way to bring more equality into the mariage. On the other hand, men can use *misyar* to take advantage of women, such as pressuring a bride into giving up her Islamic right to financial support or else not get married at all. Worse, when combined with the *fiqh* rules that allow men to have multiple spouses, *misyar* can be used as a loophole to have extramarital affairs. That is, *misyar* with a second wife would enable a husband to have sex with another woman but have no financial obligations toward her that normally come with marrying a second wife. If he does this without informing the first wife, the potential harm to these women—a *misyar* wife and the first wife—can be devastating. (More on polygynous marriage and secrecy in the next section.)

[296] Yusouf, S, and Yusouf-Sadiq N. (2022). Temporary Pleasure, Permanent Effects: Practical Advice on Mut'a Marriage. in Ali, Kecia, ed. *Tying the Knot: A Feminist/Womanist Guide to Marriage in America.* Boston: OpenBU. https://hdl.handle.net/2144/44079.

[297] It apparently emerged in Saudi Arabia in the 1980s/1990s as cited in Jurdi, S. (2001) Misyar Marriage. *Al-Raida*, Vol XVIII-XIX, 93-94. Available at: file:///Users/nmohajir/Downloads/528-Article%20Text-1040-1-10-20160727.pdf; also see Badran, S and Turnbull, B. (2019). Contemporary Temporary Marriage: A Blog analysis of First-Hand Experiences. *Journal of International Women's Studies.* (20)2: 241-256.

[298] Hasannia, A., & Masoudian, M. (2021). *Temporary Marriage Among Shiite and Sunni Muslims: Comparative Study of 'Istimtā', Mut'ah, and Misyār. In Temporary and Child Marriages in Iran and Afghanistan,* (pp. 31-45). Springer, Singapore.

[299] Jurdi, S. (2001). Misyar Marriage. *Al-Raida.* Vol XVIII-XIX, 93-94.

TRY IT OUT

Questions to Ask if You are Considering an Alternative Marriage

If you are being asked to be in an alternative marriage such as *mut'a* or *misyar*, use this space to assess if it is a choice for you.

- Have all parties freely consented to being in the arrangement?
- What are both partners' reasons for such an arrangement?[300]
- Do you have all the information you need about all parties involved?
- Is the relationship being kept a secret? If so, why?
- Do you feel pressured to participate in this arrangement?[301]
- If the relationship is temporary, what are the reasons to keep it temporary?
- Do you have support of trusted people in your life that can help support if you have any concerns about your relationship?
- Have the partners discussed the boundaries and parameters of the agreement?[302]
- Have partners discussed whether finances or other assets will be shared and divided?
- Are all partners (and any children resulting) being treated with justice and equity?
- Do you feel safe with all partners involved?
- If this is a misyar marriage, are you fully informed about the rights you are waiving?

Polygyny

Polygamy is a type of marriage where there are more than two spouses. Polygyny is a type of polygamy where a husband has more than one wife; polyandry is a marriage where a wife has more than one husband. Both were practiced in pre-Islamic times; Islam put restrictions on polygyny and prohibited polyandry.

The Quran regulated polygyny by allowing it, but with the condition that all wives must be treated equally and also limited the number of concurrent wives to four.[303] Others have taken this further to argue that equal treatment includes other conditions such as:

> (1) if the wife(s) has no objection about polygamy during or before the marriage contract and if the husband disregards that, the wife has the right to raise that to the Islamic court, (2) If a man can offer equitable treatment to all the wives, (3) if the man is wealthy enough to fulfill all their financial needs, and (4) if women are unable to produce children.[304]

A polygynous marriage does not in and of itself violate the RIDHA framework; with care, it is possible to be in a polygynous marriage that is aligned with the RIDHA principles. That being said, while the Quran does allow polygyny, it also discourages the practice by reminding men that it is almost impossible to treat all wives equally and justly.[305] Because of this, some scholars argue that "a man's marriage to a second wife normally falls under the ethical category of disfavored, not the permissible."[306] Research studies have also explored that when polygyny is not practiced with care, it can also be interwoven with abuse.[307]

[300] Yusouf, S, and Yusouf-Sadiq N. (2022). Temporary Pleasure, Permanent Effects: Practical Advice on Mut'a Marriage. in Ali, Kecia, ed. *Tying the Knot: A Feminist/Womanist Guide to Marriage in America.* Boston: OpenBU. https://hdl.handle.net/2144/44079

[301] Ibid.

[302] Ibid.

[303] Husain, R. Ahmad, A. Kara, S., and Alwi, Z. (2019). Polygamy in the Perspective of Hadith: Justice and Equality among Wives in A Polygamy Practice. Madania: *Jurnal Kajian Keislaman.* 23, 93. 10.29300/madania.v23i1.1954.

[304] Alamgir, A. (2014). Islam and Polygamy: A Case Study in Malaysia. *Procedia-Social and Behavioral Sciences*, 114, 889-893.

[305] Quran 4:3 "If you fear that you might not treat the orphans justly, then marry the women that seem good to you: two, or three, or four. If you fear that you will not be able to treat them justly, then marry (only) one, or marry from among those whom your right hands possess. This will make it more likely that you will avoid injustice."

[306] Fadel, M. H. (2016). Not All Marriages are Equal: Islamic Marriage, Temporary Marriage, Secret Marriage and Polygamous Marriage. *AltMuslimah*. Retrieved from http://www.altmuslimah.com/2016/03/not-marriages-equal-islamic-marriage-temporary-marriage-secret-marriage-polygamous-marriage/.

[307] Hassouneh-Phillips, D. (2001). Polygamy and Wife Abuse: A Qualitative Study of Muslim Women in America. *Health Care for Women International*, 22(8), 735-748.

Many have theorized why the Quran continued to allow polygyny, one view being protection of women rather than a sexual privilege for men. As Asma Barlas puts it:

> Although the Quran permits polygyny in certain cases, it is not because it privileges males, but strange as it may sound to us today, because it wishes to ensure justice for the most vulnerable women in society: the orphans...these verses are said to have been revealed after a battle in which many Muslim men lost their lives and many women were left as widows and orphans. It is the Quran's desire to protect these women, left without support in a predatory/tribal/patriarchal society, that fuels its sanction for polygyny which is, nonetheless, made contingent on three criteria: it is restricted to orphans, its purpose is to ensure justice for them, and it is not right if it results in injustice to the wife. That injustice may be inherent in a polygynous situation is clear not only from the last line of this verse, but also from another verse which warns men that 'you will not be able to be equitable between your wives, be you ever so eager.' Yet another verse reminds men that 'God has not made for any man two hearts,' implying that a man cannot love two women equally.' Together, then, these verses can be read as presenting a case against polygyny, which is never presented as catering to men's sexual needs or as a universal male prerogative.[308]

Also notably, the Prophet Muhammad (peace be upon him) took very seriously the feelings of first wives who did not want to be in a polygynous marriage. Perhaps the most profound example is the situation of his own daughter, Fatima (may God be pleased with her), when Ali (may God be pleased with him) wanted to take a second wife.[309] Fatima (may God be pleased with her) strongly opposed the idea, and the Prophet (peace be upon him) validated her feelings by going to Ali (may God be pleased with him) and saying "what hurts Fatima hurts me."[310]

Unfortunately, some interpretations of *fiqh* rules do not always prioritize the feelings of the first wife—most allowing a husband to marry a second wife even against the wishes of the first. However, it does allow wives to protect themselves against this situation by adding a clause in the marriage contract stating that the marriage will be monogamous as being the individual being directly impacted by polygyny.[311] Thus, this is one of the important conversations to have before signing the marriage contract—talk about polygyny and understand your partner's views about it, and then memorialize your mutual agreement in the marriage contract.[312] If you are already married and this is not in your contract, it might still be very useful to talk about it, to make sure both parties are fully aware of each other's feelings on the subject.

Polygamy is illegal in every state in the United States, and this has several implications for Muslim Americans. First, a polygamous husband might be prosecuted, but that doesn't have any impact on the marriage itself. Second, because it is illegal, any wife after the first has no marital rights under US law—such as healthcare benefits, inheritance rights, and so on. Some have argued that this makes polygyny Islamically impossible in the US because of the requirement that all wives be treated equally.[313]

308 Barlas, A. (2001). Muslim Women and Sexual Oppression: Reading Liberation from the Quran. *Macalester International:* Vol. 10, Article 15. Available at: http://digitalcommons.macalester.edu/macintl/vol10/iss1/15.

309 According to the Shia tradition, this story is fabricated to discredit Ali (may God be pleased with him). See Husayn, Nabil. (2021). *Opposing the Imam: The Legacy of the Nawasib in Islamic Literature.* Cambridge University Press.

310 Majah, S. I. (1999). The Chapters on Marriage Chapter (56): Jealousy. Sunnah.com The chapters on marriage, sayings and teachings of Prophet Muhammad. Retrieved from https://sunnah.com/ibnmajah:1999; Rohman, Arif.(2013). "Reinterpret Polygamy in Islam: A Case Study in Indonesia." *International Journal Humanities & Soc Science Inv*, 2(10), 68-74.

311 Rohman, A.(2013). Reinterpret Polygamy in Islam: A Case Study in Indonesia. *International Journal Humanities & Soc Science Inv*, 2(10), 68-74.

312 Ahmad, N., Ghazali, N. M., Othman, R., & Ismail, N. S. (2019). Women's Rights in Marriage: Between Quranic Provision and Malpractice. *Pertanika Journal Of Social Science And Humanities.* 27 (4): 2721 - 2730.

313 HG.Org. (2022). *Is Polygamy Illegal in the United States?* Hg.org. Retrieved from https://www.hg.org/legal-articles/is-polygamy-illegal-in-the-united-states-31807.

POINT OF INTEREST

Polygyny is a common practice.

Despite the restrictions previously discussed, polygyny is practiced in some Muslim families, even in the United States, and some Muslims are comfortable participating in such marriages. American Muslim scholar Debra Majeed, who has documented polygyny in African American communities, argues for a de-stigmatization of polygamy in order support healthy relationships for those who choose it for themselves—for people to "live polygyny of liberation or choice."[314] She recommends:

1. widespread and open dialogue and education on the forms of marriage and their application in the US.
2. that local mosques and Islamic organizations keep track of (civil and religious) marriage registrations (to prevent secret marriages).
3. that women exercise their agency by stating clearly in their contracts the kind of marriage they want
4. that first and potential subsequent wives are consulted prior to any multiple-wife marriage.
5. any courting or conversations with prospective wives are with the full knowledge of the first wife.
6. that marriage ceremonies that occur without the knowledge of the husband's current wife or wives should not be socially accepted in Muslim communities.[315]

 TRY IT OUT

If you are part of polygamous arrangement or are being asked to be in one, use this space to assess if it aligns with the RIDHA framework.

- Have all parties consented to being in the polygamous arrangement?
- Do you have all the information you need about all parties involved?
- Are all partners (and any children resulting) being treated with justice and equity?
- Do you feel safe with all partners involved?
- How is the arrangement being affirmed in commitment? Is your marriage known to the public?
- How will your partner ensure all partners are provided for fairly?
- If you are a subsequent wife, have you been able to speak to the first wife to reach an understanding of the marital and familial arrangement?

---

[314] Majeed, D. (2015). Afterword from Polygyny: What It Means When African American Muslim Women Share Their Husbands. *Half of Faith: American Muslim Marriage and divorce in the Twenty-first century.* Boston: OpenBU.
[315] Ibid.

Secret Relationships

Sometimes a marriage or relationship is kept secret from the general public, as well as family and friends. This is often true of temporary *mut'a* and *misyar* marriages (because of the stigma of such marriages in the Muslim community), as well as polygamous marriages (because of their illegality under U.S. law). A secret marriage or relationship could be monogamous—where it is only the public who is unaware; or it could be polygynous, creating the possibility that one (or more) wife does not know about the other(s). In recent years, there appears to be a profound rise in the prevalence of secret marriages among Muslim Americans, especially polygynous secret marriages.

The motivation for secret relationships are many. Couples may find themselves in a romantic relationship that is leading to sexual activity, and they do not want to engage in *zina* (extramarital sex), or they are experiencing resistance from their family members toward the relationship. As such, they find themselves in a relationship or getting married in secret to avoid disapproval or even hostility from family and/or community members. For situations like this, there are many variables to navigate, and every situation is different. Not all secret relationships are unhealthy, and sometimes, the secrecy is necessary to prevent further harm from the family or larger community. As it becomes more common to have more honest and realistic discourse about relationships, perhaps the expectations by parents, community, and couples will come into closer alignment, and these situations won't push these couples to secrecy quite so often.

Deception

Secrecy is not the same as deception. Sometimes the motivation for a secret marriage or relationship is one party's deception of another partner, such as hiding the relationship from another partner or spouse, or promising that the relationship will be made public in the future, but never intending to do so. Even more egregious is when the secret marriage is combined with spiritual abuse, where one partner misuses their religious power and authority to take sexual advantage of another, and keep keep it secret from the public.

Unfortunately, because polygyny is permissible in Islam, many Muslim men justify keeping their second (and third and fourth) marriages (either permanent or temporary) secret from their first wives on the grounds that they are permitted to do so by the *fiqh*. This is dangerous. As Mohammad Fadel has put it:

> it is easy for a lay Muslim to confuse the legal rules regulating marriage as a worldly institution in Islam, with the ideals about marriage as a religious institution. When this confusion occurs, even validly contracted marriages can be, at a minimum, deficient from the religious perspective, and in the worst case, immoral, and be little more than a subterfuge for illicit sex.[316]

He goes on to say that polygynous marriages are "a disfavored practice in the best of circumstances, and when the second marriage is secret, it goes beyond being disfavored and enters the realm of the forbidden, as the *Mālikīs* have argued."[317] In other words, many *fiqh* scholars have concluded that polygynous secret marriages, where the second (or more) marriage that is kept a secret from an existing wife and family, is impermissible and akin to infidelity.[318] In short, as we've said before, just because you can, doesn't mean you should.

---

[316] Fadel, M. H. (2016). Not All Marriages are Equal: Islamic Marriage, Temporary Marriage, Secret Marriage and Polygamous Marriage. *AltMuslimah*. Retrieved from http://www.altmuslimah.com/2016/03/not-marriages-equal-islamic-marriage-temporary-marriage-secret-marriage-polygamous-marriage/.

[317] Ibid.

[318] Ibid.

The Harm of Deceptive Relationships

Relationships that have elements of deception and infidelity violate every aspect of the RIDHA framework because they break the very foundations of trust, pleasure, communication, equity, safety, and commitment between partners. When a partner/spouse is having a deceptive secret marriage, it can cause a lot of tangible harm by negatively impacting the sexual and mental health of all individuals involved. Similar to an extramarital affair, a deceptive secret marriage can put an existing partner at risk for sexually transmitted infections, emotional distress, and trauma, and can severely compromise the mental well being of the partners involved, and ultimately threaten the health of the relationship.

In addition to harming the betrayed partner, deceptively secret marriages can also be potentially harmful and abusive towards the partner who is kept a secret, as they may not be able to have their rights fulfilled in the marriage and in the event of a divorce.[319] As both Mohammed Fadel and Debra Majeed have argued, there are benefits to making a marriage—any kind of marriage—public, including adding a community layer of protection.[320] The hope is that the risk of abuse and neglect is reduced when others have knowledge of the union, and the partners have more trust that their rights will be honored.[321]

 Red Flags That You're in a Deceptive Secret Relationship:

- Your partner avoids any conversation about public commitment.
- Your partner is resistant to introducing you to their family, friends, and other social circles, without any reason.
- Your partner has asked you to keep your relationship a secret, indefinitely.

 Red Flags That Your Partner is Having a Deceptive Secret Relationship with Someone Else:

- Your partner doesn't seem to be interested in you sexually or otherwise, and blames you for their disinterest.
- Your partner seems emotionally absent.
- Your partner is secretive about their finances or whereabouts and gets angry when you ask questions.

Infidelity (Cheating)

Infidelity or cheating occurs when a person in a committed relationship engages in intimate acts with individuals who are not their partner, without their partner's consent or knowledge. Some of this happens in a deceptive polygynous marriages, as described above, but it can also happen as simple "cheating" with no attempt to justify it in the form of a separate marriage.

It is important to realize that infidelity can be physical or emotional. Whatever form infidelity takes, it is always a deep betrayal of trust and can permanently damage the relationship, break up families, and cause much conflict and turmoil. The discovery of infidelity can feel like a total destruction of a person's world and

[319] Nadwi, S M., (2017). On Secret Marriages. *MuslimMatters*. Retrieved from: https://muslimmatters.org/2017/10/06/ secret-marriages-dr-shaykh-mohammad-akram-nadwi/.

[320] Fadel, M. H. (2016). Not All Marriages are Equal: Islamic Marriage, Temporary Marriage, Secret Marriage and Polygamous Marriage. *AltMuslimah*. Retrieved from http://www.altmuslimah.com/2016/03/not-marriages-equal-islamic-marriage-temporary-marriage-secret-marriage-polygamous-marriage/; Majeed, Debra.(2015) "Afterword from Polygyny: What It Means When African American Muslim Women Share Their Husbands" in Kecia Ali, ed., *Half of Faith: American Muslim Marriage and Divorce in the Twenty-First Century* (Boston: OpenBU, 2021). https:// hdl.handle.net/2144/42505.

[321] Ibid.

in addition to a relationship betrayal, it can also feel like a spiritual betrayal and the breaking of sacred vows. Not only is the trust in the relationship weakened or diminished, but you may trust yourself less as well. The betrayed partner may start to doubt their self-worth as a partner and as a person. The shock the betrayed partner may feel can trigger many emotions and trauma responses, and can also result in post-traumatic stress disorder.

If you have experienced betrayal, being kind and patient with yourself, getting therapy, and surrounding yourself with a strong support system can all be critical to navigating this difficult time and determining how you want to move forward. In addition to the emotional pain, infidelity puts individuals at risk for STIs, and both partners should schedule STI screenings.

Despite all of this, it is possible to overcome infidelity, and couples who are able to work through infidelity can emerge with stronger bonds than they initially had. At the same time, not everyone works through infidelity. Relationships often end if there is cheating or a history of cheating. Every person is different with respect to what they believe is something they can forgive and move on and what they can't. Working to move forward (with or without one's partner) after discovering infidelity can also be a process of self-discovery and growth for the betrayed partner: they may revisit one's commitment to themselves and how they want to be in a relationship moving forward.

DIVORCE

There are several types of divorce in Islam, and the differences are important.

There is a *hadith* that is often used to discourage divorce, stating that divorce is the "most hated" of the Islamically lawful things.[322] The misuse of this *hadith*, as well as the linguistic meaning that is lost in translation, has resulted in far too many spouses—particularly wives—feeling compelled to remain in challenging, harmful, and oppressive marriages.

First, some say this *hadith* has a weak chain of narration.[323] But even if you believe it to be valid, it is important to note that the *hadith* is referring to a specific type of divorce, the *talaq*, which is a divorce that can be initiated by the husband unilaterally and without the wife's consent. In other words, if this *hadith* is taken at its word, this particular type of divorce is "hated by God likely because of its unilateral and irrevocable nature."[324] Moreover, this hadith does not refer to wife-initiated divorces at all—those are called *khul* or *faskh*. Therefore to use this hadith to shame women who want to pursue divorce is unfair and unjust.[325]

Classical *fiqh* on divorce is complicated and nuanced, and we don't have time or space to detail it all here. In brief summary, there are three types of Islamic divorce:[326]

Talaq: a divorce initiated by the husband, which does not require the wife's consent, making it unilateral. It is executed by the husband pronouncing divorce and then waiting for three menstrual cycles (also known as *idda*, or waiting period) to pass without any sexual contact. The *idda* period is

322 Abu Dawud 2178, Bayhaqi, al-Sunan al-Kubra, Vol. 7. P. 322, Ibn Addi, al-Kamil, Vol.6, p. 2453).

323 Gamal Ahmed. (2019). *Is the Hadith Stating Allah Dislikes Divorce Authentic?* Islamaqate. Retrieved https://www.islamiqate.com/3252/is-the-hadith-stating-allah-dislikes-divorce-authentic#.

324 Ayubi, Z. (2021). What to consider if you're getting a divorce. in Kecia Ali, *Half of Faith: American Muslim Marriage and Divorce in the Twenty First Century.* Boston: OpenBU.

325 Ibid.

326 Ibid.

used to determine whether the wife is pregnant, and she is not allowed to remarry during that time. The *idda* period is also a period during which the husband can change his mind and take her back; although he is only allowed to do that twice. Pronouncing divorce for a third time finalizes the divorce and makes it irrevocable.

Khul': a divorce initiated by the wife, in which the wife initiates, and the husband agrees, an end to the marriage. This can all be done extra-judicially, without any need to go to a third party. In such divorces it is typical for the husband to ask for the wife paying back her *mahr* in exchange for the divorce. *Khul'* divorces are irrevocable, and the couple cannot reconcile during the *idda* period.

Faskh: a wife-initiated divorce where the husband has not agreed, so she approaches a third party (such as a *qadi*, or Islamic judge) who then determines whether grounds for divorce have been met; depending on the school of *fiqh*, these grounds could be failure to provide maintenance, or abandonment or harm. In a *faskh* divorce, the wife retains her *mahr*.

Although unilateral divorce (*talaq*) is a right held by men only, it can also be delegated to women with a clause in the marriage contract. Including a "delegated *talaq*" clause in a marriage contract means that a wife has a unilateral right to divorce according to whatever terms are put in the delegation. This could be as widely open as the husband's *talaq* right, limited to certain events, such as the husband choosing to marry additional wives. Delegated talaq sometimes adds power to key conditions in the marriage contract because, as Kecia Ali points out, it is often hard to hold a husband accountable to contractual stipulations. When a husband delegates his power of repudiation however, he gives his wife the right to decide the next course of action for their marriage when stipulations are not followed.[327]

Living in the U.S., navigating the Islamic laws on divorce can feel challenging, especially given that there are no Islamic courts, and therefore no *qadis* to adjudicate a divorce case according to Islamic principles and then enforce it with the power of the state. For those who want to seek divorce through the U.S. civil court system, this is also an equally valid route and many scholars have deemed a civil divorce according to the law of the country one lives in as sufficient to be Islamically divorced as well. Under traditional islamic jurisprudence, Islamic marriage contracts are considered a civil contract. This means that these marriages can be dissolved through the U.S. court system.[328] Unfortunately, this is not well-known, and not all scholars agree with this ruling, which may complicate divorce proceedings for couples, especially if the husband does not want to agree to an Islamic divorce. As such, the experience of seeking divorce will vary from person to person, depending on family traditions, personal beliefs, and what they need moving forward. There is a wealth of knowledge on Islamic marriage and divorce which we have included in the footnotes throughout this chapter.

---

[327] It is important to note that there are differences in opinion as to how long a wife can keep her right to delegated divorce. For more information, read: Kecia Ali, "Progressive Muslims and Islamic Jurisprudence: The Necessity for Critical Engagement with Marriage and Divorce Law," in Kecia Ali, ed., *Half of Faith: American Muslim Marriage and Divorce in the Twenty-First Century* (Boston: OpenBU, 2021), pp. 34-51. https://hdl.handle.net/2144/42505.

[328] Alkhateeb, M. (2012). *Islamic Marriage Contracts: A Resource Guide for Legal Professionals, Advocates, Imams, and Communities.* Peaceful Families Project, Asian & Pacific Islander Institute on Domestic Violence, and Battered Women's Justice Project.

POINT OF INTEREST

Secular is not always better.

Despite common belief, secular U.S. law may not always be more beneficial to women. For example, under Islamic law "a Muslim man's property is not wholly his, whereas a woman's property (of all sorts, whether land, money, personal assets, etc.) is exclusively her own."[329] This means that Islam does not obligate a wife to share her wealth with her husband, while the husband is obligated to financially provide (food, housing, basic needs) for her and their children. As such, there is no such thing as "community property" in which everything either spouse earns during a marriage is equally owned by both spouses. In a Muslim divorce, the wife keeps all her income and assets as her own, wheras in a community property state in the United States today, a wife might be surprised that her separate bank account or other assets solely in her own name are actually 50% owned by her husband - a rude awakening when those assets are divided in the event of a divorce![330] If preservation of your separate property is important to you, consider writing a prenuptial agreement to avoid losing your wealth in the event of a divorce. (Note: most states have specific requirements for a prenuptial agreement to be enforceable. Be sure to consult a lawyer.)

---

[329] Quraishi-Landes, A. (2013). Secular is Not Always Better: A Closer Look at some Woman-Empowering Features of Islamic Law. *ISPU Policy Brief.* Available at: https://www.ispu.org/secular-is-not-always-better-a-closer-look-at-some-women-empowering-features-of-islamic-law/.
[330] Ibid.

Chapter 5 Key Resources

This list is not comprehensive, and for full citations please see the works-cited at the end of the book.

Centering Pleasure and Safety

- *Kunyaza: The Secret to Female Pleasure* (book). By Habeeb Akande Available on Amazon.
- @TheVillageAuntie on Instagram and twitter.
- *Dr. Shaakira Abdullah @thehalalsexpert on Instagram.*
- *The complete illustrated Kama Sutra.* Available online at Amazon.
- *Pleasure Activism* by Adrienne Marie Brown. Available online.
- *The Perfumed Garden: Based on the Original Translation* by Sir Richard Burton. Available online on Abebooks.com and Amazon.

Sex Addiction and Pornography

- Sex Addicts Anonymous: https://saa-recovery.org/
- Purify Your Gaze: **www.purifyyourgaze.com**
- Counseling Today Article: "It's Not About Sex" by Stacy Notaras Murphy. **https://ct.counseling.org/**
- COSA: **https://cosa-recovery.org/**
- Sexual Recovery Anonymous: **www.sexualrecovery.org**
- Porn Addiction Toolkit by Family and Youth Institute: The toolkit can be accessed at **https://mailchi.mp/thefyi/porntoolkit**

National Hotlines for Immediate Support While Experiencing Violence

- National Sexual Assault Hotline: **1-800-656-HOPE**
- Rape Crisis Hotline: **1-888-293-2080**
- AMALA Hopeline: **1-855-95-AMALA**
- National Suicide Prevention Lifeline: **1-800-273-8255**
- National Alliance on Mental Illness: **1-800-950-6264**
- National Child Abuse Hotline: **1-800-422-4453**
- Love is respect: **1.866.331.9474**

National Organizations Focused on Educating About Sexual and Domestic Violence

- National Sexual Violence Resource Center: **www.nsvrc.org/**.
- Rape, Abuse, & Incest National Network: **www.rainn.org/**.
- YWCA: **www.ywca.org**.
- Stop It Now!: **https://www.stopitnow.org/**.
- Love is respect: **1.866.331.9474**.
- National Domestic Violence Hotline: **https://thehotline.org/**.

Specialty Organizations on Violence that Work with Muslims:

- Peaceful Families Project; Domestic violence within Muslim families: **www.peacefulfamilies.org**.
- KARAMAH, Muslim Women Lawyers for Human Rights: **http://karamah.org**.
- HEART Women & Girls, Sexual health education & sexual violence awareness: **www.hearttogrow.org**.
- The Hurma Project, Spiritual abuse within Muslim spaces: **https://hurmaproject.com/**.
- FACE, **facetogether.com**.
- Muslim Women's League. (1995). **https://www.mwlusa.org/**.

Domestic and Sexual Violence:

- "The Best of you will not Strike:" Al-Shafi on Quran, Sunnah, and Wife-Beating" article by Kecia Ali in *Comparative Islamic Studies*.
- "Does the Koran Allow Wife-Beating? Not If Muslims Don't Want It To." by Ayesha Chaudhry in *The Globe and Mail*.
- "An Islamic Perspective on Domestic Violence" By Azizah al-Hibri.

Safety Planning and Violence Prevention:

- *Create a safety plan.* Available at: **https://www.thehotline.org/plan-for-safety/create-a-safety-plan/**.
- *Creative Interventions Toolkit A Practical Guide to Stop Interpersonal Violence.* Available at **https://www.creative-interventions.org**.

For Finding Psychologists and Therapists

- Psychology Today: https://www.psychologytoday.com/us.
- Good Therapy: https://www.goodtherapy.org/find-therapist.html.
- Theravive: https://www.theravive.com/.
- TalkSpace: https://www.talkspace.com.
- BetterHelp: https://www.betterhelp.com/.
- Open Path Psychotherapy Collective: https://openpathcollective.org.

Grounding

Brief breathing and mindfulness exercises to support you:

- Living Well: https://www.livingwell.org.au/well-being/mental-health/grounding-exercises/.
- Headspace: https://www.headspace.com/meditation/breathing-exercises.
- Health Line: https://www.healthline.com/health/grounding-techniques.
- Medical News Today: Please check out Jenna Fletcher's article "How to use 4-7-8 breathing for anxiety" on www.medicalnewstoday.com. Published February 12th, 2019.
- Five Minute Mindful Breathing: Please check out the 5-minute mindful breathing video by Epworth Healthcare on YouTube.

Marriage and Divorce

- *Tying the Knot: A Feminist/Womanist Guide to Muslim Marriage in America.* https://hdl.handle.net/2144/44079.
- *Half of Faith: American Muslim Marriage and Divorce in the Twenty-First Century* edited by Kecia Ali
- "Marriage in Classical Islamic Jurisprudence: A Survey of Doctrines 11-42" by Kecia Ali in *The Islamic Marriage Contract: Case Studies in Islamic Family Law* (Vogel & Quraishi, ed.s).
- "Progressive Muslims and Islamic Jurisprudence: the necessity for critical engagement with marriage and divorce law." by Kecia Ali in *Progressive Muslims on justice, gender, and pluralism, edited by O. Safi.*
- "A Meditation on Mahr, Modernity, and Muslim Marriage Contract Law." by Asifa Quraishi-Landes In *Feminism, Law, and Religion* (1st ed).
- 100 Questions by Imam Magid https://www.rahmaa.org/resources/100-questions-by-imam-magid/.

Conclusion

This book has been years in the making. It began as a vision for a pocketbook, and since then has evolved over time to become a long interactive workbook, journal, and library of resources to learn more. It was originally intended to be co-authored by two or three staff writers, but has now evolved into a collaborative effort by more than twenty volunteers and advisors.

Our hope is that this book serves as a resource to help Muslims learn and talk about sex, reproductive health, relationships, and violence in healthy and productive ways. Sex and relationships are life experiences that impact nearly every human being. It is a natural part of life that Islam embraces and for which it provides healthy guidelines. We believe it is time that contemporary Muslims committed to regularly having conversations about this important part of life in a nuanced and intersectional manner. Whether you read this book cover to cover, skipped around to relevant sections, or used it as a place for journaling, we hope your journey to learn more about your body and your needs is a continuing one of which this book is just one part.

However you engaged with this book, we thank you. We appreciate you taking the time and energy to learn from our research and we are confident that you will learn more about your body and how to engage in healthier sexual practices as you continue to grow your knowledge around these topics. For people who have not had sex yet, we hope that you were able to gain enough information to be able to understand your body better for when you do have sex for the first time, and we pray that you have a spiritually and physically fulfilling sex life when the time is right. If you've already had sex, we are optimistic that this book has offered either confirmation or new knowledge to equip you to make informed decisions about sex and relationships and have even more fulfilling experiences in the future. If you are, or someday will find yourself, in an unhealthy or abusive relationship, we pray that the resources and information provided here also serve as a way to accurately recognize that and how to get help. For all our readers, we hope you put down this book with a renewed motivation and commitment to have open conversations about sex, your body, and your faith whenever you find it appropriate.

At HEART, we are committed to keeping this critical conversation going. As we celebrate and surpass more than ten years of working to increase the sexual health literacy of Muslim communities, we look forward to the next decade and beyond. InshaAllah, in the days and years to come, you will find us on social media engaging with our followers on many topics. You will find us hosting our interactive workshops—virtually and in person—across the country. And you will find us working in partnership with our communities to deepen our understanding of Muslims' needs pertaining to sexual health and violence. Ultimately we envision a world where all Muslims are safe and exercise self determination over their reproductive lives in communities where they live, work, and pray, and we have dedicated our work toward trying to realize that vision. This book is an important part of that work, and we are so grateful that you have joined us in this part of our journey. We began this book in the Name of God, and we end this book calling upon God one more time: May God continue to guide and bless us all with goodness in this life and the next.

Glossary

Abortion: a method of terminating pregnancy that involves taking a medication (also known as a medication abortion or the abortion pill) or undergoing a procedure (also known as a surgical abortion or in-clinic abortion).

Abstinence: The active decision to not have sex. Someone who has had sex can decide to practice abstinence at any point.

Abusive Relationship: a relationship in which one or both of the partners seek to hurt, manipulate, abuse or otherwise exert control over the other. It is typically signified by physical abuse but can consist of mental or psychological abuse as well.

Adalah: Arabic word for quality and justice.

Amanah: Arabic word that refers to trust, which has a broader Islamic meaning: the moral responsibility of fulfilling one's obligations due to Allah and fulfilling one's obligations due to Allah's slaves.

Anus: The opening where feces exit the body.

Asexual: A person who does not experience sexual attraction or sexual desire. Being asexual does not mean that you are not attracted to your partner, it means that you may find them attractive in other ways such as aesthetically pleasing, just not sexually.

Basal Body Temperature Method: A method of fertility awareness that focuses on basal body temperature, your body's temperature when your body is at rest. When a person ovulates, their basal body temperature rises slightly.

Boundary: A personal boundary is a certain limitation defined by an individual that defines what they are and are not comfortable with. An example of defining a boundary can be as simple as someone requesting you do not hug them. That is a personal boundary and should be respected.

Cesarian Delivery (C-Section): A surgical procedure used to deliver a baby that involves making incisions in the abdomen and uterus.

Calendar Method: A method of fertility awareness that predicts fertile days through tracking one's menstrual cycle lengths.

Cervical Cancer: Cervical cancer is a type of cancer that occurs in the cells of the cervix.

Cervical Mucus Method: A method of family planning that focuses on tracking the changes in color, texture and thickness of cervical mucus to track the stages of your menstrual cycles.

Cervix: A narrow passage at the bottom of the uterus connecting to the vaginal canal.

Cisgender: Denoting or relating to a person whose sense of personal identity and gender corresponds with their birth sex.

Clitoris: a small and nerve-dense tissue located between labia minora which connects underneath the clitoal hood.

Coercion: A tactic used to intimidate, trick or force someone to have sex without resorting to physical force. Examples include: constantly putting pressure on someone and refusing to take a no for an answer, implying sex is owed in return for financial favors, making someone feel guilty for not engaging in sex, etc.

Colostrum: Fluid released by mammals that have recently given birth, before breast milk production begins.

Communication: In terms of relationships, communication is about making your partner aware of your needs and wants. It is not only verbal but can also be physical or written.

Consent: Granting permission for something to happen. In terms of relationships, consent is always specific to that point in time, can always be revoked, and should always be respected, it can never be assumed and should always be respected.

Consummation of Marriage: When a newly married couple has sex for the first time. In some cultures, the expectation is for the consummation of the marriage to be on the first night, this does not have to be the case and may be preferable for some couples to delay their first experience with one another.

Decision-Making: When thinking about sex, decision - making is to actively consider your choices and enact your bodily, physical and life autonomy.

Demisexuality: A type of sexuality or sexual orientation. Demisexual people need to feel a strong emotional bond or connection with their partners first to feel sexual attraction.

Depression: A common and serious medical illness that negatively affects how you feel, the way you think and how you act. Depression causes feelings of sadness and/or a loss of interest in activities you once enjoyed.

Digital abuse: The use of technology and/or social media to control the victim. Some examples include: telling the victim who they can or can't be friends with on Facebook, uses email, social media, and tweets to harass, threaten, or insult them, and looks through their phone frequently.

Dysphoria: A state of feeling very unhappy, uneasy, or dissatisfied.

Economic abuse: The use of financial assets to control the victim. Some examples include: denying access to money, preventing the victim from viewing or having access to bank accounts, stealing money from the victim or their family and friends.

Ejaculation: When a sticky liquid substance (ejaculate/cum/semen) shoots out of the penis when it gets hard and is sexually aroused. Often before ejaculation, another natural fluid called pre-ejaculate or pre-cum is secreted when sexually aroused. Pre-ejaculate may contain sperm and could cause pregnancy.

Embryo: A human offspring during the period from approximately the second to the eighth week after fertilization.

Emergency Contraceptive: A method to prevent pregnancy after unprotected sex. Often called the morning-after pill, emergency contraceptive pills (ECPs) are pills that can be taken up to 120 hours (5 days) after having unprotected sex.

Emotional abuse: Can come in the form of degradation, ignoring, isolating, terrorizing, corrupting, exploiting, or controlling.

Endometriosis: A disorder where endometrial tissue (the type of tissue that lines the uterus) grows outside the uterus leading to sometimes excruciating pain. As surrounding tissue becomes aggravated leading to scarring and the development of fibrous tissues that can cause tissue and organs to stick to one another abnormally. Symptoms include, but are not limited to infertility, pain during intercourse, and painful periods.

Episiotomy: A cut (incision) through the area between the vaginal opening and the anus. This procedure is done to make one's vaginal opening larger for childbirth.

Epidural: A procedure that injects a type of medicine used to temporarily numb a part of one's body into the space around the spinal nerves in the lower back. It is also a type of pain relief for women in labor or who are having a cesarean section.

Erectile Dysfunction: The inability to get or keep an erection firm enough to have sexual intercourse. It can also be called impotence.

Erection: When blood flows to the penis faster than it flows out, and makes the spongy tissue in the penis swell (making it hard).

Erogenous zones: Sensitive areas on the body that causes sexual arousal when it is touched.

Fallopian Tubes: Slender tubes that connect the ovaries to the uterus. Eggs pass from the ovaries, through the fallopian tubes, to the uterus.

Female Genital Mutilation: Refers to cutting or removal of some parts or all of the outer parts of the female genitalia for non-medical reasons.

Fertility: The physical ability to be able to conceive, either as an individual or as a partnership, without medical or external aid.

Fidelity: In a relationship fidelity is about remaining loyal to your significant other and is a key foundation in a successful relationship. Infidelity or cheating can be physical or emotional.

Fiqh: Islamic rules of behavior.

> **Five Categories of Human Behavior:** In Islam, every human behavior can be identified as either required (*wajib*), recommended (*mandub*), neutral (*mubah*), discouraged (*makruh*) or prohibited (*haram*).

Foreplay: Activities leading up to sex, typically for sexual excitement or pleasure.

Foreskin: Fold of skin which covers the head of the penis.

Fuqaha: Arabic word for Muslim legal scholars.

Gaslighting: A type of psychological abuse in which the abuser denies the victim's reality, causing them to question themselves, their memories, or their perceptions.

Gender: How society thinks we should look, think, and act as girls and women, and boys and men. Each culture has beliefs and informal roles about how people should act based on their gender. For example, many cultures expect and encourage men to be more aggressive than women.

Gender Identity: How one expresses their gender, usually through behavior and personal appearance.

Gender non-conforming: Term given to people who don't conform with the gender norms.

Gendered violence: - Refers to harmful acts directed at an individual based on their gender.

Genital Warts: A common type of sexually transmitted infection that affects the moist tissues of the genital area. They can look like small, flesh-colored bumps or have a cauliflower-like appearance.

Gestational Diabetes: A type of diabetes that can develop during pregnancy in women who don't already have diabetes.

Grey-Asexuality: Also known as gray asexuality, gray-a, gray-ace, or grey-ace — is a term to describe people who identify as asexual but don't fit into the main types of asexuality. The three major types are: sex-repulsed, sex-neutral, and sex-positive.

Hadith: A record of the traditions or sayings of the Prophet Muhammad (peace be upon him).

Halal: Arabic word for permissible

Haram: Arabic word for impermissible

Heteronormative: Denoting or relating to a world view that promotes heterosexuality as the normal or preferred sexual orientation.

Human Papillomavirus (HPV): A type of virus that can cause abnormal tissue growth (for example, warts) and other changes to cells.

Hurma: Arabic word for sacred inviolability.

Hymen: A thin membrane that covers part of the vaginal opening and is commonly associated with virginity. The phrase "popped cherry" refers to the hymen being torn which causes bleeding. A hymen is not indicative of virginity. It also could be torn from riding a bike or several other physical activities.

Iblis: Arabic word referring to Satan/the devil in the Quran.

Ijtihad: Arabic word for interpretation of the Quran and Sunnah.

Ilm: Arabic word for knowledge.

Imam: Refers to the head of a mosque or a person who leads prayers.

Infertility: The inability to conceive children.

Infidelity: Refers to when a person in a committed relationship engages in intimate acts with individuals who are not their partner, without their partner's consent or knowledge. Infidelity can be physical or emotional.

Intimacy: Close familiarity or friendship; closeness.

Islamic Ethics: A system of belief and approaching religious guidance that is based on understanding morals, good or bad and builds principles based on those morals.

Islamic Law: A system of belief and approach to religious law, often rigid and vague but set as guidelines not to be used or understood alone but rather in combination with Islamic ethics.

Karamah: Arabic word for dignity.

Labia Majora: The "large lips", the labia majora surrounds and protects the external organs.

Labia Minora: The "small lips"; just inside the labia majora, the labia minora surrounds the opening of the vagina.

Madhab: Arabic word for a school of Islamic jurisprudence.

Mahr: A dowry that is paid by the potential spouse to the potential bride. It can be monetary, in-kind or a gift and belongs solely to the bride, neither her family nor the groom should have access to it.

Mammogram: An X-ray picture of the breast. Doctors use a mammogram to look for early signs of breast cancer.

Marriage Contract: Islamically, a marriage contract is a religious document that can be upheld in U.S. courts that outlines the terms of agreement of marriage between the partners. When signed, the marriage contract officiates the marriage.

Martyr: A person who is killed because of their religious or other beliefs.

Menstrual Cycle: Hormonal and physical cycle those with vaginas undergo, typically with a duration of 21-40 days. Over the course of the cycle, the uterus prepares for a potential pregnancy, undergoes ovulation and eventually the shedding of the uterine lining (commonly called a period).

Miscarriage: Refers to the loss of a pregnancy during the first 20 weeks.

Monogamy: The practice or state of being married to one person at a time.

Orgasm: The "peak" or pinnacle of sexual feeling or arousal usually accompanied by ejaculation for those with a penis.

Ovary: Typically there are two ovaries on either side of the uterus that are oval shaped and produce eggs and hormones in the female reproductive system.

Ovulation: The release of an egg (ovum) from an ovary into the fallopian tube. While the egg waits in the fallopian tube for potential sperm, the uterus accumulates blood and tissue where the egg and sperm will potentially attach.

Pap Smear: Also called a Pap test, is a procedure to test for cervical cancer in women. A Pap smear involves collecting cells from your cervix — the lower, narrow end of your uterus that's at the top of your vagina and those cells are analyzed for abnormalities.

Patriarchy: Social organization marked by the supremacy of the father in the clan or family, the legal dependence of wives and children, and the reckoning of descent and inheritance in the male line.

Pelvic Inflammatory Disease: An infection of one or more of the upper reproductive organs, including the uterus, fallopian tubes and ovaries.

Penis: The primary external organ of the reproductive system through which semen travels during ejaculation.

Physical Abuse: The intentional use of force or threats of force on another person in an attempt to control behavior and/or intimidate the victim. Examples include hitting, slapping, punching, strangulation, shoving, throwing, pulling hair.

Polyandry: A marriage or state with one woman having multiple husbands.

Polycystic Ovary Syndrome (PCOS): A hormonal condition that affects someone with a vagina's reproductive cycle and functions. Some common symptoms are irregular periods and polycystic ovaries. Some other symptoms and complications include obesity, excess androgen, infertility, depression, anxiety among numerous other potential symptoms.

Polygamy: The practice or custom of having more than one wife or husband at the same time.

Polygyny: A marriage or state with one man having multiple wives.

Postpartum Depression: Also called Peripartum Depression, refers to depression occurring during pregnancy or after childbirth. The use of the term peripartum recognizes that depression associated with having a baby often begins during pregnancy.

Post-Traumatic Stress Disorder: (PTSD)- is a psychiatric disorder that may occur in people who have experienced or witnessed a traumatic event.

Prostate: A gland the size of a walnut in the front of the rectum.

Qadi: An Arabic word for a Muslim judge who interprets and administers the religious law of Islam.

Quran: Islamic holy book.

Rahma: Arabic word for compassion.

Rape Culture: Refers to the ways in which society blames victims of sexual assault and normalizes male aggression and sexual violence. It is a complex set of beliefs that portrays violence as sexy and sexuality as violent.

Reproductive justice: SisterSong defines Reproductive Justice as the human right to maintain personal bodily autonomy, have children, not have children, and parent the children we have in safe and sustainable communities. Reproductive justice is the concept that all people deserve:

- the right to live, work, and pray in communities that are free from sexual violence,
- communities that sustain and support them, not those that oppress and harm them,
- the right to make decisions about their bodies,
- the right to decide whether to have children or not,
- the right to decide how to parent their children, if they have them,
- to be treated like the sacred beings that they are,
- access to sexual health resources and services that meets them where they are, and
- to make these choices in a way that aligns with their personal, political, and faith values.

Revenge Porn: The distribution of nude and/or sexually explicit photos and/or videos of an individual without their consent. In many cases, the pictures or footage are obtained by a partner during a relationship and posted after a break-up. Posts can also be made by acquaintances, former partners or hackers hacking into someone's personal electronic device(s).

Ridha: Arabic word for fullness of choice.

RIDHA: HEART has developed the RIDHA framework as a useful aid to identify healthy (sexual) relationships that are rooted in choice, consent, pleasure, communication, and spiritual well-being. Please see below for the acronym definition.

RIDHA Framework

- Respond by listening
- Affirm and believe
- Honor cultural and religious context and values
- Maintain anonymity and privacy
- Assist with providing resources and information

Scrotum: External sack of skin that holds the testis.

Secrecy: In the context of marriage, secrecy is not about keeping personal information or experiences private, it is about purposefully hiding details or information that violate trust in a partnership and that your partner would not be comfortable with, if they knew.

Secret Marriages: The practice of getting married and then keeping the marriage secret from the general public, as well as family and friends.

Sex: A label that's usually first given by a doctor based upon the genes, hormones, and body parts (like genitals) you're born with. It goes on your birth certificate and describes your body as female or male.

Sex Therapy: Couples therapy that focuses on overcoming sexual dysfunction limitation and psychological responses and limitations to sex.

Sex-neutral: Someone who isn't repulsed by sex but also doesn't actively seek it out. These people may still have sex if, for example, they're in a relationship and want to please their partner.

Sex-positive: A positive attitude towards human sexuality that views all consensual sexual activities as healthy and pleasurable. Being sex positive also means being respectful of other people's sexual presences.

Sex-repulsed: Someone who is repulsed by or completely disinterested in the idea of sex.

Sexual dysfunction: Occurs when a person has a problem that prevents them from wanting or enjoying sexual activity.

Sexual Empowerment: This type of empowerment is extremely personal and specific to each person. It is about any decision made regarding sex—such as being abstinent or deciding to engage in sexual activity.

Sexual intimacy: When people engage in sensual or sexual activities.

Sexual Violence: All unwanted sexual acts — whether harassment, abuse, or assault - committed against another person, without that person's freely given consent, is sexual violence and a could be prosecuted as a crime.

Sharia: Arabic word for Islamic canonical law based on the teachings of the Quran and the traditions of the Prophet (Hadith and Sunna), prescribing both religious and secular duties and sometimes retributive penalties for lawbreaking.

Shirk: Arabic word for associating another with God.

Spiritual abuse: Using religion to manipulate, control, and bully through the guise of religion, religious principles, or claims to spirituality. This includes using religion for personal gain, such as sexual or financial.

Standard Days Method: A method of fertility awareness similar to the calendar method, but can only be used if your cycle is 26-32 days in length.

Stealthing: The act of deliberately removing a condom during sex without your partner's knowledge or consent.

Stillbirth: A miscarriage after 20 weeks.

STIs: Infections transmitted through sexual contact and are caused by bacteria, viruses, or parasites.

Sunnah: The life example of the Prophet Muhammad, peace be upon him.

Syphilis: A bacterial infection usually spread by sexual contact. The disease starts as a painless sore — typically on the genitals, rectum or mouth. Syphilis spreads from person to person via skin or mucous membrane contact with these sores.

Testis: Commonly referred to as testicle, testis produce sperm and hormones.

Toxic Relationship: A toxic relationship is not just about being unhappy within a partnership but about a repeated cycle of behaviors exhibited by one or both of the partners that undermines, manipulates or causes stress to the other partner. A toxic relationship happens out of a lack of self control on the part of the toxic individual. It is different than an abusive one where an individual intends to hurt another, but the line between the two can often be blurry.

Transgender: An umbrella term for persons whose gender identity, gender expression or behavior does not conform to that typically associated with the sex to which they were assigned at birth.

Trichomoniasis (Trich): A very common sexually transmitted illness which is caused by infection with a protozoan parasite called Trichomonas vaginalis.

Types of Divorce in Islam:

> **Faskh:** A wife-initiated divorce where a religious authority such as a qadi, or judge determines the husband's consent is unnecessary. There are some conditions around which such a divorce is granted. It may also be determined that the marital gift does not need to be returned.

> **Khul:** A divorce initiated by the husband, in which the wife asks for the husband's consent to end the marriage. Islamic law does require the wife to pay her mahr, or marital gift, back to her husband in

exchange for the divorce. This is irrevocable and the couple cannot reconcile during the iddah period.

Talaq: A divorce initiated by the husband, and does not require the wife's consent, making it unilateral.

Urethral Opening: The opening of the urethra in the female where urine is excreted.

Urinary Tract Infection: An infection in any part of your urinary system—your kidneys, ureters, bladder and urethra.

Uterus: Commonly referred to as the womb, the uterus holds the developing fetus during pregnancy.

Vagina: The entry canal that connects the uterus to the outside of the body.

Vaginal Lubrication: A natural fluid created by the vagina when sexually aroused.

Vaginismus: An involuntary tightness of the vagina during attempted intercourse because of involuntary contractions of the pelvic floor muscles.

Vas deferens: Tube that takes sperm from the testes to the penis.

Verbal abuse: The use of words to manipulate, intimidate, and maintain power and control over someone. This can include: Insults, humiliation and ridicule, silent treatment, attempts to scare, isolate, and control.

Victim blaming: This occurs when the victim of a crime or any wrongful act is held entirely or partially at fault for the harm that befell them.

Virginity: Used to describe someone who has never had sex. Typically a person's first time having penetrative or penile-vaginal sex is often described as one losing their virginity, although any kind of sexual experience can be described as losing your virginity.

Vulva: The outer part of the female genitals. The vulva includes the opening of the vagina (sometimes called the vestibule), the labia majora (outer lips), the labia minora (inner lips), and the clitoris.

Yeast Infection: A fungal infection that causes irritation, discharge and intense itchiness of the vagina and the vulva.

Zina: Islamically, zina refers to any act of illicit sexual intercourse between a man and woman.

Zygote: A fertilized ovum/egg.

Works Cited

ABC Law Centers. (2018). *Involuntary Sterilization of Disabled Americans: An Historical Overview*. Retrieved from https://www.abclawcenters.com/blog/2018/11/06/involuntary-sterilization-of-disabled-americans-an- historical-overview/.

Abu Dawud 2178, Bayhaqi, al-Sunan al-Kubra, Vol. 7. P. 322, Ibn Addi, al-Kamil, Vol.6, p. 2453.

Abugideiri, S. E. (2010). *A Perspective on Domestic Violence in the Muslim Community*. Retrieved from https://www.faithtrustinstitute.org/resources/articles/DV-in-Muslim-Community.pdf.

Adam, M. I. (n.d.). *Female masturbation and Islam*. Female Masturbation and Islam. Retrieved from https:// rabaah. com/female-masturbation-and-islam.html.

Adoptive Families. (Website). www.adoptivefamilies.com/adoption-laws-by-state/.

Advocates For Youth. (Website). https://www.advocatesforyouth.org.

Ahmad, N., Ghazali, N. M., Othman, R., & Ismail, N. S. (2019). Women's Rights in Marriage: Between Qur'anic Provision and Malpractice. *Pertanika Journal Of Social Science And Humanities*.

Ahmed, G. (2019). *Is the Hadith Stating Allah Dislikes Divorce Authentic?* Islamaqate. Retrieved https://www. islamiqate.com/3252/is-the-hadith-stating-allah-dislikes-divorce-authentic#.

Ahmed, S., and Maha E. (2009). Challenges and Opportunities Facing American Muslim Youth. *Journal of Muslim Mental Health* 4(2): 159-174.

Akande, H. (2015). *A Taste of Honey: Sexuality and Erotology in Islam*. Rabaah Publishers.

Akande, H. (2018). *Kunyaza: The Secret to Female Pleasure*. Rabaah Publishers.

Akande, H. (2021). *Women of Desire: A Guide to Passionate Love and Sexual Compatibility*. Rabaah Publications.

Alahmad, G., & Dekkers, W. (2012). Bodily Integrity and Male Circumcision. *Journal of the Islamic Medical Association of North America*, 44(1). https://doi.org/10.5915/44-1-7903.

Alamgir, A. (2014). Islam and polygamy: A case study in Malaysia. *Procedia-Social and Behavioral Sciences*, 114, 889- 893.

Al-Awa, M. S. (2012). *FGM in the Context of Islam*. UNFPA Egypt. Available at: https://egypt.unfpa.org/sites/ default/files/ pub-pdf/d9174a63-2960-459b-9f78-b33ad795445e.pdf.

al-Hibri, A. (2003). An Islamic Perspective on Domestic Violence. *Fordham International Law Journal*, 27(1), 195. https://doi.org/http://ir.lawnet.fordham.edu/ilj.

al-Hibri, A. (1982). A Study of Islamic Herstory: Or How did we ever get into this mess? Women and Islam: *Women's studies International Forum Magazines*, 5.

al-Hibri, A., & Ghazal, G. (2018). *Debunking The Myth: Angels Cursing Hadith*. Karamah Muslim Women Lawyers for Human Rights. Retrieved from https://karamah.org/debunking-the-myth-angels-cursing-hadith/.

Al-Jauziayah, Ibn Qayyim. (1999). *Healing with the Medicine of the Prophet*. Dar-us-Salam Publications; First Edition. Available at: https://www.kalamullah.com/Books/Medicine.pdf.

Al-Kawthari, M. A. (2006). *Birth Control and Abortion in Islam*. White Thread Press.

Al-Matary, A and Ali, J (2014). Controversies and Considerations Regarding the Termination of Pregnancy for Foetal Anomalies in Islam. *BMC Medical Ethics*.15:10.

Al-Sheha, A. R., & Dabas, M. S. (2001). *Islamic Perspective of Sex*. Islamic Propagation Office.

Ali, K. (2002). *Same Sex Sexual Activity and Lesbian and Bisexual Women*. Feminist Sexual Ethics Project. Available at: https://www.brandeis.edu/projects/fse/muslim/same-sex.html.

Ali, K. (2003). *Marriage Contracts in Islamic Jurisprudence*. The Feminist Sexual Ethics Project Brandeis University. Retrieved from https://www.brandeis.edu/projects/fse/muslim/marriage.html.

Ali, K. (2003). Progressive Muslims and Islamic Jurisprudence: the necessity for critical engagement with marriage and divorce law. *Progressive Muslims on justice, gender, and pluralism*, edited by O. Safi. Oxford: Oneworld Publications 163-89.

Ali, K. (2006). "The Best of you will not Strike": Al-Shafi on Qu'ran, Sunnah, and Wife-Beating. *Comparative Islamic Studies*. 2(2): 143-155.

Ali, K. (2008). Marriage in Classical Islamic Jurisprudence: A Survey of Doctrines. 11-42, in *The Islamic Marriage Contract: Case Studies in Islamic Family Law* (Vogel & Quraishi, ed.s Harvard University Press).

Ali, K. (2016). *Sexual Ethics and Islam: Feminist Reflections on Qur'an, Hadith, and Jurisprudence*. Oneworld Publications; Expanded, Revised edition.

Ali, K. (2021). Acting on a Frontier of Religious Ceremony. in Kecia Ali, ed., *Half of Faith: American Muslim Marriage and Divorce in the Twenty-First Century*. Boston: OpenBU. https:// hdl.handle. net/2144/42505.

Ali, K. (2022). Making it Official: A Guide to Officiating at Muslim American Weddings. in Ali, Kecia, ed. *Tying the Knot: A Feminist/Womanist Guide to Marriage in America*. Boston: OpenBU.

Ali, K. (2022). *Tying the Knot: A Feminist/Womanist Guide to Marriage in America*. Boston: OpenBU.

Ali-Faisal, S.F. (2014). *Crossing sexual barriers: The influence of background factors and personal attitudes on sexual guilt and sexual anxiety among Canadian and American Muslim women and men*. Electronic Theses and Dissertations. Paper 5051.

Ali-Faisal, S.F. (2015). *What Does the Research Say? That Muslim Youth Need Sex Education.* Blog post. Available at: https://hearttogrow.org/what-does-the-research-say-that-muslim-youth-need-sex-education/.

All-Options. (Website). www.all-options.org.

Alkhateeb, M. (2012). *Islamic Marriage Contracts: A Resource Guide for Legal Professionals, Advocates, Imams, and Communities.* Peaceful Families Project, Asian & Pacific Islander Institute on Domestic Violence, and Battered Women's Justice Project.

American College of Obstetricians and Gynecologists (website): www.acog.org/womens-health.

Amala Hopeline – Muslim Youth Hotline. AMALA. (Website). from https://amala.mas-ssf.org.

American College of Obstetricians and Gynecologists. (Website). www.acog.org.

American Pregnancy Association. (2021). *In Vitro Fertilization.* Available at: https://americanpregnancy. org/ getting-pregnant/infertility/in-vitro-fertilization/.

Amnesty International. (N.d.). *Key Facts on Abortion.* Retrieved from: https://www.amnesty.org/en/what-we-do/ sexual-and-reproductive-rights/abortion-facts/.

Arriaga, X. B., & Agnew, C. R. (2001). Being Committed: Affective, Cognitive, and Conative Components of Relationship Commitment. *Personality and Social Psychology Bulletin, 27*(9), 1190-1203.

Asha, A. (2020). *Women And STIs.* American Sexual Health Association. Available at: http://old. ashasexualhealth. org/sexual-health/womens-health/women-and-stis/.

Asra. (2011). *'Ilm: Knowledge.* Available at: https://islamic-dictionary.tumblr.com/post/5470765752/ilm-arabic- %D8%B9%D9%84%D9%85-translates-into-knowledge.

Ayubi, Z. (2019). Muslim Biomedical Ethics of Neonatal Care: Theory, Praxis, and Authority. *Religion and Ethics in the Neonatal Intensive Care Unit.* Oxford University Press.

Ayubi, Z. (2021). What to Consider if You're Getting a Divorce. *Half of Faith: American Muslim Marriage and Divorce in the Twenty First Century.* Boston: OpenBU.

Ayubi, Z .(2022). Premarital Counseling and Nikkah Contract Writing Guide. in Ali, Kecia, ed. *Tying the Knot: A Feminist/Womanist Guide to Marriage in America.* Boston: OpenBU. https://hdl.handle. net/2144/44079.

Azmat, A. Khayr Y, Mohajir, N, Reyna, M, and Spitz, G. "They Sit with the Discomfort, They Sit with the Pain instead of Coming Forward": Muslim students' Attitudes and Challenges Mobilizing Sexual vVolence Education on Campus. Religions. Manuscript submitted for publication.

Baby Center (website): www.babycenter.com.

Badran, S. and Turnbull, B. (2019). Contemporary Temporary Marriage: A Blog analysis of First-Hand Experiences. *Journal of International Women's Studies.* (20)2: 241-256.

Barlas, A. (2001). Muslim Women and Sexual Oppression: Reading Liberation from the Quran. *Macalester International:* Vol. 10, Article 15. Available at: http://digitalcommons.macalester.edu/macintl/vol10/iss1/15.

Bedsider. (website). https://www.bedsider.org/methods.

Beckmann MM, Stock OM (2013). Antenatal Perineal Massage for Reducing Perineal Trauma. *Cochrane Database of Systematic Reviews* (4).

Bennice, J A., Resick, P A., Astin M. (2003). The Relative Effects of Intimate Partner Physical and Sexual Violence on Post-Traumatic Stress Disorder Symptomatology. *Violence and Victims* 8,(1) 87-94. doi:10.1891/vivi.2003.18.1.87.

BetterHelp. (website). https://www.betterhelp.com/.

Bhatti, W. (2018). *HEART to Heart: Breast Self-Exams & Mammograms.* HEART Women & Girls. Available at: https://www.youtube.com/watch?v=j6NHVjHh4jw&t=3s.

Bhatti, W. (2018). HEART to Heart: *Pap Smears.* HEART Women & Girls. Video. Available at: https://www.youtube.com/watch?v=50BEEDBJqR4&t=6s.

Blank, H., Corrinna, H. (2001). Innies & Outies: The Penis, Testes and More. *Scarlateen.* Retrieved from: https://www.scarleteen.com/article/bodies/innies_outies_the_penis_testes_and_more.

Boucher, S. et al (2009). Marital Rape and Relational Trauma. *Sexologies.* 18 (2): 95-97. https://doi.org/10.1016/j. sexol.2009.01.006.

Boutot, M. (2019). How Many Types of Female Orgasms are There Really? *Hello Clue.* Available at https://helloclue.com/articles/sex/researching-orgasm-how-many-types-of-female-orgasms-are-there-really.

Bowen, D L. (2006). Reproduction: Abortion and Islam - Overview, In: Joseph, S (ed.) *Encyclopedia of Women and Islamic Cultures Volume IIIL* Family, Body, Sexuality, and Health. Leiden and Boston: Brill.

Brown, A M. (2019). *Pleasure Activism: The Politics of Feeling Good.* AK Press.

Carrasco-Miró, G. (2019). Encountering the Colonial: Religion in Feminism and the Coloniality of Secularism. *Feminist Theory*, 21(1):91–109., https://doi.org/10.1177/1464700119859763.

Castleman, M. (2009). The Most Important Sexual Statistic There is Today. *Psychology Today.* Available at https://www.psychologytoday.com/gb/blog/all-about-sex/200903/the-most-important-sexual-statistic.

Ceesay, H. (2020). *HEART to HEART: STIs.* HEART Women & Girls. Available at: https://www.youtube.com/watch?v=KFELpk1wsd8&t=1s.

Centers for Disease Control and Prevention. (2022). *HPV and Men—Fact Sheet*. Available at: https://www.cdc.gov/ std/hpv/stdfact-hpv-and-men.htm.

Centers for Disease Control and Prevention. *STD Prevention Success Stories from Around the Country*. Available at: https://www.cdc.gov/std/default.htm.

Centers for Disease Control and Prevention. (N.d.). Pregnancy. Retrieved from https://www.cdc.gov/ pregnancy/during.html.

Center for Parent Information and Resources. (N.d.). *Resources Especially for Foster or Adoptive Families*. Retrieved from: https://www.parentcenterhub.org/fosteradoptive/.

Center for Young Women's Health. (2021). *Types of Hymens*. Retrieved from: https://youngwomenshealth.org/2013/07/10/hymens/.

Chapman, G. (2015). *Discover Your Love Language - The 5 Love Languages®*. Available at: https://www.5lovelanguages.com/.

Chaudhry, A. (2014). Does the Koran Allow Wife-Beating? Not If Muslims Don't Want It To. *The Globe and Mail*. Retrieved from https://www.theglobeandmail.com/opinion/its-muslims-who-give-voice-to-verse/article17684163/.

Check it Out Guys. (website). https://web.archive.org/web/20170424225956/http://checkitoutguys.ca/.

Childhelp. (Website). https://www.childhelp.org.

Cho, H., Shamrova, D., Han, J., & Levchenko, P. (2017). Patterns of Intimate Partner Violence Victimization and Survivors' Help-Seeking. *Journal of Interpersonal Violence*, 1–25.

Conwan, J.M. ed. (1979). r-d-a. *The Hans Wehr Arabic English Dictionary*. Spoken Language Services.

Corrina, H and Rotman, I. (2000). Human Reproduction: A Seafarer's Guide. *Scarlateen*. Retrieved from: https://www.scarleteen.com/article/bodies/where_did_i_come_from_a_refresher_course_in_human_reproduction.

Corinna, H. (2000). *Your First Gynecologist Visit*. Scarlateen. Retrieved from: https://www.scarleteen.com/article/bodies/your_first_gynecologist_visit.

Corrina, Hr. (2001). *Innies & Outies: The Vagina, Clitoris, Uterus and More*. Scarlateen. Retrieved from: https://www.scarleteen.com/article/bodies/innies_outies_the_vagina_clitoris_uterus_and_more.

Corinna, H. (2014). *First Intercourse 101*. Scarlateen. Retrieved from: https://www.scarleteen.com/article/sexuality/first_intercourse_101.

Corinna, H. (2019). *Condom Basics: A User's Manual*. Scarleteen. Retrieved from: https://www.scarleteen.com/article/ sexual_health/condom_basics_a_users_manual.

Corrina, H. (2021). *With Pleasure: A View of Whole Sexual Anatomy for Every Body*. Scarlateen. Retrieved from: https://www.scarleteen.com/article/bodies/with_pleasure_a_view_of_whole_sexual_anatomy_for_every_body.

Codependents Of Sex Addicts. (website). https://cosa-recovery.org/.

Creative Interventions. (2020). *Creative Interventions Toolkit A Practical Guide to Stop Interpersonal Violence*. Retrieved from https://www.creative-interventions.org/wp-content/uploads/2020/10/CI-Toolkit-Final-ENTIRE-Aug-2020-new-cover.pdf.

Danielsson, K. (2021). *How to Track Ovulation while Trying to Conceive*. Very Well Family. Available at: https://www.verywellfamily.com/how-to-track-ovulation-when-trying-to-conceive-2371830.

Daigle, C. (n.d.). *Supporting Muslim Women Dealing with Infertility: The Amal Support Group*. Amal Fertility. Retrieved from: https://muslimlink.ca/stories/supporting-muslim-women-dealing-with-infertility.

Dane, L. (2003). *The Complete Illustrated Guide of the Kama Sutra*. Inner Traditions.

Department of Health and Human Services. (Website). www.hhs.gov.

Dionne, E. (2014). I have HPV and I got the Vaccine. *Bustle*. Retrieved from: https://www.bustle.com/articles/29300-what-its-like-to-have-hpv-how-the-vaccine-failed-to-protect-me-as-a-black.

Disability Horizons. (2019). *8 Accessible Sex Toys and Aids for Anyone with a Disability*. Disability Horizons. Available at: https://disabilityhorizons.com/2019/02/8-accessible-sex-toys-and-sex-aids-for-anyone-with-a- disability/.

Dr. Shaakira Abdullah @thehalalsexpert on Instagram.

Dunn, P. (2004). *The Perfumed Garden*. Based on the Original Translation by Sir Richard Burton. Hamlyn.

Espinoza, R. (2016). 'Coming Out' or 'Letting In'? Recasting the LGBT Narrative. *HuffPost*. Retrieved from: https://www. huffpost.com/entry/coming-out-or-letting-in_b_4070273.

End FGM/C US Network. (website). https://endfgmnetwork.org/resources.

Epworth Healthcare. (2019). *Five Minute Mindful Breathing*. Video. Retrieved from: https://www.youtube.com/watch?v=I-SFdhVwrVA.

Exhale. (Website). www.exhaleprovoice.org.

FACE. (Website). www.facetogether.com.

Fadel, M. (1998). Reinterpreting the Guardian's Role in the Islamic Contract of Marriage: The Case of the Maliki School. *J. Islamic Law.*, 3, 1.

Fadel, M. H. (2016). *Not All Marriages are Equal: Islamic Marriage, Temporary Marriage, Secret Marriage and Polygamous Marriage.* Alt Muslimah. Retrieved from http://www.altmuslimah.com/2016/03/not-marriages- equal-islamic-marriage-temporary-marriage-secret-marriage-polygamous-marriage/.

Family and Youth Institute. (n.d.). *Premarital Sex Among Muslim Youth.* Infographic. Retrieved from: https://www.thefyi.org/ infographics/pre-marital-sex-among-muslim-youth/.

Family and Youth Institute. (2022). *Porn Addiction Toolkit.* Retrieved from: https://mailchi.mp/thefyi/porntoolkit.

Familydoctor.org editorial staff. (2019). *Sexually Transmitted Infections (STIs).* Retrieved from: https://familydoctor.org/ condition/sexually-transmitted-infections-stis/.

Farooq, M. (2019). *Walayah (Guardianship) and Kafa'a (Equality) in Muslim Marriage verses the Woman's Consent.* Available at SSRN: https://ssrn.com/abstract=3497607.

Fletcher, J. (2019). How to Use 4-7-8 Breathing for Anxiety. *Medical News Today.* Retrieved from: https://www.medicalnewstoday.com/articles/324417#:~:text=The%204%2D7%2D8%20breathing,help%20people%20get%20to%20sleep.

Fletcher, J. (2021). Demisexuality: What to Know. *Medical News Today.* Retrieved from: https://www.medicalnewstoday.com/articles/327506.

Free Clinics. (Website). https://www.freeclinics.com/.

Freefrom. (2021). *Prioritizing Financial Security in the Movement to End IPV: A Roadmap.* Retrieved from: https:// www.freefrom.org/wp-content/uploads/2021/07/Prioritizing_Financial_Security_Report.pdf.

Futures without Violence. (2017). *Safety Card for Muslim Youth on Healthy Relationships.* Developed by HEART, Advocates for Youth and Futures Without Violence, available at https://hearttogrow.org/resources/beyond- halal-and-haram-muslims-sex-and-relationships-safety-card/.

Get Tested | National HIV, STD, and Hepatitis Testing. Centers for Disease Control and Prevention. Retrieved from https://gettested.cdc.gov.

Ghazzālī, & Farah, M. (1995). *Marriage and Sexuality in Islam: A Translation of al-Ghazali's Book on the Etiquette of Marriage from the Ihya'.* UMI Books on Demand.

Gillette, H. (2021). *What Is Sex Addiction?* Psych Central. Retrieved from https://psychcentral.com/lib/what-is- sexual-addiction.

Good Therapy. (Website). https://www.goodtherapy.org/find-therapist.html.

Guttmacher Institute. (Website). www.guttmacher.org.

Guttmacher Institute. (N.d.). *Emergency Contraception.* Retrieved from: https://www.guttmacher.org/state-policy/ explore/emergency-contraception.

Guttmacher Institute. (N.d.). *Induced Abortion in the United States*. Retrieved from: https:// www. guttmacher.org/fact-sheet/induced-abortion-united-states?gclid=Cj0KCQiAJWOBhDRARIsANymNOY nCM5TFEaufUwhIvjK9rITNM3g4CqXojHr9UfSgGvOKKMCPMUKT6EaAvZFEALw_ wcB.

Guttmacher Institute. (2017). *Abortion is Increasingly Concentrated Among Poor Women*. Retrieved from: https:// www.guttmacher.org/news-release/2017/abortion-common-experience-us-women-despite-dramatic-declines-rates.

Guttmacher Institute. (N.d.). *Table 1: Percentage Distribution of U.S. Women Obtaining Abortions in Nonhospital Settings and of All U.S. Women Aged 15-44, and Abortion Index, by Selected Characteristics, 2014 and 2008*. Retrieved from: https://www.guttmacher.org/sites/default/files/ report_downloads/us-abortion-patients-table1.pdf.

Hammer, J (2019). *Peaceful Families: American Muslim Efforts against Domestic Violence*. Princeton: Princeton University Press.

Hammer, J. (2020). Queer Love, Abrahamic Morailty, and (the Limits of) American Muslim Marriage. *Theology & Sexuality* 27(1): 20-43.

Hammer, J. (2021). Weddings: Love and Mercy in Marriage Ceremonies. in Kecia Ali, ed. *Half of Faith: American Muslim Marriage and Divorce in the Twenty-first Century*. Boston: Open BU, 4-16.

Hasannia, A., & Masoudian, M. (2021). Temporary Marriage Among Shiite and Sunni Muslims: Comparative Study of 'Istimtā', Mut'ah, and Misyār. *In Temporary and Child Marriages in Iran and Afghanistan* (pp. 31-45). Springer, Singapore.

Hassouneh-Phillips, D. (2001). American Muslim Women's Experiences of Leaving Abusive Relationships. *Health Care for Women International*, 22, 415–432.

Hassouneh-Phillips, D. (2001). Polygamy and Wife Abuse: A Qualitative Study of Muslim Women in America. *Health Care for Women International*, 22(8), 735-748.

Hassouneh-Phillips, (2003). Strength and Vulnerability: Spirituality in Abused American Muslim Women's Lives. *Issues in Mental Health Nursing*, 24(6–7), 681–694.

Headspace. (Website). https://www.headspace.com/meditation/breathing-exercises.

Health Insurance Marketplace. (Website). https://www.healthcare.gov/.

Health Line. (Website). https://www.healthline.com/health/grounding-techniques.

HEART Women & Girls. (Website). www.hearttogrow.org.

HEART. (2020). *What's that Stuff Coming Out of my Vagina?* Instagram Post. Retrieved from: https://www. instagram.com/p/CFKxZFIDE2_/?igshid=YmMyMTA2M2Y=.

HEART Women & Girls (2020). *HEARTfelt Conversation series with Community Health Compass*. Retrieved from: https://www. youtube.com/watch?v=0JoemhgDM8U&feature=youtu.be.

HEART Women & Girls. (2011). *Let's Talk about Sex Education: A Guide for Effective Programming for Muslim Youth.* Retrieved from: https://hearttogrow.org/resources/lets-talk-about-sex-education-a-guide-to-effective- programming-for-muslim-youth/.

HG.Org. (2022). *Is Polygamy Illegal in the United States?* Retrieved from https://www.hg.org/legal-articles/is-polygamy-illegal-in-the-united-states-31807.

Hoel, N., & Shaikh, S. D. (2013). Sex as Ibadah: Religion, Gender, and Subjectivity among South African Muslim Women. *Journal of Feminist Studies in Religion*, 29(1): 69-91.

Husain, R., Ahmad, A., Kara, Si & Alwi, Z. (2019). Polygamy in the Perspective of Hadith: Justice and Equality among Wives in A Polygamy Practice. *MADANIA: JOURNAL KAJIAN KEISLAMAN.* 23. 93. 10.29300/madania.v23i1.1954.

Hussein, J. &. Ferguson, L. (2019). Eliminating Stigma and Discrimination in Sexual and Reproductive Health Care: A Public Health Imperative. *Sexual and Reproductive Health Matters*, 27(3): 1-5.

The Hurma Project, Spiritual Abuse within Muslim Spaces. (Website). https://hurmaproject.com/.

Ibrahim, N., & Abdalla, M. (2010). A Critical Examination of Qur'an 4: 34 and its Relevance to Intimate Partner Violence in Muslim Families. *Journal of Muslim Mental Health*, 5(3), 327-349.

Ireland, L. (2019.) Who are the 1 in 4 American Women who Choose Abortion? *For the Conversation.* Retrieved from: https://www.umassmed.edu/news/news-archives/2019/05/who-are-the-1-in-4-american-women-who- choose-abortion/.

Iqbal, R. (2015). *A Thousand and One Wives: Investigating the Intellectual History of the Exegesis of Verse Q4:24.* Dissertation. Georgetown University.

Jaafar-M I and Lehmann, C. (2011). Women's Rights in Islam Regarding Marriage and Divorce. *Journal of Law and Practice:* Vol. 4, Article 3.

Jessica Zucker, Ph.D. (Website). https://drjessicazucker.com.

Jurdi, S. (2001). *Misyar Marriage.* Al-Raida. Vol XVIII-XIX, 93-94. Available at: file:///Users/nmohajir/Downloads/528-Article%20Text-1040-1-10-20160727.pdf.

Kaiser Family Foundation. (Website). www.kff.org.

KARAMAH, Muslim Women Lawyers for Human Rights. (Website). http://karamah.org.

Katz, P., Showstack, J., Smith, J. F., Nachtigall, R. D., Millstein, S. G., Wing, H., Eisenberg, M. L., Pasch, L. A., Croughan, M. S., & Adler, N. (2011). Costs of Infertility Treatment: Results from an 18-month Prospective Cohort Study. *Fertility and sterility*, 95(3), 915–921. https://doi.org/10.1016/j.fertnstert.2010.11.026.

Khan, A A. (2017). *Marrying Without the Consent of the Wali (a Case Study of Pakistan) Compatibility of Pakistani Family Laws with UDHR.* Available at SSRN: https://ssrn.com/abstract=3067457.

Kiely-Froude, C and Abdul-Karim, S. (2009). Providing Culturally Conscious Mental Health Treatment for African American Muslim Women Living with Spousal Abuse. *Journal of Muslim Mental Health*, 4:175– 186.

Korstmit K, Jatlaoui TC, Mandel MG, et. al (2020). *Abortion Surveillance—United States—2018. Surveillance Summaries.* 69(7);1–29 retrieved from: https://www.cdc.gov/mmwr/volumes/69/ss/ss6907a1.htm.

Kugle, S. (2010). *Homosexuality in Islam: Critical Reflection on Gay, Lesbian, and Transgender Muslims.* OneWorld Publications. England.

Kugle, S. (2013). *Living Out Islam: Voices of Gay, Lesbian, and Transgender Muslims.* NYU Press. New York.

Lang, N. (2020). How Do You Celebrate Coming Out Day When You Can't Be Out?. *Them.* Retrieved from: https://www. them.us/story/coming-out-day-2020-fawzia-mirza-interview?fbclid=IwAR3fGuhayKHF M6Os-4H12SJb5h2u fUvfxuIMt2AMLaptkeWezdv-BiR4agw.

Lavendar, N. (2019). *Here's how Emergency Contraception Actually Works.* Self. Retrieved from: https://www.self.com/story/how-emergency-contraception-works.

Laws, M. (2020). Why we Capitalize 'Black' (and not 'white'). *Columbia Journalism Review.* Available at https://www.cjr.org/analysis/capital-b-black-styleguide.php.

Lawson, W. (2005). *Sex, Sexuality and the Autism Spectrum.* Jessica Kingsley Publishers.

Learn About Sex and Disability. *Come As You Are.* (2022). Retrieved from https://www.comeasyouare.com/blogs/sex-information/sex-and-disability.

Learn Islam. (n.d.). *Intimacy in Islam.* Retrieved from https://learn-islam.org/class3-intimacy-in-islam.

Lindsey-Ali, A. (2020) *A Quick & Dirty Guide to Ghusl!* Part 2. Retrieved from: https://www.instagram.com/tv/B8w00Vag5HP/?igshid=pir41zlfeqtd.

Living Well. (Website). https://www.livingwell.org.au/well-being/mental-health/grounding-exercises/.

Love Is Respect. (Website). https://www.loveisrespect.org.

Majah, S. I. (1999). *The Chapters on Marriage Chapter (56):* Jealousy. Sunnah.com The chapters on marriage, sayings and teachings of Prophet Muhammad . Retrieved from https://sunnah.com/ibnmajah:1999;

Majeed, D. (2015). Afterword from Polygyny: What It Means When African American Muslim Women Share Their Husbands. *Half of Faith: American Muslim Marriage and divorce in the Twenty-first century.* Boston: OpenBU.

Masjid Al Rabia. (Website). https://masjidalrabia.org.

Mattson, I. (2018). Gender and Sexuality in Islamic Bioethics. *Islamic Bioethics: Current Issues and Challenges.* Vol 2: 57–83.

Mattson, I. (2021). *Spiritual Abuse and the Hurma Project.* Muslim Network TV. Retrieved from: https://www. facebook.com/MuslimNetworkTV/videos/451356129512697/.

Mayo Clinic. (Website). www.mayoclinic.org.

Mayo Clinic Staff. (2020). *Vulvodynia.* MayoClinic.org. Retrieved from: https://www.mayoclinic.org/diseases- conditions/vulvodynia/diagnosis-treatment/drc-20353427.

Mayo Clinic Staff. (2021). *Female Infertility.* MayoClinic.org. Available at: https://www.mayoclinic.org/diseases-conditions/female-infertility/symptoms-causes/syc-20354308.

Mayo Clinic Staff. (2022). *Erectile Dysfunction.* MayoClinic.org. Retrieved from: https://www.mayoclinic.org/diseases- conditions/erectile-dysfunction/symptoms-causes/syc-20355776.

Mayo Clinic Staff. (2022). *Painful Intercourse (Dyspareunia)—Symptoms and Causes.* MayoClinic.org. Retrieved from: https://www.mayoclinic.org/diseases-conditions/painful-intercourse/symptoms-causes/syc-20375967.

McRuer, R., & Mollow, A. (2012). *Sex and Disability.* Duke University Press.

Mernissi, F. (1975). *Beyond the Veil: Male-Female Dynamics in Modern Muslim Society.* Schenkman Pub. Co.

Mills, B, and Turnbull, G. (2004). Broken Hearts and Mending Bodies: The Impact of Trauma on Intimacy. *Sexual and Relationship Therapy.* (19): 3. Retrieved from: https://www.recoveryonpurpose.com/upload/ Broken%20Hearts%20and%20Mending%20Bodies%20The%20Impact%20of%20Trauma%20 on%20Intimacy. pdf.

Mir, S. (2014). *Muslim American Women on Campus: Undergraduate Social Life and Identity.* University of North Carolina, Chapel Hill.

Mirza, S and Issra K. (2022). *3 Things You Should Know about Porn Addiction.* Retrieved from: https:// www.thefyi.org/3-things-about-porn-addiction/.

Miscarriage Matters Inc. (Website). www.mymiscarriagematters.org.

Mohajir, N and Pickett, K. (2020). *HEARTfelt Conversations with Kamilah Pickett, Part One: Foundational Public Health Concepts.* Available at: https://www.youtube.com/watch?v=0JoemhgDM8U&t=1s.

Mohajir, N and Qureshi, S. (2020). *Responding with RAHMA: Removing Roadblocks for Muslim Survivors.* Hurma Project Conference. Retrieved from: https://hurmaproject.com/wp-content/ uploads/2021/03/Responding-with-RAHMA-Removing-Roadblocks.pdf.

Mohammed, M. (2022). *100 Questions by Imam Magid.* https://www.rahmaa.org/resources/100-questions-by-imam-magid/.

Muladhat, U. (2018). *The Muslimah Sex Manual: A Halal Guide to Mind Blowing Sex.* Self Published.

Mu'Min, K. (2019). *I'm Proud to be Black, I'm Proud to be Muslim. I'm Good, but Everybody Else is Trippin'!: Identity & Psychological Well-Being among Black American Muslim Emerging Adults.* Ph.D. dissertation, Chestnut Hill College, Philadelphia, Pennsylvania, USA.

Murphy, Stacey. (2011). *It's not about the Sex.* Counseling Today. Retrieved from: https://ct.counseling. org/2011/12/its- not-about-sex/.

Musallam, Basim F. (1983). *Sex and Society in Islam: Birth Control before the Nineteenth Century.* Cambridge: Cambridge University Press.

Muslim Alliance for Sexual and Gender Diversity (MAGSD). (Website). http://www.muslimalliance.org/.

Muslim Women's League of America. (Website). https://www.mwlusa.org/.

Muslim Women's League. (1995). *An Islamic Perspective on Violence against Women.* Retrieved from: https:// www. mwlusa.org/topics/violence&harrassment/violence.html.

Muslim Women's League. (1995). *Sex and Sexuality in Islam.* Retrieved from: https://www.mwlusa.org/topics/ sexuality/ sexuality.html.

Muslim Women's League. (2001). *Female Sexual Dysfunction.* Pamphlet. Retrieved from: https://www. mwlusa.org/ topics/health/fsd.pdf.

Muslim Women's League. (2001). *Birth Control and Islam.* Retrieved from: https://www.mwlusa.org/topics/ health/ contraception.pdf.

Nadwi, S M., (2017). On Secret Marriages. *MuslimMatters.* Retrieved from: https://muslimmatters. org/2017/10/06/ secret-marriages-dr-shaykh-mohammad-akram-nadwi/.

Nagoski, E. (2014). *Unwanted Arousal: it Happens. What Science Says About those Times your Genitals Respond to Sexual Violence.* Available at: https://enagoski.medium.com/unwanted-arousal-it-happens-29679a156b92.

Naphtali, K., MacHattie, E., Krassioukov, A., & Elliott. (2009). *PleasureABLE: Sexual Device Manual For Persons With Disabilities.* Disabilities Health Research Network.

National Alliance on Mental Illness. (Website). https://www.nami.org/Home.

National Coalition for Sexual Health. (Website). www.nationalcoalitionforsexualhealth.org.

The National Domestic Violence Hotline. (Website). https://www.thehotline.org/.

National Domestic Violence Hotline. Create a safety plan. Available at: https://www.thehotline.org/plan-for-safety/create-a-safety-plan/.

National Health Services UK. (Website). www.nhs.uk.

National Network of Abortion Funds (website). www.abortionfunds.org.

National Sexual Assault Hotline. Rainn.org. (Website). https://www.rainn.org/resources.

National Suicide Prevention Lifeline. Suicide Prevention Lifeline. (Website). https://suicidepreventionlifeline.org.

National Sexual Violence Resource Center. (Website). www.nsvrc.org/.

Neighmond, P. (2019). *Why Racial Gaps in Maternal Mortality Persist.* NPR. Retrieved from: https:// www. npr.org/sections/health-shots/2019/05/10/722143121/why-racial-gaps-in-maternal-mortality-persist?t=1586793409588.

Office on Women's Health. Endometriosis. Retrieved from: https://www.womenshealth.gov/a-z-topics/endometriosis.

Office on Women's Health. (N.d.). PCOS. Retrieved from: https://www.womenshealth.gov/a-z-topics/polycystic-ovary-syndrome.

Office of Victim Assistance. (n.d.). *The Difference Between Healthy, Unhealthy and Abusive Relationships.* Office of Victim Assistance. Retrieved from https://www.colorado.edu/ova/sites/default/files/attached-files/ova_ knowthedifference_flyer.pdf.

Omari, H. K., & Chamwama, E. K. (2019). *Comprehensive Sex Education in Kenya: Islamic Perspective.* 2nd Annual International Conference Machakos University, Kenya. Machakos University.

Open Path Psychotherapy Collective. (Website). https://openpathcollective.org.

Oyewuwo-Gassikia, O. B. (2016). American Muslim Women and Domestic Violence Service Seeking: A Literature Review. *Affilia*, 31(4), 450−462. doi:10.1177/0886109916654731.

Oyewuwo-Gassikia, O. B. (2020). Black Muslim Women's Domestic Violence Help-Seeking Strategies: Types, Motivations, and Outcomes. *Journal of Aggression, Maltreatment & Trauma*, 29:7, 856-875, DOI: 10.1080/10926771.2019.1653411.

Parent Center hub. (Website). www.parentcenterhub.org.

Paul, Pamela. (2006). *Pornified. How Pornography is Damaging our Lives, our Partnerships, and our Families.* St. Martin's Griffin; First edition.

Peaceful Families Project. (n.d.). *Power and Control in Muslim Families.* Peaceful Families. Retrieved from https:// www.peacefulfamilies.org/uploads/1/1/0/5/110506531/providers%E2%80%99_fact_sheet_.pdf.

Pemberton, B. (2021). *What is Stealthing and is Removing the Condom During Sex Assault?* The Sun. Retrieved from https://www.thesun.co.uk/living/3488839/what-is-stealthing-sexual-trend-assault-risks/.

Petrosky, E., Blair, J. M., Betz, C. J., Fowler, K. A., Jack, S. P., & Lyons, B. H. (2017). Racial and Ethnic Differences in Homicides of Adult Women and the Role of Intimate Partner Violence − United States, 2003−2014. *MMWR. Morbidity and Mortality Weekly Report*, 66(28), 741-746. doi:10.15585/mmwr.mm6628a1.

Parvez, V. (2017). *HEART to Heart: Birth Control FAQs.* HEART Women & Girls. Retrieved from: https://www. youtube.com/watch?v=aLknFhVO7b4&t=32s.

Peaceful Families Project; Domestic Violence within Muslim Families. (Website). www.peacefulfamilies.org.

Planned Parenthood. (Website). www.plannedparenthood.com.

Planned Parenthood. (N.d.). *How Do IUDs Work as Emergency Contraception?* Retrieved from: https://www. plannedparenthood.org/learn/morning-after-pill-emergency-contraception/how-do-iuds-work-emergency-contraception.

Planned Parenthood. (N.d.). *Pregnancy Options.* Retrieved from: https://www.plannedparenthood.org/learn/ pregnancy/pregnancy-options.

Planned Parenthood. (N.d.). *STDs.* Retrieved from: https://www.plannedparenthood.org/learn/stds-hiv-safer-sex.

Planned Parenthood. (N.d.). *What's the Deal with Erections, Ejaculations, and Wet Dreams?* Retrieved from: https://www. plannedparenthood.org/learn/teens/puberty/whats-deal-erections-ejaculation-and-wet-dreams.

Planned Parenthood. (N.d.). *What Happens When You Lose Your Virginity?* Retrieved from: https://www. plannedparenthood.org/learn/teens/sex/virginity/what-happens-first-time-you-have-sex..

Planned Parenthood. (2022). What STD's Should I Get Tested For | STD Symptom Quiz. Retrieved from https:// www.plannedparenthood.org/online-tools/should-i-get-tested.

Porn Addicts Anonymous. (Website). www.pornaddictsanonymous.org.

Pregnancy and Infant Loss Support. (Website). www.nationalshare.org.

Psychology Today. (Website). https://www.psychologytoday.com/us.

Purify Your Gaze. (Website). www.purifyyourgaze.com.

Queer Crescent. (Website). www.queercrescent.org.

Quraishi-Landes, A. (1997). Her Honor: An Islamic Critique of the Rape Laws of Pakistan from a Woman-Sensitive Perspective. *Michigan Journal of International Law,* (18)287.

Quraishi-Landes, A. (2001). *Islamic Legal Analysis of Zina Punishment of Bariya Ibrahim Magazu, Zamfara, Nigeria.* Retrieved from: http://www.mwlusa.org/topics/marriage&divorce/islamic_legal_analysis_of_ zina.htm.

Quraishi-Landes, A. (2013). A Meditation on Mahr, Modernity, and Muslim Marriage Contract Law. In *Feminism, Law, and Religion* (1st ed.) p. 179-181. essay, Routledge. Retrieved from https://www.routledge. com/Feminism- Law-and-Religion/Failinger-Schiltz-Stabile/p/book/9781409444213.

Quraishi-Landes, A. (2016). Five Myths about Sharia. *The Washington Post.* Retrieved from https://www. washingtonpost.com/opinions/five-myths-about-sharia/2016/06/24/7e3efb7a-31ef-11e6-8758- d58e76e11b12_ story.html.

Quraishi-Landes, A. (2018). *Sharia and Diversity: Why Some Americans Are Missing The Point.* Institute for Social Policy and Understanding. Retrieved from https://www.ispu.org/sharia-and-diversity- why-some-americans- are-missing-the-point/.

Quraishi-Landes, A. (2018). *Advancing America Toward Justice.* (video). https://www.youtube.com/ watch?v=pSHYOm8Dwx4.

Quraishi-Landes, A. (2022). Drafting a Muslim Marriage Contract: A Summary of Mandatory and Optional Clauses. in Ali, Kecia, ed. *Tying the Knot: A Feminist/Womanist Guide to Marriage in America.* Boston: OpenBU. https://hdl.handle.net/2144/44079.

Rabbani Lubis, A. A. A. M., Muzakki, M. H., Rizal, F., & Makmun, A. R. (2021). Mut'ah Marriage: Between Human Rights and Maqashid Shari'ah. *Proceedings of the 2nd International Conference on Islamic Studies,* ICIS 2020, 27-28.

RAHMA. (Website). https://haverahma.org/.

Rape, Abuse, & Incest National Network. (Website). www.rainn.org/.

Rape Abuse Incest National Network. (N.d.). *Sexual Abuse of People with Disabilities.* Retrieved from: https://www.rainn.org/ articles/sexual-abuse-people-disabilities.

Rape Abuse Incest National Network. (2021). *Victims of Sexual Violence: Statistics. Victims of Sexual Violence: Statistics.* Retrieved from https://rainn.org/statistics/victims-sexual-violence.

Reid, J., Haskell, R., Dillahunt-Aspillaga, C., & Thor, J. (2013). Trauma Bonding and Interpersonal Violence. *Psychology of trauma.* Nova Science Publisher.

Reid, J. A., Haskell, R. A., Dillahunt-Aspillaga, C., & Thor, J. A. (2013). Contemporary Review of Empirical and Clinical Studies of Trauma Bonding in Violent or Exploitative Relationships. *International Journal of Psychology Research,* 8(1), 37.

Rocha, B.D.D., Zamberlan, C., Pivetta, H.M.F., Santos, B.Z., & Antunes, B.S. (2020). Upright Positions in Childbirth and the Prevention of Perineal Lacerations: A Systematic Review and Meta-Analysis. *Revista da Escola de Enfermagem da U S P,* 54, e03610.

Rohman, A. (2013). Reinterpret Polygamy in Islam: A Case Study in Indonesia. *International Journal of Humanities and Social Science Innovation,* 2(10), 68-74.

Roudi-Fahimi F. (2004). *Islam and Family Planning.* Population Reference Bureau. Retrieved from: https:// www.prb.org/wp-content/uploads/2004/09/IslamFamilyPlanning.pdf.

Safdar, Ayesha. (2017). *Sexual Health Knowledge and Practices of Muslim American Women.* Blog post. Available at: https://hearttogrow.org/sexual-health-knowledge-and-practices-of-muslim-american- women/.

Sahih Muslim. *Touching a Menstruating Woman Above the Izar*. Book 3, Hadith Number 2.

Sahiyo. (website). https://sahiyo.com/.

Sangor-Katz, M, Miller Claire C, and Bui Quoctrung. (2021). Who Gets Abortions in America? *The New York Times*. Retrieved from: https://www.nytimes.com/interactive/2021/12/14/upshot/who-gets-abortions-in-america.html.

Scarlateen. (Website). www.scarleteen.com.

Sex Addicts Anonymous. (Website). https://saa-recovery.org/.

Sexual Recovery Anonymous. (Website). www.sexualrecovery.org.

Shahar, Zaynab. (2022). LGBTQ Muslim Marriage Praxis and Queer Ethics of Relation. in Ali, Kecia, ed. *Tying the Knot: A Feminist/Womanist Guide to Marriage in America*. Boston: OpenBU. https://hdl.handle.net/2144/44079.

Siddiqui, S. Z. M., & Quraishi-Landes, A. (2019). Legislating Morality and Other Illusions about Islamic Government. *In Locating the Sharī'A* (pp. 182–182). essay, Brill.

Sidebottom, A.C., Vacquier, M., Simon, K., Wunderlich, W., Fontaine, P., Dahlgren-Roemmich, D., ... & Saul, L. (2020). Maternal and Neonatal Outcomes in Hospital-Based Deliveries With Water Immersion. *Obstetrics and Gynecology*, 136(4), 707-15.

Silvers, L. (2008). 'In the Book we have left out nothing': The Ethical Problem of the Existence of Verse 4:34 in the Quran. *Comparative Islamic Studies* (2)2: 171-180.

Silverberg, C and Kaufman, M. (2007). Ultimate Guide to Sex and Disability: *For All of Us Who Live with Disabilities, Chronic Pain, and Illness*. Cleis Press. San Francisco.

Skloot, Rebecca. (2010). *The Immortal Life of Henrietta Lacks*. Crown Publishing.

Stop FGM Middle East. (N.d.). *Fatwas against FGM*. Available at: http://www.stopfgmmideast.org/fatwas-against-fgm/.

Stop It Now!. (Website). https://www.stopitnow.org/.

Suleiman, O. (2017). *Islam and the Abortion Debate*. Yaqeen Institute. Available at: https://yaqeeninstitute.org/omar-suleiman/islam-and-the-abortion-debate/.

Tahseen, M. (2022). *Muslim Youth & Pornography*. The Family and Youth Institute. Retrieved from: https://www.thefyi.org/porn-findings/.

Taking Charge of your Fertility. (Website). www.tcoyf.com.

TalkSpace. (Website). https://www.talkspace.com.

The Conversation. (2019). Watching Pornography Rewires the Brain to a More Juvenile State. *Neuroscience News*. Retrieved from: https://neurosciencenews.com/neuroscience-pornography-brain-15354/ .

The Muslim Vibe. (2019). *Analyzing the so-called Wife-Beating Verse: 4:34 of the Holy Quran*. Retrieved from: https://themuslimvibe.com/faith- islam/in-practice/434-of-the-holy-quran-analysing-the-so-called-wife-beating-verse.

The National Domestic Violence Hotline (2021). *Domestic Violence Statistics*. Retrieved from https://www. thehotline.org/stakeholders/domestic-violence-statistics/.

The National Domestic Violence Hotline. (2021). *Create a safety plan*. Retrieved from https://www. thehotline.org/ plan-for-safety/create-a-safety-plan/.

Theravive. (Website). https://www.theravive.com/.

Tommy's Pregnancy Hub. (2022). *How Common is Miscarriage?* Retrieved from: https://www.tommys. org/ pregnancy-information/im-pregnant/early-pregnancy/how-common-miscarriage.

Transform Harm. (Website). https://transformharm.org/.

UN Populations Fund. (Website). www.unfpa.org.

U.S. End FGM/C Network. (2021). Resources. Available at: https://endfgmnetwork.org/resources/.

Vaginismus. (Website): www.vaginismus.com.

Van Leeuwen. T & M. Brouwer (ed.), Reid, J. A., Haskell, R. A., Dillahunt-Aspillaga, C., & Thor, J. A. (2013). Contemporary Review of Empirical and Clinical Studies of Trauma Bonding in Violent or Exploitative Relationships. *International Journal of Psychology Research*, 8(1), 37.

Village Auntie. Instagram & Twitter. @Villageauntie.

Villnes, Z. (2019). *What to Know about Vaginal Lubrication*. Medical News Today. Available at: https:// www. medicalnewstoday.com/articles/326450#_noHeaderPrefixedContent.

wadud, a. (1999). *Qur'an and Woman: Rereading the Sacred Text from a Woman's Perspective*. Oxford University Press.

Wall, S and Corrinna, H. (2019). *Quickies: Periods and the Menstrual Cycle*. Scarlateen. Retrieved from: https://www.scarleteen.com/article/disability_quickies/quickies_periods_and_the_menstrual_cycle.

Wasserman, D., Adrienne., Jeffrey B., and Daniel P. (2016). Disability: Health, Well-Being, and Personal Relationships. *The Stanford Encyclopedia of Philosophy*. Edward N. Zalta (ed.) Retrieved from: https:// plato.stanford.edu/entries/disability-health/#PerRelFamDis.

WebMD Editorial Reviewers. (2021). *What is foreplay?* WebMD. Retrieved from: https://www.webmd.com/sex/what-is-foreplay.

WebMD Editorial Contributors. (2021). *What Is Gray Sexuality?* WebMD. Retrieved from: https://www.webmd.com/ sex/what-is-graysexuality.

Weigel, G., Sobel, L., & Salganicoff, A. (2019). *Understanding Pregnancy Loss in the Context of Abortion Restrictions and Fetal Harm Laws—Glossary.* KFF. Available at: https://www.kff.org/womens-health-policy/issue-brief/ understanding-pregnancy-loss-in-the-context-of-abortion-restrictions-and-fetal-harm-laws/.

Wessiman, C. (2015). Why Porn is Exploding in the Middle East. *Salon.* Available at: https://www.salon.com/2015/01/15/why_porn_is_exploding_in_the_middle_east_partner/.

Witwer, E., Jones, R. K., Fuentes, L., & Castle, S. K. (2020). Abortion Service Delivery in Clinics by State Policy Climate in 2017. Contraception: X, 2, 100043. https://doi.org/10.1016/j.conx.2020.100043.

World Health Organization. (Website). www.who.int.

World Health Organization. (2022). *Cervical Cancer.* Retrieved from: https://www.who.int/news-room/fact-sheets/ detail/human-papillomavirus-(hpv)-and-cervical-cancer.

World Health Organization. (2022). *Types of Female Genital Mutilation.* Retrieved from: https://www.who.int/teams/sexual- and-reproductive-health-and-research-(srh)/areas-of-work/female-genital-mutilation/types-of-female- genital-mutilation.

Younis, I., Fattah, M., Maamoun, M. (2016). Female Hot Spots: Extragenital Erogenous Zones. *Human Andrology* (6)1: 20-26.

Yusouf, S. and .Yusouf-Sadiq, N (2022). Temporary Pleasure, Permanent Effects: Practical Advice on Mut'a Marriage. in Ali, Kecia, ed. *Tying the Knot: A Feminist/Womanist Guide to Marriage in America.* Boston: OpenBU. https://hdl.handle.net/2144/44079.

YWCA. (Website). www.ywca.org.

Zakaria, R. (2021). *Against White Feminism: Notes on Disruption.* W. W. Norton & Company.

Zahid, A. W., & Tabasum, M. (2012). The Islamic Era and its Importance to Knowledge and the Development of Libraries. *Library Philosophy and Practice.* Retrieved from: https://digitalcommons.unl.edu/libphilprac/718/.

Zuberi, H. (2016). Intimacy for Muslim Couples: the Anti-Climax. *Muslim Matters.* Retrieved from: https://muslimmatters.org/2016/01/05/intimacy-for-muslim-couples-the-anti-climax/.

About the Contributors

Nadiah Mohajir, M.P.H.

AUTHOR

Nadiah Mohajir is a lifelong Chicagoan, Pakistani-American-Muslim, mother of three, public health professional, reproductive justice activist, and anti-sexual assault advocate.

She is the Co-founder and Co-Executive Director for HEART Women & Girls. For over a decade, she has led the organization to provide sexual health education and sexual violence awareness programming and advocacy to thousands of individuals, organizations, and campuses across the country. Nadiah has worked in public health and reproductive justice for over twenty years in a variety of settings, including, but not limited to research, academics, policy, and community health. Her past work includes projects such as redesigning teen pregnancy programs, improving pregnancy outcomes in low-income communities in Chicago, running sex education programming for vulnerable youth, and evaluating innovative cross-sector partnerships in public health.

She earned her Master's degree in Public Health in 2009 from the University of Illinois at Chicago and her Bachelor's degree in Public Policy Studies from the University of Chicago. Nadiah has also participated in a number of fellowships, including the American Muslim Civic Leadership Institute, Germanacos Fellowship, is a recipient of the Women's Innovation Fund and most recently was selected to participate in NoVo Foundation's Move to End Violence program. She is also the recipient of numerous awards, including the 2018 Chicago Foundation for Women's Impact Award and the El Hibri Foundation's Community Builder award.

Navila Rashid, M.S.W.

AUTHOR

Navila is a Muslim, Queer, Bangladeshi-American. She's a trauma-informed forensic social worker, and community educator.

She joined HEART in 2019 full-time, and is the Manager of Training and Survivor Advocacy. Before HEART, Navila was consulting for public defenders, government agency staff, and nonprofits to support in creating safe(r) spaces for victims and survivors either through organizational programming or 1:1 case management.

Navila also Co-Founded 'The Cathartist' in 2012, a web-based platform for victims and survivors, allies, and co-conspirators to find a safe, judgment-free home for their storytelling as a part of their journey on coping and healing. Navila is also featured as a survivor in the award winning documentary, Breaking Silence, where she addresses the nuances and experiences of being a survivor of sexual violence in a Muslim and South Asian community, and the journey towards healing.

She earned her Master's in Social Work from Long Island University-Brooklyn, a Post-Baccalaureate Degree in Biology from University of North Carolina-Greensboro, and a BS in Health Science and Creative Writing from University of the Sciences in Philadelphia.

Haddijatou Ceesay, Ph.D.

AUTHOR

Haddijatou Ceesay is a Gambian Muslim, researcher, writer and social justice advocate with expertise and significant experience in research, project management and advocacy, primarily focusing on education policy, youth empowerment, public health, and gender.

She holds a doctorate from City, University of London; where her research centered on sexual and reproductive health education policy for young people. She has extensive experience working with survivors of various forms of gender-based violence (GBV) including Female Genital Mutilation (FGM), child marriages and sexual violence.

Dr Ceesay is a health educator and consultant at HEART, and has consulted for other agencies, including the United Nations Populations Fund, the Institute for Human Rights and Development in Africa, and the Population Council. Prior to this, she was part of an inter-agency committee that worked with the African Union's (AU) campaign to end child marriage, and successfully lobbied to pass a law to ban child marriage in The Gambia.

Dr Ceesay co founded the #SaveGambianWomen initiative, an online repository for documenting violence against women cases in The Gambia. She is a firm believer of activism through digital spaces for the global amplification of women's voices.

Dr. Asifa Quraishi-Landes, J.D., S.J.D.

EDITOR

Asifa Quraishi-Landes specializes in comparative Islamic and U.S.constitutional law, with a current focus on modern Islamic constitutional theory. She is a 2009 Carnegie Scholar and 2012 Guggenheim Fellow. Recent publications include "Healing a Wounded Islamic Constitutionalism: Sharia, Legal Pluralism, and Unlearning the Nation-State Paradigm (forthcoming in Transformative Constitutionalism, Boaventura De Sousa Santos, editor) and "Legislating Morality and Other Illusions about Islamic Government," (forthcoming in Locating the Shari'a: Legal Fluidity in Theory, History and Practice, Nathan French and Sohaira Siddiqui editors). Currently, she is working on a book manuscript tentatively titled "Three Pillars Constitutionalism" in which she proposes a new model of Islamic constitutionalism for today's Muslim-majority countries.

Professor Quraishi-Landes holds a doctorate from Harvard Law School and other degrees from Columbia Law School, the University of California - Davis, and the University of California - Berkeley, and has served as law clerk in the United State Court of Appeals for the Ninth Circuit. She has served as a Public Delegate on the United States Delegation to the United Nations Commission on the Status of Women, the Task Force on Religion and the Making of U.S. Foreign Policy for the Chicago Council on Global Affairs, and as advisor to the Pew Task Force on Religion and Public Life. She is past President of the National Association of Muslim Lawyers (NAML), and serves on the governing board of the Association of American Law Schools' Section on Islamic Law. She is an affiliate of the Muslim Women's League, past President and Board Member of Karamah: Muslim Women Lawyers for Human Rights, a Fellow with the Institute for Social Policy and Understanding and a member of the "Opinion Leaders Network" for the British Council's "Our Shared Future" project.

Lohitha Kethu, M.A.
ILLUSTRATOR

Lohitha is a queer, chronically ill, Telugu-American medical illustrator and artist whose award-winning work aims to be rooted in health equity, thoughtful representation of marginalized people in medical media, and increased accessibility of health education. Lohitha earned their Master's in Medical and Biological Illustration from The Johns Hopkins University School of Medicine in 2019. In 2017, they wrote and illustrated a graphic novel for children about type 1 diabetes, and used both their love of graphic novels and their own experiences of being chronically ill to inform their engaging and empathetic approach to patient education illustration.

Their illustration and research interests include cell and molecular biology, geriatric medicine, pediatric medicine, sexual health education, and the sociopolitical history of medical illustration. Lohitha believes in the power of science and health-related visual communication to help patients and communities feel more informed, empowered, and supported in their health experiences.

Mat Schramm
DESIGNER

Mat's background in creative direction is what led him to his career in photography. For the past 12 years, Mat has strategized on brand and website direction with large, national nonprofit campaigns and startup companies that focus primarily on initiatives list diversity, environmentalism, and health education. Since 2018, he has been a full time wedding photographer, capturing weddings all over the country but primarily in Colorado. His work his been featured in national media including TODAY, Huffpost, PBS, and Rocky Mountain Bride.

Mat lives in Denver with his family, which includes his wife Jenny, two rambunctious cats Jack and Mabel, and silly puppy Daisy. When he's not at his desk, you can usually find him tending to his rare houseplant collection or hiking on one of Colorado's many beautiful trails.

Made in the USA
Columbia, SC
20 September 2022

67680238R00130